R.A. AKINDELE is a Senior Lecturer in Political Science at the University of Ife, Ile-Ife, Nigeria.

The simultaneous application of the principles of universality and regionalism to the organization of world peace has created several problems in the past fifty years. *The Organization and Promotion of World Peace* is a comprehensive legal and political study of how the international community, organized under the League Covenant and the UN Charter, has attempted to tackle these problems.

R.A. Akindele first examines the legal formula devised to reconcile the competing claims of the universalist and regionalist principles, a formula which assigned concurrent but independent roles to world and regional organizations. It defined broadly their respective constitutional competences in the promotion of peace, and clearly emphasized the pre-eminent position of the world organization.

Then, with the aid of a careful analysis of selected cases, he reviews the working experience of the League and the UN to determine how the two principles have been combined in practice, and what political criteria decided the dosage of each principle actually employed in resolving disputes and promoting peace.

While the operating relationship in the period 1919-39 did not upset the constitutional balance established in the League Covenant, Akindele finds that there has been, since 1945, a *de facto* revision, in favour of regional agencies, of the UN Charter allocation of competences. Accompanying this revision has been a minimalist interpretation of the authority and jurisdiction of the United Nations. This study discusses this post-war development against the background of the division of the international community into power-camps based on antagonistic social and economic philosophies.

Students in the fields of international constitutional law, politics, and organization will find this work of scholarly interest; it will be of practical value to foreign policy makers and professional diplomats who are concerned with the search for a workable world order.

R.A. AKINDELE

The Organization and Promotion of World Peace: a study of universal-regional relationships

UNIVERSITY OF TORONTO PRESS
TORONTO AND BUFFALO

© University of Toronto Press 1976
Toronto and Buffalo
Printed in Canada

Library of Congress Cataloging in Publication Data

Akindele, R A 1939–
  The organization and promotion of world peace.

  A revision of the author's thesis, University of Alberta.
  Bibliography: p.
  Includes index.
  1. International organization.   2. Regionalism (International
  organization)   3. United Nations.   4. League of Nations.   I. Title.
  JX1954.A37   341.2   74-79987
  ISBN 0-8020-5314-9

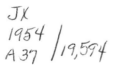

To
Olumide

The principal task of the student of international organization is not to waste more time debating over regionalism versus universalism but to study the ways in which, in concrete cases, the two principles can be utilized in combination and the standards to be applied in determining the dosage of each to be adopted.

Pitman B. Potter

Contents

Foreword

It gives me great pleasure to respond to Dr Akindele's request that I write the Foreword to his book, *The Organization and Promotion of World Peace*, which has grown out of a University of Alberta Ph D dissertation entitled 'Regional Organizations and World Order.'

Despite the great hopes for universalism expressed at the creation of the United Nations in 1945, and the paeans of praise that accompanied its twenty-fifth birthday in 1970, it became apparent at an early date that regionalism was far from being supplanted. In the first place, the Charter itself recognized the significance of regional distribution and the importance of regional arrangements if world peace was to be maintained or enforcement measures were to be successfully carried through. In addition to this, national states soon made it clear that, because of such things as the veto, they were not prepared to put their faith in the new universal organization, but sought to strengthen their regional ties, doing so through the medium of the traditional type of alliance and by way of new institutions.

It is the merit of Dr Akindele's work that he has analysed the relationship between the United Nations and the more important regional institutions seeking to establish the role that each may play in the promotion of world peace and security. In doing so, he has made a major contribution to the law and politics of international organization.

L.C. GREEN
Edmonton, Alberta

Preface

The world community has had half a century of experience in trying to cope with problems arising from the simultaneous application of the principles of universality and regionalism to the organization of international security and promotion of world peace. This book is a comprehensive review of that experience. The issue of the relationship between the United Nations and regional organizations has become a major problem, the essential nature of which is less constitutional than political. Fundamentally rooted in the decentralized character of the international system, it is consequently least susceptible to a purely legal solution.

A comparative study of the League of Nations and the United Nations reveals that the relationship between universal and regional organizations tended to be less problematic between 1920 and 1939 than since 1945. At the heart of the problem today is the division of the international community into power-camps based on antagonistic social and economic philosophies. This has resulted in the tendency of principal regional organizations to develop mainly within, instead of across, the boundaries of the ideologically structured power-camps. The policy pursued by the two super-powers of excluding each other from participation in the maintenance of peace in their respective hemispheres has imposed a de facto geographical limitation on the territorial scope of the United Nations' jurisdiction. In addition, the policy of 'competitive exclusion' and of 'hegemonial intervention' has tended to reduce the influence and effectiveness of the world organization. The constitutional history of the United Nations shows that there has been a de facto revision of the Charter law of universal-regional relationships in favour of greater autonomy for regional organizations.

The principal argument for placing an expansive construction on the competence of regional organizations is that the Security Council, originally conceived as the nerve-centre of the UN mechanism for the maintenance of international peace and security, has not been as effective as was envisaged. The political argument is indeed persuasive. Less convincing is the claim, made during the Cuban missile crisis in 1962, that the naval quarantine imposed by the independent initiative of the United States and the Organization of American States is 'the kind of action by regional organizations to keep the peace envisaged in Chapter VIII of the Charter and contemplated by Article 52(1).'[1] Such manipulation of legal argument in order to make the increasing autonomy of regional organizations look as if it entails no extension of the limits of regional action defined in the UN Charter is a good example of the abuses inherent in political interpretation of rules of international law.

Given the political structure of contemporary international society, disharmony between the forces of universality and those of regionalism is to be expected and, in fact, does not admit of any permanent solution, which would surely require a radical transformation of the organization of the international system towards imperial universality. Short of this, the precise relationships between the United Nations and regional organizations will continue to be worked out pragmatically as cases arise in light of policy considerations deemed relevant.

The material presented in this book was in its original form submitted to the University of Alberta in partial fulfilment of the degree of Doctor of Philosophy. At the University of Alberta, I was most fortunate to study under Professor L.C. Green who was a stimulating teacher and an extremely able research supervisor. His advice and constructive criticisms did much to improve the quality of my doctoral dissertation. Professor Green has equally been helpful to me in the revision of the manuscript for publication. While acknowledging my immense debt of gratitude to him, I hold myself alone responsible for whatever weaknesses there may be in the treatment of the subject-matter presented in the book.

I owe special thanks to my wife, Ann Dupe Pinheiro, who proof-read and corrected the manuscript at many stages during its preparation for publication, to the editors and publishers of the *Canadian Yearbook of International*

1 Abram Chayes in L.M. Tondel Jr, ed. *The Inter-American System and The Cuban Crisis* (Dobbs Ferry, New York: Oceana Publications, 1964), 46

Law, the *Indian Journal of International Law*, the *Malaya Law Review*, the *Egyptian Review of International Law*, and the *Israel Law Review*, for permission to use materials from my articles which have appeared in the pages of their journals, and to Lydia Burton of the University of Toronto Press for her outstanding editorial work. The Index was prepared by Mr Dapo Bello of the University of Ife Library.

The book has been published with the help of a grant from the Social Science Research Council of Canada, using funds provided by the Canada Council, and a grant to the University of Toronto Press from the Andrew W. Mellon Foundation.

R.A.A.
The University of Ife, Ile-Ife, Nigeria

ABBREVIATIONS

AFDI	*Annuaire Français de Droit International*
AJIL	*American Journal of International Law*
APSR	*American Political Science Review*
ASIL	American Society of International Law
BYBIL	*British Year Book of International Law*
CJIA	*Columbia Journal of International Affairs*
CJTL	*Columbia Journal of Transnational Law*
CYBIL	*Canadian Yearbook of International Law*
CLP	*Current Legal Problems*
FRUS	*Foreign Relations of the United States*
GAOR	*General Assembly Official Records*
Recueil des Cours	*Recueil des Cours de l'Academie de Droit International*
ICJ	International Court of Justice
ICLQ	*International and Comparative Law Quarterly*
ILA	International Law Association
ILM	*International Legal Materials*
IYBIA	*Indian Year Book of International Affairs*
IJIL	*Indian Journal of International Law*
JMAS	*Journal of Modern African Studies*
LNOJ	*League of Nations Official Journal*
LNMS	*League of Nations Monthly Summary*
LNTS	*League of Nations Treaty Series*
NLJ	*Nigerian Law Journal*
NSIL	Nigerian Society of International Law
PCIJ	Permanent Court of International Justice
RIIA	Royal Institute of International Affairs
SCOR	*Security Council Official Records*
TGS	*Transactions of the Grotius Society*
UCLA	University of California, Los Angeles
UN	United Nations
UNCIO	United Nations Conference on International Organization
YBWA	*Year Book of World Affairs*
REDI	*Revue Egyptienne de Droit International*
RGDIP	*Revue Générale de Droit International Public*
WPQ	*Western Political Quarterly*

THE ORGANIZATION AND PROMOTION OF
WORLD PEACE

1
Universality and regionalism in international organization

World peace, like war, has tended to become indivisible. International organization for the promotion of peace and security nevertheless continues to be based on the principle of division and imperfect co-ordination of responsibilities between universal and regional agencies. Promoting world peace might have been less troublesome than it now is if the international system had been either hierarchically organized or based upon a strictly federal foundation. As it is, the global system is largely a decentralized structure in which universal and regional systems of international co-operation are precariously superimposed upon the nation-state system.

The problem arising out of the simultaneous resort to the principles of universality and regionalism in furthering world order, and out of the increasing reliance placed on regional organizations after World War II, was cogently formulated by Dag Hammerskjold:

[D]evelopments outside the organizational framework of the United Nations, but inside its sphere of interest, do give rise to certain problems which require serious consideration. In the short view, other approaches than those provided by the United Nations machinery may seem expedient and convenient, but in the long view, they may yet be inadequate. To fail to use the United Nations machinery on those matters for which Governments have given to the Organization a special or primary responsibility under the Charter, or to improvise other arrangements without overriding practical and political reasons – to act thus may tend to weaken the position of the Organization and to reduce its influence and effectiveness, even when the ultimate purpose which it is intended to serve is a United Nations purpose. The balance to be struck here must be struck with care.[1]

This study is organized around the concepts of universality, regionalism, and universal-regional relationships. A technical discussion of these concepts provides an introduction to the practical application of them in international organization.

THE LEAGUE AND THE UN AS UNIVERSAL ORGANIZATIONS

The concept of universality in international organization has two dimensions: membership and territorial extent of jurisdiction. An international organization composed of all the sovereign states of the world community will ipso facto be global in its area of operation. But an international organization which aims at (but has not yet achieved) absolute universality of membership, and claims competence in maintaining peace in any part of the world may also be called a universal organization if its membership is sufficiently comprehensive and has a non-exclusive character. It is in the latter sense that the League of Nations and the United Nations may justifiably be placed in that category.

The constitutional provisions dealing with admission of nations into the League concealed the fact that the world organization was originally conceived as an international organization of only 'democratic' states.[2] Lord Cranborne has pointed out that '[t]aking the Covenant as a whole, on the basis of its actual wording, what seems to have been contemplated was a powerful, but not necessarily a universal, League; a League strong enough to enforce its will on an aggressor, but also strong enough to dispense with the assistance of some, even powerful, States, without having its action thereby paralyzed. In brief, the framers of the Covenant seemed to have assumed great, even overwhelming, strength, but not necessarily universal membership.'[3] Thus, for instance, when in 1920, the Government of Argen-

1 'Annual Report of the Secretary-General on the Work of the Organization, 1 July 1953 – 30 June 1954,' in *GAOR*, 9th Sess., Suppl. no 1, A/2663 (1954), xi
2 According to Georg Schwarzenberger (*The League of Nations and World Order*, London, 1936, chap. iii), the League of Nations Commission as a whole 'favoured the idea of universality to be modified by qualifications of constitutional homogeneity' (p. 35).
3 Lord Cranborne, 'Participation of all States in the League of Nations,' *Report of the Special Main Committee Set Up to Study the Application of the Principles of the Covenant* (Geneva, 1938), 46

tina proposed amendment of the admission provisions of the Covenant such that 'all sovereign States recognized by the community of nations be admitted to join the League of Nations in such a manner that if they do not become Members of the League, this can only be the result of a voluntary decision on their part,'[4] the League Assembly overwhelmingly rejected the proposal on the ground that it 'aims at a radical transformation of the actual character of the League of Nations' and further, that 'the condition of some States renders them unfit for admission, even should they request it.'[5]

The League subsequently abandoned a membership policy reflecting the 'democratic' conception of the world organization in order 'to repair those decisions of the early post-war period which had been based less on the needs of the future League than on the political wishes of the Allied and Associated Powers at that time omnipotent,'[6] but it never attained the ideal of universal membership. As a number of states began to withdraw from the world organization, it was soon realized that the problem of universal membership was not merely how to increase membership but also how to stem the outflow of members from the organization. Convinced that non-cooperation on the part of a state which was technically a member might be indistinguishable in its practical effects from non-membership, many supporters of the League began to regard universal membership merely as a necessary but not a sufficient condition for enhancing the capacity of the world organization to perform its functions effectively. During discussions on League Reform between 1936 and 1939, when members of the organization tended to link poor performance of the League in the years after 1930 with its non-universal character, it was still generally admitted that a membership policy based on indiscriminate admission of states was in the long-run capable of compromising the effectiveness of the world organization.[7]

The authors of the United Nations Charter, like those of the League Covenant, viewed universality of membership as 'an ideal toward which it was proper to aim but which was not practicable to realize at once.'[8] They therefore rejected proposals seeking to make membership in the organization automatic and obligatory for all independent states while hoping that some day all the nations of the world would become members participating in the

4 League of Nations, *Records of the First Assembly, Meeting of the Committee* II (1920), 224; F.P. Walters, *A History of the League of Nations* (London, 1967), 124

5 League of Nations, *Records of the Second Assembly, Plenary Meetings* (1921) 684

6 Schwarzenberger, *The League of Nations and World Order*, 72

7 S. Engel, 'League Reform: An Analysis of Official Proposals and Discussions, 1936-1939,' *Geneva Studies* XI (1940), 69

8 UNCIO, *Documents* VII, 326

collective effort to maintain world order. The authors of the Charter deliberately refrained from either expressly permitting or prohibiting withdrawal from the world organization, although they recognized in an interpretative commentary that a member could withdraw under 'exceptional circumstance.'[9] For instance, when Indonesia left the United Nations in 1965 and resumed membership in 1966, the UN Secretariat, with the tacit approval of the Security Council and the General Assembly, appeared to have treated the case as absence from and a cessation of co-operation with the world organization rather than as a withdrawal.[10] Membership in the United Nations has expanded from the fifty-one states which signed the Charter in 1945 to one hundred and thirty-eight states in 1974. In the first decade of the United Nations, admission of new members was viewed by the leaders of both East and West more from the narrow perspective of the effect of the admission of a particular state on the voting strength of the Eastern and Western camps within the General Assembly than on the future needs of the world organization.[11] Not surprisingly, progress toward universal membership moved at a snail's speed until the package deal of 1955. The conscious drive towards universality of membership as a means of enhancing the UN's image in international affairs became more pronounced in the 1960s when a large number of African states, on becoming independent, joined the world body.[12] Probably the most profound success recorded by the advocates of universal representation was the vote in 1971 to seat the Government of Communist China in the world organization. Moreover, recent developments in relations between East and West Germany made the admission of both countries into the world organization possible in 1973 – another triumph for the United Nations. Although the

9 *Ibid.*, 557; Nagendra Singh, *Termination of Membership in International Organization* (New York, 1957), 92 *et seq.*; Hans Kelsen, *The Law of the United Nations* (New York, 1950), 127
10 Egon Schwelb, 'Withdrawal from the United Nations: The Indonesian Intermezzo,' *AJIL* LXI (1967), 661-72; L.C. Green, 'Indonesia, the UN and Malaysia,' *Journal of Southeast Asia History* VI (1965), 71-86; Frances Livingston, 'Withdrawal from the United Nations – Indonesia,' *ICLQ* XIV (1965), 637-46; William R. Harris, 'Legal Aspects of Indonesia's Withdrawal from the United Nations,' *Harvard International Law Club Journal* VI (1964-5), 172-88; Y.Z. Blum, 'Indonesia's Return to the United Nations,' *ICLQ* XVI (1967), 522-31
11 Inis Claude Jr, *Swords into Plowshares* (3rd ed. rev., New York, 1964), 81-6; John G. Stoessinger, *The United Nations and the Superpowers* (New York, 1965), 21-6; L.C. Green, 'Membership in the United Nations,' *CLP* II (1949), 258-82; Nathan Feinberg, 'L'Admission de nouveaux membres à la Société des Nations et à l'Organisation des Nations Unies,' *Recueil des Cours* LXXX (1952), part I, 279-389
12 David Kay, *The New Nations in the United Nations* (New York, 1973)

United Nations does not yet include all the sovereign states of the world, its membership is now sufficiently comprehensive and world-wide to justify the claim that the organization is a universal one.

The second dimension of the concept of universality is the territorial limit of authority. Both the League and the UN were conceived as supreme guardians of peace for the entire community of nations. The League claimed competence to deal with any matter within the sphere of action of the League or affecting the general peace of the world. The Covenant accordingly declared war or threat of war to be a matter of concern to the whole League.[13] Similarly, there is hardly any international problem of which the General Assembly of the UN is not competent to take cognizance and discuss. The UN Security Council, which has primary responsibility for the maintenance of world peace, is empowered to determine the existence of any threat to the peace of the world and to decide what measures are necessary to maintain or restore order.[14]

Clearly, the relationship between the peace agency and non-members is the crux of the claim to supervise the promotion and maintenance of peace throughout the world. This relationship was formulated principally in Article 17 of the Covenant and in Article 2(6) of the Charter (sea appendices).

The Covenant required non-members of the League to conduct their international relations in such a manner that international peace would not be endangered or they would face the collective sanctions of the League. In the words of the authoritative British commentary on the Covenant, 'Article 17 asserts the claim of the League that no State, whether a member of the League or not, has the right to disturb the peace of the world till peaceful methods of settlement have been tried. As in early English law any act of violence, wherever committed, came to be regarded as a breach of the King's peace, so any and every sudden act of war is henceforth a breach of the peace of the League which will exact due reparation.'[15] If it is a rule of international law that no sovereign state can without its consent be obligated to submit its disputes with another state to any form of peaceful settlement,[16]

---

13 Sir John F. Williams, *Some Aspects of the Covenant of the League of Nations* (London, 1934); T.P. Conwell-Evans, *The League Council in Action* (London, 1929), Chap. ii; Alfred Zimmern, *The League of Nations and the Rule of Law 1918-1935* (London, 1936)

14 Kelsen, *The Law of the United Nations*, 193-218, 279-95; F.A. Vallat, 'The General Assembly and the Security Council of the United Nations,' *BYBIL* XXIX (1952), 63-104

15 Cmd 151 (London, 1919), 17

16 'Status of Eastern Carelia Case,' PCIJ, Series B, no 5 (1923), 27; M.O. Hudson, *World Court Reports, I, 190*

then the claim of Article 17 is at least legally questionable.[17] There is, however, no doubt that Articles 3(3), 4(4), 11, and 17 of the Covenant were indicative of the high hopes that the League would develop as a truly universal organization possessing jurisdiction over a world-wide area, even if its membership did not include all the sovereign states of the international community.

Under Article 2(6), the UN Charter imposes on members of the organization the duty to ensure that those states which are not members of the United Nations act consistently with the principles of the Charter so far as may be necessary for the maintenance of peace. Adopted without dissent at San Francisco, the provision expressed international interest in, and UN responsibility for, the preservation of peace.[18] The duty imposed by Article 2(6) nowhere gives the United Nations an all-encompassing authority: the authority of the United Nations has been restricted to the maintenance of peace.[19]

Most scholars agree that Article 2(6) does not impose obligations on non-members,[20] but non-members can hardly be unaware of the possible political consequences that may result in the event of a breach of Article 2(4) of the Charter.[21] If UN members are willing to carry out the obligations assumed under Article 2(6), no non-member can disturb world peace and hope to escape sanctions by the UN on the strength of the claim that it is not or has ceased to be a member of the United Nations.[22] The effectiveness of the claim of the UN Charter to be the law of the entire international commu-

---

17 Kelsen, 'Legal Technique in International Law: A Textual Critique of the League Covenant,' *Geneva Studies* x (1939), 139. Kelsen considers Article 17 as 'an attempt to introduce a new juridico-political principle into international law' (p. 139). Schwarzenberger is of the opinion that Article 17 is compatible with international law 'only with regard to non-members which were signatories of the Peace Treaties' (see *The League of Nations and World Order*, 118).

18 Richard Falk, *The Authority of the United Nations over Non-Members* (Princeton, 1965)

19 Josef Kunz, 'General International Law and the Law of International Organizations,' *AJIL* XLVII (1953), 456-62; Alfred Verdross, 'The Charter of the United Nations and General International Law,' in G. Lipsky, ed., *Law and Politics in the World Community* (Berkeley, 1953), 153-61

20 For a dissenting opinion, see Ian Brownlie, *Principles of Public International Law* (Oxford, 1966), 530-1; Kelsen, *The Law of the United Nations*, 106-10. 'In Article 2, paragraph 6, the Charter shows the tendency to be the law not only of the United Nations but also of the whole international community' (p. 109).

21 P.C. Jessup, *A Modern Law of Nations* (Hamden, 1968), 135; N. Bentwich and A. Martin, *A Commentary on the Charter of the United Nations* (2nd ed., London, 1969), 14

22 This was pointed out by some UN members in connection with the withdrawal of Indonesia from the United Nations in 1965 (see UN Docs A/5910, A/5914, and S/6356)

nity depends partly on the readiness of the Great Powers to enforce Article 2(4) whenever it is disregarded by any state. They have the power to determine whether the Security Council will take measures to ensure that powerful non-members conduct their international relations in a peaceful manner.

REGIONALISM AND REGIONAL ORGANIZATIONS

In an international system which already has a universal organization to perform world-wide functions, the ideal is to have regional organizations which actually are regional in their membership, areas of operation, and significance, and which confine their activities to well-defined areas corresponding to their circles of membership. The principles of regionalism and universality might then be simultaneously applied to the organization of world peace with a minimum of conflict of competence and jurisdiction.[23]

With respect to 'membership' and 'area of operation,' it is not necessary that the territories of members of a regional organization be geographically contiguous. In international relations, a region is defined by a cluster of interests – economic, political, ideological, linguistic, etc. – which are perceived to be common among some but not all states, and which are significant enough to warrant collective expression in permanent institutional forms. As Padelford has pointed out, 'in speaking of "regional" organization . . . we are thinking of those spatial areas which [have] come to be spoken of as "regions" as a result of usage stemming from the practices of states . . . the utterances of statesmen, or the terms of treaties and agreement between groups of states.'[24] The territories of members of many of the existing principal regional organizations are not propinquous. In any case, considerations bearing upon the principle of territorial propinquity have not figured predominantly in the calculations of statesmen who wanted to establish regional systems of international co-operation.

The requirement that regional organizations (like the North Atlantic Treaty Organization and the Warsaw Treaty Organization led by the United States and the Soviet Union respectively) be regional in their significance has been the most problematic of the three elements specified above. Both NATO and the Warsaw Pact were established to deal with the situation created by the cold war and the resulting loss of confidence in the

23 Pitman B. Potter, 'Universalism versus Regionalism in International Organization,' *APSR* XXXVII (1943), 854
24 N.J. Padelford, 'Recent Developments in Regional Organizations,' ASIL, *Proceedings* (1955), 25

ability of the UN Security Council to perform the managerial functions assigned to it; it is hardly surprising, therefore, that both organizations have tended to assume the function of collective security of world-wide significance. What gives certain regional organizations their trans-regional political significance is the membership of super-powers with global strategic interests who have tended to use those organizations less as impartial instruments for the management of regional peace than as instruments of world policy against the rival world power camp. The Committee of Three on Non-Military Co-operation in NATO sounded a note of warning in its 1957 Report:

NATO should not forget that the influence and interests of its members are not confined to the area covered by the Treaty, and that common interests of the Atlantic Community can be seriously affected by developments outside the Treaty area. Therefore, while striving to improve their relations with each other, and to strengthen and deepen their own unity, they should also be concerned with harmonising their policies in relation to other areas taking into account the broader interests of the whole international community.[25]

One aspect of the problems associated with the concept of regionalism often raised in the context of the League Covenant and the UN Charter is the meaning of the term 'regional arrangements.' The authors of the Covenant and the Charter deliberately refrained from placing any explicit construction on the meaning of the term.[26] Discussion in the Crillon Commission which drafted the Covenant and the formulation of Article 21 of the Covenant failed to recognize a necessary distinction between an understanding concerning a region held by one state and a regional understanding among some states of a particular region.[27] The Munroe Doctrine, the focus of the heated debate leading to the insertion of Article 21 into the Covenant, is not an understanding among the states of the Western Hemisphere. It is an understanding by the United States concerning the Western Hemisphere. The unintended ambiguity and confusion in the formulation of Article 21 probably resulted from the fact that the substance of what finally became Article 21 was originally proposed as an amendment to a

25 US Dept of State, *Bulletin* XXXVI (1957), 20
26 D.H. Miller, *The Drafting of the Covenant* I (New York, 1928) 443; UNCIO, *Documents* XII, 701-2
27 Boutros Boutros-Ghali, *Contribution à l'Etude des Ententes Régionales* (Paris, 1949), 41-4; John H. Spencer, 'The Monroe Doctrine and the League Covenant,' *AJIL* XXX (1936), 410, Jean Ray, *Commentaire du Pacte de la Société des Nations* (Paris, 1930), 575

different provision of the draft Covenant. In any event, the term 'regional arrangements' appearing in Article 21 was interpreted in practice to mean arrangements entered into by a number of states for the purpose of maintaining regional peace.[28]

At San Francisco in 1945, the Egyptian delegation urged the authors of the Charter to recognize a distinction between military alliances and regional arrangements, arguing that the former are the outcome of 'fortuitous political circumstances' whereas the latter are generally based on 'affinities.' The Egyptian delegation proposed the following definition of a regional organization:

There shall be considered as regional arrangements organizations of a permanent nature grouping in a given geographical area countries which, by reason of their proximity, community of interests or cultural, linguistic, historical or spiritual affinities, make themselves jointly responsible for the peaceful settlement of any disputes which may arise between them and for the maintenance of peace and security in their region, as well as for the safeguarding of their interests and the development of economic and cultural relations.[29]

The idea of an explicit definition of regionalism and the consequent discrimination between types of regional arrangements was rejected. But the UN Charter, like the League Covenant before it, takes cognizance of regional arrangements largely and explicitly in the field of peace maintenance. The issue of what constitutes a regional arrangement was again raised in the course of discussion on the proposal to invite the Secretary-General of the Organization of American States, the League of Arab States, and the Organization of African Unity to attend meetings of the General Assembly as observers. The General Assembly on three occasions avoided passing judgment on whether or not those regional organizations are agencies in the context of Article 52 of the UN Charter.[30]

Scholarly discussion on the issue has centred around the Beckett-Kelsen argument concerning whether or not NATO, a collective defence organiza-

28 J. Paul-Boncour, 'Report on Regional Pacts of Mutual Assistance,' *Report of the Special Main Committee Set Up to Study the Application of the Principles of the Covenant* (Geneva, 1938), 118-23. See also J.R. Arregui, 'Le Régionalisme dans l'Organisation internationale,' *Recueil des Cours* LIII (1935), part III, 1-93; Axel von Freytagh-Loringhoven, 'Les Ententes Régionales,' *Recueil des Cours* LVI (1936), part II, 589-671.
29 UNCIO, *Documents* XII, 850, 857
30 L.M. Goodrich, E. Hambro, and A.P. Simons, *Charter of the United Nations Commentary and Documents* (3rd and rev. ed., New York, 1969) 356-7

tion set up under Article 51 of the UN Charter, is a regional organization within the meaning of Chapter VIII of the UN Charter.[31] Sir Eric Beckett advanced the thesis that NATO is not a regional arrangement in the context of Articles 52-54 of the UN Charter. First, Beckett argued that the subject-matter regulated by Articles 52, 53, and 54 does not include collective self-defence. In reply, Hans Kelsen explained that matters relating to the maintenance of peace and security appropriate for regional action do not exclude self-defence and, in any event, self-defence is a measure relating to peace and security. Second, Beckett contended that whereas the use of force by a collective self-defence organization does not require prior authorization from the Security Council, legitimate enforcement measures by a 'regional arrangement' must have been approved by the Security Council. Kelsen's rejoinder was that the term enforcement action cannot refer exclusively to measures decided on or approved by the Security Council in as much as no approval of the Security Council is required to validate a regional enforcement action by the Great Powers against an 'enemy' state of World War II. Third, Beckett observed that collective self-defence arrangements are generally directed against extra-regional aggressors, but maintained that the hall-mark of a regional arrangement is the assumption of responsibility for enforcement action under the authority of the Security Council against a member of the regional organization which resorts to war or threatens international peace. Kelsen in return argued that since neither the formulation of Article 51 of the UN Charter nor the wording of Article 5 of the North Atlantic Treaty expressly rules out the possible use of NATO to deal with an aggressor which is also a NATO member, there is no reason why a collective self-defence organization like NATO cannot be used to maintain internal peace.

In a sense, the Beckett-Kelsen controversy, as Bowett has pointed out, 'arises from an attempt to characterize organizations by form rather than by function, as being either organizations in collective self-defence or regional arrangements.'[32] If a functional interpretation were brought to bear on Articles 51-54 of the UN Charter, the character of any limited-membership organization dealing with matters of peace and security appropriate for regional action would be defined by the specific function the organization is

31 Sir Eric Beckett, *The North Atlantic Treaty, the Brussels Treaty and the Charter of the United Nations* (London, 1950); Kelsen, *The Law of the United Nations*, 918-26. The Beckett view is accepted by Julius Stone, *Legal Controls of International Conflict* (New York, 1959), 247ff; J.G. Starke, *The ANZUS Treaty Alliance* (Melbourne, 1965) 78-82; A.L. Goodhart, 'The North Atlantic Treaty of 1949,' *Recueil des Cours* LXXIX (1951), part II, 207-9
32 D.W. Bowett, *Self-Defence in International Law* (Manchester, 1958), 222

performing at a given time. Thus, there is ample justification for employing a broad interpretation of the term 'regional arrangements' to include regional arrangements under Article 52-54 and collective self-defence arrangements under Article 51.

MODELS OF UNIVERSAL-REGIONAL RELATIONSHIP

Two general models of universal-regional relationship may be identified, depending on 1/ whether the world organization is built upon and derives its authority from regional organizations, or 2/ whether regional organizations are welded into the global agency which derives its authority directly from individual states. In Paris in 1919, the Crillon Commission did not even consider the first model; it adopted the second by default. Although both models were considered during World War II, the Moscow Declaration of 1943 appeared to have sounded the death knell of the idea of a regionalized world organization.[33] The authors of the Covenant and the Charter further recognized that a general model of universal-regional relationship under which subordinate regional organizations are built into the superior world organization can still take varying forms. They carefully and deliberately avoided putting the League and the United Nations in a position which would have permitted those world organizations to decide at pleasure whether a regional organization should exist in the first place, and if it is already in existence, whether it should be allowed to continue to function. Neither in 1919 nor in 1945 was the formation of regional organizations made to require the prior consent of the universal organization. In fact, the Czechoslovak proposals which sought to amend Article 21 of the Covenant in such a way that regional organizations 'may be not only approved by the [League] Council or the [League] Assembly, but also promoted by these bodies and negotiated under their auspices'[34] were not favourably received. Similar proposals put forward at the United Nations Conference on International Organization at San Francisco in 1945, which would in effect have made regional organizations exist at the pleasure of the United Nations and under its benevolent paternalism, were rejected.[35] But on both occasions, while regional organizations were made structurally independent of the world organization, they have nevertheless been function-

---

33 US Dept of State, *Charter of the United Nations: Report to the President on the Results of the San Francisco Conference* (Washington, 1945), 22
34 *LNOJ* (May 1921), 252
35 UNCIO, *Documents* III, 488

ally integrated with the world peace agency in a supplementary and subordinate capacity.

Under the model of universal-regional relationship that was adopted in 1919 and 1945, a perfect state of reciprocal equilibrium between universal and regional organization is believed to exist 'when the scope of their respective functions correspond to their geographic scope, the composition of their membership, and the needs they are to serve,' and when 'the two forms . . . mutually reinforce each other by a proper differentiation of their functions on the one hand, and their reciprocal integration under the over-all control of the more inclusive body on the other.'[36]

As employed in this study, the terms 'universality' and 'regionalism' define the formal structure for the search for world peace rather than the processes of international community-building, although it is recognized that international community-building at the universal and regional levels clearly has some bearing on the relationship between organizations which themselves reflect the levels of integration attained in the international society. An effective universal organization for the promotion of peace presupposes the existence of a high degree of integration in the world community. Ideological pluralism poses a great threat to an effective universal legal and political order.[37] At the same time, the search for peace in a world which is too heterogeneous to support an effective universal organization is bound to proceed along a non-universal plane where a sense of regional solidarity is presumably stronger. In terms of the perspective in this study, the relevant question posed by the processes of international community-building is whether regional organization constitutes a building block for an effective world community.

It has been said that regional organization is an intermediate step in the transition from nationalism to universalism.[38] Adherents of this view point out that the basic trend in the evolution of political communities has been in the direction of expansion, amalgamation, and consolidation by consent

36 George Liska, *International Equilibrium* (Cambridge, Mass., 1957), 134
37 H.A. Smith, *The Crisis in the Law of Nations* (London, 1947), 17-32; C.W. Jenks, *The Common Law of Mankind* (London, 1958), ch 2; Oliver Lissitzyn, 'International Law in a Divided World,' *International Conciliation*, no 542 (March 1963); Rosalyn Higgins, *Conflict of Interest: International Law in a Divided World* (London, 1965), 101ff; G.I. Tunkin, 'Coexistence and International Law,' *Recueil des Cours* XCV (1958), part III, 5-78
38 See, for example, E.H. Carr, *Nationalism and After* (London, 1965), 45; Bart Landheer, *On the Sociology of International Law and Society* (The Hague, 1968), 17-26, 65-73; Gladwin Jebb, *Halfway to 1984* (New York, 1966), 89

or conquest. The increasing permeability of the hard shell of the territorial state and, hence, its conditional viability[39] insures that this evolution of political communities into larger units will continue. In a strong warning against an 'uncritical acceptance of [this] comfortable principle of gradualness,' Schwarzenberger has persuasively asserted: 'In relation to the overriding issue of world power politics *versus* world community, proposals for federations inside either of the world's two halves are irrelevant. In other respects, such federations may be highly beneficial. They leave, however, the character of the present-day world politics unchanged.'[40] Or as Russett puts it, '[t]he choice about what to do for *global* unity will determine whether regional blocs will build a stable political edifice for man, or merely a shaky temple he can pull down upon his head.'[41]

The implications of regionalism for the emergence of an effective universal organization are a matter of empirical determination. This point has been well made by Etzioni:

Regional and bloc organizations should . . . not be judged *a priori* as anti-United Nations or as undermining other global organizations. They might be stepping stones to a global community. The main question is not whether there are initially intermediary bodies or not, but what orientation they take toward global organization. Do they see the bloc organization as the ultimate superior body, and are they jealous of its functions and powers? Or do they orient positively to the more encompassing global structure? Do they attempt to block, to slow down, or to accelerate the process of upward transfer [of power and responsibility] to the global level?[42]

My purpose in this book is to seek answers to such questions in the light of the half-century of experience undergone by the world community since it decided, in 1919 and 1945, to combine the principles of universality and regionalism in designing the legal and political structure for the promotion of international peace. The over-all research strategy is to compare the standards that statesmen have found politically convenient to adopt when deciding how much of each principle is to be applied in specific cases with those

---

39 John H. Herz, 'The Rise and Demise of the Territorial State,' *World Politics* IX (1957), 473-93; Kenneth Boulding, *Conflict and Defense: A General Theory* (New York, 1962), 272
40 Schwarzenberger, *Power Politics* (3rd ed., London, 1964), 527; and also 'Reflections on the Law of International Institutions,' *CLP*/XIII (1960), 258
41 Bruce M. Russett, *International Regions and the International System* (Chicago, 1967), 232 (emphasis in the original)
42 Amitai Etzioni, 'Atlantic Union, the Southern Continents and the United Nations,' in Roger Fisher, ed., *International Conflict and Behavioral Science* (New York, 1964), 197

standards that the authors of the Covenant and the Charter considered to be most desirable. Basically, therefore, this is a study of the *political* interpretations of the carefully formulated *law* of universal-regional relationships as contained principally in Article 21 of the Covenant and Articles 51-54 of the Charter. The chief subjects of the study are the two world peace organizations, the League of Nations and the United Nations, and a number of carefully selected regional organizations. Among the comparatively fewer number of regional organizations that existed during the League period, the Little Entente, the Locarno Pact, and the Inter-American System have been chosen for study in order to examine the on-going relationships in three different situations. These involve 1/ a regional organization composed of small states (the Little Entente); 2/ a regional organization composed of the big powers (the Locarno Pact); and 3/ a regional organization composed predominantly of small states but dominated by a single major power. In order to test the operation of the UN Charter law of universal-regional relationships, the following regional organizations were selected: 1/ the Organization of American States, the Warsaw Pact, and the North Atlantic Treaty Organization, each of which contains a super-power; and 2/ the League of Arab States and the Organization of African Unity both of which are regional organizations composed mainly of new small states. The selection has of course also been influenced by the availability of cases which provide the necessary raw material for observing the developing relationships between the superior and subordinate organizations for the maintenance of world peace. The guiding consideration for selecting cases was the need to pick, as much as possible, many relevant ones with varying degrees of political intensity. Thus, the list ranges from the most obscure Szent-Gotthard incident (1928), involving three small Little Entente members in a 'dispute' with Hungary, to probably the most acute and politically serious crisis since World War II, the Cuban missile crisis (1962), featuring a direct confrontation between the two super-powers.

2
The League experience

Discussions on the organization of international peace and security after World War I rested clearly upon an assumption, indeed a conviction, that international peace would be best maintained or promoted by a world-wide organization.[1] The dogmatic veneration for the principle of universality prevented the planners of the post-war peace machinery from initially recognizing the relevance of the principle of regionalism to the organization of world peace. Not surprisingly, neither the influential Phillimore Plan, the Hurst-Miller Draft, nor even the Draft Covenant of 14 February 1919 contained any reference to regionalism and regional organizations. Perhaps such omission would in any case have been of no consequence in view of the general principle formulated in the *SS Lotus* case that international law permits what it does not expressly prohibit.[2] Nevertheless, political thinking about the collective organization of international peace between 1915 and 1919 was very much in universalistic terms. The principle of regionalism was admitted into the League Covenant through the back door, as a product of a determined effort to include a reference to the Monroe Doctrine in the Covenant. The primary formulation of the legal foundation of regionalism is contained in Article 21 which states: 'Nothing in this Covenant shall

1 See generally, H.R. Winkler, *The League of Nations Movement in Great Britain, 1914-1919* (Metuchen, 1967); Theodore Marburg, *The Development of the League of Nations Idea* (New York, 1932); L.S. Woolf, ed., *The Framework of a Lasting Peace* (London, 1917)
2 M.O. Hudson, *World Court Reports* 2 (New York, 1935), 20 at p. 45

be deemed to affect the validity of international engagements, such as treaties of arbitration or regional understandings like the Monroe doctrine, for securing the maintenance of peace.' What became Article 21 was originally an amendment sponsored by President Woodrow Wilson of the United States to Article 10 (see Appendix A).

The formulation of Article 21 provides an illuminating study of the interaction between domestic and international political processes. The Wilson amendment to Article 10 was, in the first instance, a political response to the demands of influential Senate and press opinion in the United States for an explicit recognition of the Monroe Doctrine in the Covenant. In 1919, there was the possibility, though not the certainty, that the United States might refuse to ratify a Covenant which did not contain a reference to the Monroe Doctrine. From the point of view of the Allied Powers in Europe, membership of the United States in the world organization was at least desirable and essential if not imperative. It was against the background of this belief that discussion of the Wilson amendment took place in the Crillon Commission. While the ensuing discussion centred on whether the Monroe Doctrine alone should be singled out for explicit mentioning in the Covenant, there was a strong underlying presumption that regional arrangements could coexist with the League only as supplementary adjuncts to the world organization.

The reception of the Wilson amendment by members of the Crillon Commission which drafted the Covenant was, as one may expect, dictated by considerations of national interest. The British spokesman, Lord Robert Cecil, in welcoming the amendment, let it be known that His Majesty's Government had important reasons for urging the retention of the all-embracing word 'understandings' in the Wilson amendment. According to him, 'so far as the British Empire is concerned, there *are* other understandings. For example, there is the ancient understanding concerning Arabia, and the new understanding with regard to the Kingdom of Hedjas, whereby Great Britain is to direct their foreign relations.'[4] In fact, about a decade later, the British Government was to declare in its reservation on the Kellogg-Briand Pact of 1928 that 'there are certain regions of the world the welfare and integrity of which constitute a special and vital interest of our peace and security' and that the defence of those interests would justify resort to legitimate use of force.[5] The initial French opposition to the Wilson

---

3 D.H. Miller, *The Drafting of the Covenant* I (New York, 1928), 276ff; D.F. Fleming, *The United States and the League of Nations* (New York, 1932), 118-71

4 Miller, *The Drafting* I, 446

5 Cmd 3109 (London, 1929), 25

amendment clearly reflected France's insecurity at the end of World War I. Believing that Article 10 under which members of the League undertook to respect and preserve the territorial integrity of the signatory states against external aggression constituted the backbone of the Covenant, the French Government feared that the Wilson amendment would create uncertainty about the prompt and faithful execution of the Article 10 obligation. The French delegate, Larnaude, read into the amendment a possible excuse for the continuation of the United States policy of indifference to and non-participation in European affairs, and its simultaneous policy of military in-tervention in Latin America. He charged that '[e]very time liberty had been threatened, either in America or in Europe, the United States had either acted upon the [Monroe] Doctrine or had reserved the right to intervene.'[6] The French Government sought firm assurance that the Monroe Doctrine, whenever employed as a guide to the United States foreign policy, would by no means be allowed to prevent the United States from actively participat-ing in European affairs. If France was concerned with the anachronism of American isolationist foreign policy in regard to Europe, Portugal showed interest in the possibility that the explicit mentioning of the Monroe Doc-trine in the Covenant might be interpreted as providing justification for a US policy of excluding the new world organization from promoting peaceful settlement of disputes between the League's Latin American members.[7]

The French and the Portuguese positions clearly reflected the view that the permissibility of regional arrangements and understandings should be understood neither as restricting in any way the obligations of League membership (particularly in the field of collective security) nor as imposing limitations on the geographic area of operation of the League. The Chinese reaction to the Wilson amendment was inspired by a different type of con-sideration. The Chinese delegate, Wellington Koo, cautioned the Crillon Commission against the use of so broad an expression as 'understandings,' arguing that the amendment might create an unfortunate impression that understandings which had in fact become obsolete were still valid.[8] The Chinese objection should be placed in a proper political context: in 1917, following an exchange of notes between the US and Japan, the former rec-ognized what amounted to a Japanese Monroe Doctrine in relation to China. The United States accepted (1917) but later denounced (1921) the Japanese claim that Japan's territorial proximity to China placed the former

6 Miller, *The Drafting* II, 369
7 *Ibid.*, 370
8 *Ibid.*, 371

in a special position similar to that enjoyed by the United States in relation to Latin America.[9] By contending that it was sufficient to mention only the Monroe Doctrine in the amendment, the Chinese Government sought to ensure that the Covenant contained no loophole which might legitimatize the declaration of a Japanese Monroe Doctrine for Asia. It is obvious that discussion on regionalism, regional arrangements, and regional understandings failed to recognize a necessary distinction between a regional understanding among states of a particular region and an understanding held by one state concerning a region. The Monroe Doctrine upon which discussion focused 'states a case of the United States *vs* Europe, and not of the United States *vs* Latin America.'[10]

As the Crillon Commission rejected demands for an authoritative definition of the Monroe Doctrine on the grounds that any attempt at definition might have the effect of either extending or limiting the application of the Doctrine, the question arises concerning the status of the Doctrine and regional understandings like it. Was their existence merely formally recognized or did the Wilson amendment give them legal validity as being compatible with the principles of the Covenant? Lord Robert Cecil's explanation seemed to have been accepted. The Wilson amendment 'gave to these engagements no sanction or validity which they had not previously enjoyed. It accepted them as they were . . . It did not make [the] substance of the [Monroe] Doctrine more or less valid.'[11] But, as the British delegate further added, 'it would not be common sense to deny that such a doctrine has existed, has been acted upon, and has been accepted by other states.'[12] President Wilson held to the view that the inclusion of a reference to the Monroe Doctrine was 'nothing but a recognition of the *fact* that it was not inconsistent with the terms of the Covenant'[13]; he was at every turn willing to give assurances to allay whatever fear France and Portugal might have harboured.

Wilson assured the Crillon Commission that 'if, for any reason, the Monroe Doctrine should take a line of development inconsistent with the principles of the League, the League would be in a position to correct this tendency,'[14] and that 'the Covenant takes precedence of the Monroe Doc-

---

9 C.C. Hyde, 'Legal Aspects of the Japanese Pronouncement in Relation to China,' *AJIL* XXVIII (1934), 431-43; George Blakeslee, 'The Japanese Monroe Doctrine,' *Foreign Affairs* XI (1932-33), 671-81; Yasaka Takaki, 'World Peace Machinery and the Asian Monroe Doctrine,' *Pacific Affairs* V (1932), 941-53
10 US Dept of State, *Memorandum on the Monroe Doctrine* (Washington, 1930), xxiv
11 Miller, *The Drafting* II, 370
12 *Ibid.*
13 *Ibid.*, 373
14 Miller, *The Drafting* I, 442

trine, not only because it is subsequent to it, but because it is a body of definite obligations which the United States cannot explain away even if it wanted to explain.'[15] The authoritative British commentary on the Covenant suggests that the presumption of superiority in favour of the League did exist even outside the meaning and context of Article 20. It states: 'Should any dispute as to the meaning of the latter [i.e., the Monroe Doctrine] ever arise between America and European Powers, the League is there to settle it.'[16] President Wilson reinforced the belief that the explicit recognition of understandings like the Monroe Doctrine was in no way intended to limit the competence of the League to settle disputes among Latin American states which were members of the world organization. The following summary of part of the discussion at the Fifteenth Meeting of the Crillon Commission is especially illuminating:

Mr. Kramar asked whether in the case of a dispute between Paraguay and Uruguay the League of Nations would have the right to come to the aid of whichever of the two States was supported by the decision of the Executive Council.

President Wilson replied in the affirmative.

Lord Robert Cecil believed that the Munroe Doctrine would in no wise prevent the forces of an European State from going to America in order to defend the rights of the oppressed ... The idea that the Monroe Doctrine would prevent the Executive Council, in the execution of an unanimous decision, from acting in Europe, America, Africa or Asia, was a perversion of the Monroe Doctrine, and the citizens of the United States would be the first to disclaim it. President Wilson agreed.[17]

The Wilson amendment to Article 10 was accepted and became Article 21 of the Covenant. The actual text of a legal document like the Covenant may not be overridden by debates and discussions preceeding the document, although it is generally agreed that where the text of a treaty is not sufficiently clear in itself, historical interpretation is permissible so long as it is not allowed to form the sole basis of interpretation.[18] It is therefore appropriate to consider whether the language of Article 21 bears out the claim that there was a clear intention to subordinate regional arrangements and understandings to the League.

In his textual critique of the Covenant, Kelsen maintained that the Monroe Doctrine involved 'a limitation of the field of application of the Coven-

15 *Ibid.*, 459
16 Cmd 151 (London, 1919), 18
17 Miller, *The Drafting* II, 383
18 Lord McNair, *The Law of Treaties* (Oxford, 1961), 411-23; The Vienna Convention on the Law of Treaties, Art. 32, text in *AJIL* LXIII (1968), 875

ant' and concluded that 'the real concordance of these [regional] engagements with the Covenant . . . is only superficially guaranteed.'[19] According
to this scholar, Article 21 carried the following simple message: 'If the
United States of America joins the League of Nations, it shall only benefit
from the provisions of the present Statute or shall only be obligated by it in
so far as the provisions are consistent with the principles of the Monroe
Doctrine.'[20] Kelsen's interpretation is excessively logical. It springs from the
attempt to examine the provision of Article 21 without reference to and independently of other relevant Articles of the Covenant, and from the questionable assumption that Article 21 was a reservation on the entire Covenant. Admittedly, the English text of the Covenant appears to subordinate
the Covenant to the Monroe Doctrine while the French text seems to subordinate the Monroe Doctrine to the Covenant[21]; but it is also true that both
texts were official and authentic. With respect to treaties drafted in more
than one language, the Law of Treaties places the various texts on the level
of equality unless the treaties themselves provide otherwise.[22] As the League
was established to maintain peace not merely among its members but also
within the entire international community, the acceptance of Kelsen's interpretation cannot but have the absurd effect of denuding Articles 3(3), 4(4),
11, and 17 of their intentions. In addition, Article 21 enjoys no special immunity from the provision of Article 20.

Failure to examine Article 21 in the context of and in relation to Articles
3(3), 4(4), 11, 12, 13, 15, 17, and 20 underlies the superficial view that the
Covenant provided little or no aid towards an understanding of the constitutional model of universal-regional relationship outside the provision of
Article 21. The responsibility of the League in the promotion of world peace
was laid down in those Articles, and they by no means gave the world organization an exclusive jurisdiction in the field of peace maintenance. To
have done so would have been to nullify the provision of Article 21. The division of responsibility and competences between the League and regional
arrangements was not based upon any principle of functional specialization
and differentiation. On the contrary, the Covenant seemed to have given

19 Hans Kelsen, 'Legal Technique in International Law: A Textual Critique of the League
   Covenant,' *Geneva Studies* x (1939), 152, 153
20 *Ibid.*, 154-5
21 Sir John F. Williams, *Some Aspects of the Covenant of the League of Nations* (London,
   1934), 63; Dexter Perkins, *A History of the Monroe Doctrine* (rev. ed., Boston, 1958), 297;
   Ray, *Commentaire du Pacte de la Société des Nations* (Paris, 1930), 571-8
22 McNair, *The Law of Treaties*, 432-5; The Vienna Convention on the Law of Treaties, Art.
   33(1)

the League and regional arrangements concurrent jurisdiction in the promotion of peace subject of course to the rule of paramountcy of the obligations of League membership expressly recognized in Article 20. Under this Article, a regional treaty which imposed obligations inconsistent with those of the Covenant was considered abrogated, and any League member signatory to the said treaty was duty bound to procure its release from such obligations immediately. The substance of Article 20 was agreed to unanimously and without any suggestion of amendment.[23] The authors of the Covenant did not consider it necessary to designate the organ competent to determine the question of inconsistency, despite the fact that in the discussion in the Crillon Commission, a concensus appeared to have emerged in favour of a ruling by the League Council.[24] Lauterpacht has pointed out that Article 20 which established the Covenant as the higher law in relation to regional treaties to which League members might adhere 'is not a knife blunted by the cutting of the dead wound of inconsistent treaties in force when states enter the League. It is a perpetual source of legal energy possessed of a dynamic force of its own and calculated to ensure the effectiveness of the Covenant unhampered by any treaties between members whenever concluded.'[25]

EVOLUTION OF THE COVENANT AND THE RISE OF
REGIONAL SECURITY PACTS

The evolution of the principles of the Covenant had great influence on the development of regional arrangements for peace and security. The first of two significant events which encouraged early resort to regional security arrangements was the interpretative resolution on Article 10 of the Covenant sponsored by the Canadian Government. The substance of the draft resolution was that each League member was alone competent to decide to what extent it was willing to employ its military forces in defence of the independence and territorial integrity of a member of the League.[26] Although the negative vote of the Persian delegate prevented the adoption of the draft resolution, the President of the League Assembly did not declare the inter-

23 Miller, *The Drafting* I, 199
24 *Ibid.*
25 Hersch Lauterpacht, '*The Covenant as the* "Higher Law,"' *BYBIL* XVII (1936), 58-9
26 *LNOJ*, Special Suppl., no. 13 (1923), 96; F.H. Soward, 'Canada and the League of Nations,' *International Conciliation*, no. 283 (1932), 359-95; F.P. Walters, *A History of the League of Nations* (London, 1967), 258-9; C.A. Manning, *The Policies of the British Dominions in the League of Nations* (London, 1932), 29-33, 58 *et seq.*

pretative resolution rejected because 'it cannot be argued that in voting as it has done, the Assembly has pronounced in favour of the converse interpretation.'[27] A second related development was the interpretative resolution (adopted by the League Assembly on Article 16) which stipulated that it was the duty of each member of the League to decide for itself whether a breach of the Covenant had occurred and whether it was willing to adopt the measures specified under Article 16.[28] The net effect of the interpretations placed on Articles 10 and 16 was to encourage a minimalist interpretation of the relevant League obligations and hence to undermine the credibility of the collective security system of the League of Nations.[29] It is not difficult to understand why regional arrangements were established mainly in the field of security during the League era.[30] But it is important to bear in mind that the advocacy of regional security pacts between 1920 and 1939 was not a manifestation of an anti-League posture indicating an abandonment of the universal organization. On the contrary, it was conceived as a means of rapidly applying the general system of security, particularly as a resolution of the League Assembly in 1921 had stated that 'agreements between Members of the League, tending to define or complete the engagements contained in the Covenant for the maintenance of peace or the promotion of international co-operation, may be regarded as of a nature likely to contribute to the progress of the League in the path of practical realizations.'[31]

THE LITTLE ENTENTE, HUNGARY, AND THE LEAGUE

A product of political expediency, the Little Entente was the creation of three bilateral treaties called 'defensive Conventions' between Yugoslavia and Czechoslovakia, Rumania and Czechoslovakia, and Rumania and Yugoslavia.[32] As successor states to the Austro-Hungarian Empire, Rumania, Czechoslovakia, and Yugoslavia had a common interest in preventing Hungarian revisionism, the Habsburg monarchical restoration, and the subversion of the Treaty of Trianon and the Treaty of Neuilly. Each of the de-

---

27 *LNOJ*, Special Suppl. no. 13 (1923), 87
28 League of Nations, *Records of the Second Assembly, Minutes of the Committees* I, (1921), 355; S.S. Jones, *The Scandinavian States and the League of Nations* (Princeton, 1939), 217-20
29 Bruce Williams, *State Security and the League of Nations* (Baltimore, 1927), 120ff; W. Rappard, *The Quest for Peace Since the World War* (Cambridge, Mass., 1940), 219ff
30 *Report of the Special Main Committee Set Up to Study the Application of the Principles of the Covenant* (Geneva, 1938).
31 League of Nations, *Records of the Second Assembly, Plenary Meetings* (1921), 833
32 Robert Machray, *The Little Entente* (London, 1929)

fensive Conventions specifically identified Hungary as the state against which the alliances were directed, while the Rumania-Yugoslavia Treaty mentioned Bulgaria in addition. Under the series of bilateral alliances, provision was made for the co-ordination of the foreign policy of the signatory states vis-à-vis Hungary. Perhaps the most important provision in each of the three treaties is Article 2 under which the signatories agreed to come to the aid of each other in the event of an unprovoked attack from Hungary and/or Bulgaria.

In contrast to contemporary defence organizations, the Little Entente lacked permanent institutions in the early 1920s for regular consultation and long-range planning. Notwithstanding this institutional deficiency, the Little Entente was clearly an organization with a great sense of solidarity and purpose. Until 1928, it remained basically a defensive military alliance with a purely external orientation, but in that year, the three states concluded a Treaty of Conciliation and Arbitration along the lines of the model treaty elaborated by the League. This was followed by a major institutional innovation in 1934 when the Little Entente powers transformed their regional organization into something close to a diplomatic federation with a Permanent Council, a Permanent Secretariat, and an Economic Council.[33]

Critics of the Little Entente have asked how an alliance system directed against a specified antagonist could really be peaceful in its relation towards such an enemy in conformity with the obligations of membership of the more inclusive organization to which they all belonged.[34] But there is considerable force in the arguments that regional pacts directed against an aggressor state fitted most accurately into the framework of the League and conformed most closely to its principles, and that a state is not encircled by a group pledged to mutual defence when it can join that group if it so desires.[35] Edward Benes apparently had these arguments in mind when he wrote in 1922: 'It is true that there is one gap in the structure [of the Little Entente]. Hungary still stands outside. She has excluded herself by virtue of her policy, directed as it is against the security of her neighbours. There is no doubt that the isolation cannot be permanent, and that Hungary too will one day take the place in this Central European peace bloc which is hers both politically and economically.'[36]

The relationship between the League of Nations and the Little Entente

---

33 *LNTS* CXXXIX, 233
34 Count Stephen Bethlen, *The Treaty of Trianon and European Peace* (London, 1934), 145ff
35 J. Paul-Boncour, 'Regional Pacts of Mutual Assistance,' in *Report of the Special Main Committee Set Up to Study the Application of the Principles of the Covenant* (Geneva, 1938), 118-23
36 Edward Benes, 'The Little Entente,' *Foreign Affairs* I (1922), 70

can be seen in the manner in which three complaints by the Little Entente powers against Hungary were handled and resolved by the League Council. The peaceful resolution of the issues raised by these incidents through the procedures and machinery of the League shows that the Little Entente did not operate in practice as a competitive rival to the League of Nations.

The Szent-Gotthard incident

On 1 January 1928, some five wagonloads of machine guns, falsely declared as machine parts and clandestinely being transported from Verona in Italy ostensibly to Warsaw in Poland, were uncovered by Hungarian railway officials in Szent-Gotthard at the Austro-Hungarian border.[37] As the shipment had no valid 'transit' permit, the Hungarian authorities proceeded to treat the incident in accordance with customs and railway regulations. The war materials were sold or destroyed despite the fact that the Hungarian authorities had not only been officially notified by the acting President of the League Council that the matter had already been placed on the Council's agenda but had also been advised to suspend action as the matter was shortly to be considered by the League Council.

In a joint declaration, the Little Entente powers announced that the strategy they would follow in dealing with the situation would be based on respect for the duties and responsibility of the League Council in the promotion of world peace.[38] In the spirit of this declaration, the Little Entente powers called upon the League Council to investigate the complaint. When the Council met on 7 March 1928, it set up a Committee of Three to study the complaint, to investigate the incident, and to report back to the full Council. Since the Committee reached the conclusion that there was no evidence that the final destination of the war material was Hungary as alleged by Rumania, Czechoslovakia, and Yugoslavia,[39] the League Council terminated discussion on the complaint by adopting a resolution which amounted to a censure of the manner in which the Hungarian authorities had dealt with the incident.[40] The Little Entente powers were no doubt gratified that international attention was focused upon a question which affected the security of their states and the peace of Europe. Supporters of the League were similarly delighted that the pre-eminence of the universal organization was recognized by the use made of the procedures established under the League machinery.

37 Machray, *The Little Entente*, 330-7; Walters, *A History of the League of Nations*, 400-2
38 *LNOJ* (April 1928), 393
39 *LNOJ* (July 1928), 905
40 *Ibid.*, 909-10

The Hirtenberg affair

The Little Entente powers received information in January 1933 that a large consignment of arms had been delivered from Italy to the cartridge factory at Hirtenberg in Lower Austria. Contending that the importation of arms contravened the terms of Articles 132 and 134 of the Treaty of St Germain which constituted the state of Austria, and dissatisfied with the explanation offered by the Austrian Government, the Little Entente powers accepted the good offices of the Governments of Britain and France which undertook to clear up the matter through diplomatic channels. Significantly, the Little Entente powers, while agreeing to this procedure, indicated to Britain and France that the three powers merely 'postponed the carrying out of their decision to bring the matter before the Council of the League of Nations.'[41]

The political demands of the Little Entente powers were that the arms from Italy should be sent back to the consignor. If the consignor refused to take delivery, the Austrian Government should destroy them and provide evidence that it did so. Moreover, the three Little Entente powers also wanted assurance that no part of the arms had crossed over to Hungary and that similar incidents would not occur again. Fortunately, the Anglo-French negotiation with the Austrian Government led to an agreement under which Austria undertook to send back, and Italy to receive, the controversial war material. The Little Entente powers accepted this settlement, but fearing that the procedure might constitute a precedent for the future, brought the matter to the attention of the Secretary-General of the League of Nations with the request that he communicate the terms of the settlement effected to members of the League Council for their information.[42]

The investigation and settlement of the complaint by the Little Entente powers were conducted outside the League framework, but certainly not against its principles. This procedure was appealing to Britain and France which did not want to embarrass Italy politically. The Little Entente powers themselves could not realistically turn down the offer of good offices from the two leading League members, especially from France which had since 1920 given strong diplomatic backing to Rumania, Czechoslovakia, and Yugoslavia. It is, however, significant that the basic attachment of the Little Entente powers to the procedures and ideals of the League of Nations made it necessary for them not only to expressly reserve their right to ask the League Council to consider the matter at the time they accepted the Anglo-

41 *LNOJ* (March 1933), 398
42 *Ibid.*

French intervention, but also to consider it a matter of utmost importance that the League Council be notified officially of the settlement of the affair.

The Marseilles tragedy
The crisis arising from the assassination in October 1934 of King Alexander I of Yugoslavia and Louis Barthou, the French Minister of Foreign Affairs, provided yet another occasion for testing the respect that the Little Entente powers had for the obligations of League membership. On this occasion, as in others, the three powers took their case before the League Council. Yugoslavia supported by Rumania and Czechoslovakia charged Hungary with complicity in the assassination and in the general terrorist activities directed against the Yugoslav state. They requested the League to investigate the odious crime which not only adversely affected relations between Yugoslavia and Hungary but also threatened to disturb international peace.[43]

The League Council's consideration of the Yugoslav request in December 1934 provides an example of how differences of opinion on the part of the major powers had great bearing on the manner in which crises were resolved. France placed its full diplomatic support behind Yugoslavia. Laval, the French representative on the League Council, considered the assassination and the revisionist policy pursued by Hungary as serious threats to European peace.[44] While generally condemning terrorism and political assassination, Aloisi of Italy upheld the revisionist demand by Hungary as legitimate and urged the League not to ignore it.[45] Eden of Britain attempted to mediate the views of Laval and Aloisi. Not surprisingly, he was unanimously appointed as Rapporteur. After reviewing the evidence before him, the British Representative concluded that certain Hungarian officials, through negligence, might have incurred responsibilities in connection with the preparation of the assassination.[46] The League Council resolution directed the Hungarian Government to punish those of its officials whose culpability might be established by an official inquiry and to report the steps taken to the Council. As supporters of an effective League, the Little Entente powers called upon the universal organization to take cognizance of and responsibility for defusing a crisis which had all the potentialities of

---

43 *LNOJ* (December 1934), 1766. See generally J.S. Pacy, 'Hungary, the League of Nations and the Assassination of King Alexander of Yugoslavia: A Case Study of the Resolution of an International Political Crisis,' unpublished Ph.D thesis, The American University, 1971
44 *Ibid.*, 1730-1
45 *Ibid.*, 1732
46 *Ibid.*, 1759

generating war between the three allied powers of the Little Entente on the one hand and Hungary, their neighbour, on the other.[47]

In a Memorandum dated 9 February 1925, the German Government proposed the establishment of a regional security pact and a comprehensive arbitration treaty among those powers interested in the Rhine, particularly among Britain, France, Italy, and Germany.[48] The German Memorandum was conspicuously silent on the relationship between the proposed security system and the League of Nations. The response to the German initiative drafted by France on behalf of her allies stipulated certain conditions which had to be satisfied before the German proposals could be seriously considered.[49] The first of three major conditions was that the search for regional guarantees of security should involve no modification of the peace treaties. The second stipulated that nothing in the proposed pact should affect the rights and obligations of League membership under the Covenant. The third demanded that the regional agreement must base itself completely on the principles, actual mechanisms, and procedures of the League. Thus, right from the very beginning of the new venture in regional security arrangement, the leadership of the League was careful not to compromise the position of the League as the dominant international instrument for the preservation of peace. At Locarno, the following treaties and conventions were concluded: a Treaty of Mutual Guarantee between Germany, Belgium, France, Britain, and Italy (the Rhine Pact); arbitration Conventions between Germany and Belgium, Germany and France, Germany and Czechoslovakia, Germany and Poland; a Treaty between France and Poland, France and Czechoslovakia; a Collective Note to Germany Regarding Article 16 of the Covenant of the League of Nations, and a Final Protocol of the Locarno Conference.[50]

The preamble to the Rhine Pact claimed that the purpose of the treaty was to give the signatory powers 'supplementary guarantees within the framework of the Covenant of the League of Nations.' This claim is amply borne out by a careful analysis of other provisions of the Rhine Pact. For

---

47 *Ibid.*, 1760
48 Cmd. 2435 (London, 1925). See generally P.B. Wehn, 'Germany and the Treaty of Locarno – 1925,' unpublished Ph.D thesis, Columbia University, 1968
49 *Ibid.*
50 Cmd 2525 (London, 1925); *AJIL*, Suppl. xx (1926), 21

instance, the obligation undertaken not to resort to war against each other exempted actions in pursuance of Article 16 of the Covenant (Article 2). In cases where two parties to a dispute failed to accept the recommendations of a conciliation commission, the Pact required that the matter be brought before the League Council which would then deal with it in accordance with Article 15 of the League Covenant (Article 3). In addition, any allegation by a signatory of the Rhine Pact that Article 2 of the Pact, Article 42 or 43 of the Treaty of Versailles had been violated was to be brought before the Council of the League (Article 4). Article 7 expressly recognized the paramountcy of League obligations. In fact, the Rhine Pact empowered the League to terminate the entire Locarno regional security arrangement once the League was satisfied it had acquired sufficient strength to enable it to protect any of the Rhine Pact powers from external aggression (Article 8). The provisions of the Rhine Pact were so completely subordinated to the principles, obligations, laws, and procedures of the League and its Covenant that their implementation depended ultimately on action by the League Council.[51] Sir Austen Chamberlain was quite sincere when, on the occasion of the deposit of the Locarno Treaties in the Archives of the League, he remarked that 'in placing these documents under the guardianship of the League and attributing to the League all the authority which is therein specified . . . we have made a contribution which . . . will be acceptable to the League towards the support and increase of its authority and strength.'[52]

While no one expected the Little Entente or the Balkan Entente as regional organizations composed of small and less powerful states to be capable of posing a real challenge to a League of Nations supported firmly and genuinely by political heavyweights like Britain, France, Germany, and Italy, the same view cannot be held in regard to the Locarno system composed of the most powerful members of the world organization. A historian of the League, reflecting on the consequences of the use made of the Locarno regional arrangement, has observed that 'the Covenant itself seemed to be in danger of oblivion. The Locarno group was to some extent a re-embodiment of the old Concert of Europe; it reached its conclusions, not by respecting the principles, nor by using the methods, of the League, but by finding diplomatic compromises between the wishes and interests of the

---

51 Walters, *A History of the League of Nations*, 291; Arregui, 'Le Régionalisme dans L'Organisation Internationale,' *Recueil des Cours* LII (1935), part III, 49-50; W.R. Bisschop, 'The Locarno Pact,' *TGS* XI (1925), 79-112; Edward Benes, 'After Locarno: The Problem of Security Today,' *Foreign Affairs* IV (1926) 62-72
52 *LNOJ* (February 1926), 179

great powers.'[53] There is much to be said for this indictment of the Locarno security system; but the charge hides an important truth. The establishment of the Locarno system was not responsible for the oligarchical domination of the League by the Great Powers. At best, what could be said is that the Locarno arrangement provided a convenient machinery for great power management of the League of Nations system which had existed since 1920. It is certain that if the Locarno system had not existed, the Great Powers would have invented alternative machinery for the management of the League system. Therefore, when castigating the Locarno system for anti-Covenant behaviour, it is necessary, though difficult, to distinguish between the behaviour of Great Britain, France, Germany, and Italy as leading members of the League, and the collective behaviour of the same major powers as members of the Locarno regional system.

The Permanent Court of International Justice was being realistic when it observed in the *Mosul* case that '[i]t is hardly conceivable that resolutions on questions affecting the peace of the world could be adopted against the will of those amongst the Members of the [League] Council who, although in a minority, would, by reason of their political position, have to bear the larger share of the responsibilities and consequences ensuring therefrom.'[54] In an international system of uneven distribution of power among competing nation-states, agreement or disagreement among the most powerful states has always provided the major critical issue bearing upon the nature of international politics. In the League days, great power disagreement was no less important than great power agreement. Yet there has been a tendency to overemphasize the degree of unity existing among the Locarno powers, which predisposes commentators to interpret the anti-League behaviour of the Great Powers as a manifestation of the Locarno front *against* the League. However, as members of the Locarno group, Britain and France placed different interpretations on the significance of the Rhine Pact. From the British point of view, the guarantees offered under the Rhine Pact were far from being the centre of the agreement, but merely an incidental part of a broad policy of reconciliation of Germany with France in particular and with the League members in general.[55] But the Locarno Pact did not give France a full sense of security because Britain was prepared to commit herself only to the defence of the West and not of the East of the Rhine. This

53 Walters, *A History of the League of Nations*, 342
54 Hudson, *World Court Reports* 1, 741
55 Alfred Wolfers, *Britain and France Between Two Wars* (Hamden, 1963), 254ff

may explain why France never really ceased to regard the League as another instrument for keeping Germany in her place.[56] The Locarno group was certainly much less cohesive than the Little Entente, and it is hardly surprising that this regional security system ceased to exist, for all practical purposes, after the German remilitarization of the Rhineland in 1936.

During the crises which developed in Europe in the middle of 1930s, Britain and France abandoned the League's rules and principles and left the authority of the League undeveloped. This was not for the purpose of revitalizing the Locarno system but rather for appeasing Germany and Italy to whom the Locarno arrangement had become politically irrelevant by 1936. The foreign policy of the major powers clearly reflected an opportunism which showed little respect for either the League obligations or the Locarno principles. To deny that there was a Locarno front against the League is not to fail to take cognizance of the obvious fact that the League, in spite of the democratic tenor of its Covenant, was dominated in practice by an oligarchy of Britain, France, Germany, and Italy – all signatories to the Locarno Pact.

THE INTER-AMERICAN SYSTEM, THE UNITED STATES, AND THE LEAGUE

The Inter-American System, now better known as the Organization of American States, has since 1890 been a regional organization in the Western Hemisphere dominated by the United States.[57] Two considerations have great bearing on the character of the relationship between the League and the Inter-American System in the promotion of pacific settlement of disputes in Latin America. The first is that the United States was not a member of the League. The vote for ratification of the Covenant on 19 March 1920 did not secure the necessary two-thirds majority in the Senate. Washington, however, participated in many of the League's non-political activities.[58] In the Fifth Reservation of the US Senate on the Covenant, the US Government reserved the right to oppose and prevent the League from extending its jurisdiction to the Western Hemisphere. The Senate reservation stated: 'The United States will not submit to arbitration or to inquiry

56 *Ibid.*, 155, 180
57 A.P. Whitaker, *The Western Hemisphere Idea: Its Rise and Decline* (Ithaca, 1954); A. van W. Thomas and A.J. Thomas, *The Organization of American States* (Dallas, 1963); Gordon Cornell-Smith, *The Inter-American System* (London, 1966); F.V. Garcia-Amador, *The Inter-American System* (Dobbs Ferry, 1966)
58 D.F. Fleming, *The United States and World Organization 1920-1933* (New York, 1938)

by the [A]ssembly or by the [C]ouncil of the League of Nations . . . any questions which in the judgment of the United States depend upon or relate to its long-established policy, commonly known as the Monroe Doctrine; said [D]octrine is to be interpreted by the United States alone and is hereby declared to be wholly outside the jurisdiction of the said League of Nations and entirely unaffected by any provision contained in the . . . treaty of peace with Germany.'[59] From a strictly legal point of view, a Senate reservation like this cannot alter an international agreement,[60] but such pronouncement by a major power occupying a dominant position in the Western Hemisphere could not in practice be ignored. Second, a great majority of the Latin American republics sought membership in the League partly as a means of diluting the enormous influence of the United States in Latin America.[61]

The Chaco conflict
The boundary dispute between Bolivia and Paraguay provides the most illuminating study of the relationship between the League of Nations and the Inter-American System in the promotion of peace.[62] The League faced a dilemma when called upon to act. As Arthur Sweetser put it, '[i]f it did, there was a risk, though not the certainty, of antagonizing the United States; if it did not, there was the certainty of alienating and perhaps losing Latin America.'[63] As far as the League was concerned, its assertion of competence was the lesser of the two evils. Commenting on the significance of the League's bold decision to intervene, the delegate from Uruguay, Antuna, observed:

The Council's action deserves to be emphasized, implying as it does a recognition of the fact that Latin America constitutes an integral part of the League. This serves to dissipate what was felt to be a very real anomaly, in that, despite the American countries' membership of the League, the latter appeared to take no action where

---

59 Henry C. Lodge, *The Senate and the League of Nations* (New York, 1925), 186
60 See Reservations to the Convention on Genocide, Advisory Opinion, *ICJ Reports* (1951), 15; Vienna Convention on the Law of Treaties, Art. 21(2), text in *AJIL* LXIII (1968), 875
61 W.H. Ketchner, *Latin American Relations With the League of Nations* (Boston, 1929)
62 Margaret La Foy, *The Chaco Dispute and the League of Nations* (Ann Arbor, 1946); William R. Garner, *The Chaco Dispute: A Study in Prestige Diplomacy* (Washington, 1966); Bryce Wood, *The United States and Latin American Wars, 1932-1942* (New York, 1966); Walters, *A History of the League of Nations*, 526-36
63 Arthur Sweetser, 'The Practical Working of the League of Nations: A Concrete Example,' *International Conciliation*, no. 249 (1929), 201

problems affecting America were concerned . . . The frank and timely intervention of the Council at its Lugano session established a precedent of the greatest significance both for Latin America and for the League. This action . . . had the effect of binding Latin America more closely to the League, now that the League's apparent hesitation in regard to American question due perhaps to the over-rigid interpretation of Article 21 of the Covenant has been disproved.[64]

The general satisfaction of Latin American leaders at the unprecedented assertion of League compete'nce over a dispute between two of its Latin American members was understandable. The first decade of the League of Nations had been characterized by an over-rigid interpretation of Article 21 of the Covenant. It was generally believed in Latin America that the influence of the United States had prevailed upon the League and had prevented the latter from asserting its lawful competence to take cognizance of the Tacna-Arica dispute (1920) between Chile, Peru, and Bolivia, and the Panama-Costa Rica boundary conflict (1921). In connection with the Tacna-Arica dispute, the United States requested Brazil to transmit to the League Council 'a suggestion that the Council of the League of Nations do not take cognizance at the present time of the Tacna-Arica which Bolivia is reported to have referred to the League of Nations.'[65] Under pressure from the United States, Peru, which had requested the League to revise the Treaty of 1883 between herself and Chile, withdrew the request. The League itself disclaimed competence to intervene on the grounds that 'the Assembly of the League of Nations cannot itself modify any treaty, the obligation of treaties lying solely within the competence of the contracting States.'[66] In the Panama-Costa Rica boundary case, Panama appealed to the world organization for intervention; but the League stood helpless while a dispute between two of its members was settled by a partisan non-League member, the United States.[67] The basis of us policy was the Monroe Doctrine. But the Latin American leaders had not forgotten that Salvador received no satisfactory answer when in 1920, she asked Washington for the authentic interpretation of the Monroe Doctrine as the us government then understood it.[68] Again, the official League reply to the Costa Rican request for the interpretation placed by the League of Nations on the Monroe Doc-

64 *LNOJ*, Special Suppl., no. 75 (1928), 35
65 *FRUS* 1 (1920), 341
66 League of Nations, *Records of the Second Assembly, Plenary Meetings*, 1921, p. 466
67 Gordon Ireland, *Boundaries, Possessions, and Conflicts in Central and North America and the Caribbean* (Cambridge, Mass., 1941), 33-42
68 *FRUS* 1 (1920), 225

trine and the scope given to that Doctrine when it was included in Article 21 of the Covenant did nothing more than restate the substance of Lord Robert Cecil's remarks in 1919 which at that time satisfied no one.[69] The period between 1920 and 1928 was clearly characterized by excessive deference on the part of the League to the the Monroe Doctrine.

When the Bolivia-Paraguay conflict first broke out (1928), the League initially hesitated to intervene but subsequently acted when it became clear that Washington's first reaction to the League's intervention was milder and more friendly than was anticipated from a nation that had declared she would not tolerate non-American intervention in Latin America. Kellogg, the US Secretary of State, made it known from the beginning that 'while the Government of the United States is of course always willing to lend its good offices in the cause of international harmony, it does not wish at the present time . . . to be placed in the position of undertaking to settle the boundary dispute between Bolivia and Paraguay, either by arbitration or other procedure.'[70] What Ambassador Lodge (at the time of the Guatemalan affair in 1954) called the fundamental question of venue arose when Bolivia, charging Paraguay with aggression in breach of the provisions of Articles 10 and 13 of the Covenant, called for League intervention, and at the same time joined Paraguay in accepting the mediation of the International Conference of American States on Conciliation and Arbitration.[71] The determination of the League to assert its competence was clearly indicated in an aide-memoire of 18 December 1928 handed down to Argentina and the United States. The Note stated inter alia:

If, in the next few days, the two Governments do not, in some form or the other, accept such mediation as will afford a likelihood of the settling by the pacific methods of the request for reparation submitted by the Bolivian Government – thereby excluding the possibility of further hostilities – the Council will, in such an eventuality, have to consider what measure should be taken, either because war has broken out – or because it is on the point of breaking out – between two Members of the League, neither of which appears to recognize any common contractual obligation not to resort to war other than that arising under the League Covenant, by which they are both bound.[72]

69 *LNOJ* (1928), 1608. Lord Robert Cecil had expressed the view in 1919 that 'any attempt at definition [of the Monroe Doctrine] might extend or limit its application.' See Miller, *The Drafting* II, 369-70
70 *FRUS* I (1928), 672
71 *Ibid.*, 695
72 *LNOJ* (February 1929), 266

The United States did not, however, over-react to the readiness of the League to extend its jurisdiction to the Western Hemisphere probably because, as Wilson, the us Minister in Switzerland, observed in a telegram to Kellogg on 11 December 1928, the League 'had . . . borne deeply in mind the relation of the United States to this question and had endeavored so to frame the message that it could not be interpreted as contravening the Monroe Doctrine or conflicting with any possible action on our part.'[73]

During the first phase of the dispute, the burden of finding a peaceful settlement fell squarely on a five-member Neutral (McCoy) Commission of Inquiry and Conciliation established by the International Conference of American States on Conciliation and Arbitration. The League confined itself mainly to supporting the efforts of the McCoy Commission. Neither the regional nor the universal organization made efforts to co-ordinate its activities with the other between 1929, when a temporary cessation of hostility was secured, and 1932 when renewed fighting broke out.

In a Note to the us Minister in Switzerland, the State Department declared that the strategy of the us Government was that of 'staving off any independent action on the part of the League in the matter,' but that 'if either Bolivia or Paraguay makes a request of the [League] Assembly . . . to study the matter, it [the League Assembly] will have to do so.'[74] The us Government further expressed the hope that the League 'will continue not to get into the matter any more than it absolutely has to, and that if it has to take action, it will use its influence to support what the Neutral Commission in Washington is doing.'[75] Washington conceded that it could not stop the League from entertaining a request for action from either of the parties to the conflict. Almost simultaneously, Geneva was making it unmistakably clear that in as much as the situation was one which might disturb the peace or the good understanding between two members of the League, the other members could not regard the situation with indifference.[76] A League Committee of Three established to keep an eye on the Latin American situation promptly announced that it would give all possible support to the endeavours of the Neutral Commission and requested that Commission to keep the Committee informed of whatever peace initiatives were being taken.[77] Although the United States did not expound the thesis of *exclusive* Inter-American regional competence over the Bolivia-Paraguay conflict, she

73 *FRUS* i (1928), 686
74 *FRUS* v (1932), 222
75 *Ibid.*, 226
76 *LNOJ* (1932), 1575
77 *LNOJ* (December 1932), 1924

openly declared her preference for the use of the regional peace machinery. White, the Assistant Secretary of State, made it abundantly clear in November 1932 that the US Government had no objection to keeping the members of the League Council informed of the activities of the Neutral Commission 'so long as they play the game with us,' and warned that 'the Neutral Commission cannot afford . . . to be put in the position that is subordinate to the League,' and that the League 'can only work through it or as permitted by it.'[78] Thus, for instance, when the League's Committee of Three first proposed the establishment of a Military Commission to be dispatched to Chaco on a fact-finding mission, the Neutral Commission immediately informed Sir Eric Drummond, the Secretary-General of the League, that the Neutral Commission believed that the nations of America, working in common accord, were capable of preserving peace in the Western Hemisphere and indeed were planning a new peace offensive.[79]

The increasing frustration experienced by the Neutral Commission and the formal declaration of war by Paraguay on 10 May 1933 led the United States to accept, probably grudgingly, the necessity for establishing a Military Commission of the League of Nations. Washington then proposed that any commission which the League might send to the Chaco should appropriately be composed entirely of Latin American states.[80] With this in mind, the Neutral Commission persuaded Argentina, Brazil, Chile and Peru – the so-called ABCP group – to act as mediators. The acceptance of this role by the ABCP Powers paved the way for withdrawal of the Neutral Commission from the scene.

Experience has shown that if there is more than one center of negotiation confusion and lack of agreement are the inevitable results. The Commission therefore feels that it can best contribute to peace on this continent by withdrawing from negotiations. Thus negotiations can be centered in Geneva, if other peace agencies will take a similar attitude, allowing the League Committee to work with universal support for peace.[81]

In view of the above statement, it is not clear why the parties to the conflict should have urged the League to confer upon the ABCP Powers a wide mandate to intervene in place of the League's Military Commission.[82] However,

78 *FRUS* v (1932), 245
79 *Ibid.*, 258, 259
80 *FRUS* iv (1933), 340
81 *Ibid.*, 343-4
82 *LNOJ* (September 1933), 1083

the League Council reluctantly acquiesced and accordingly requested the ABCP Powers to submit a formula for the settlement of the conflict. The failure of the ABCP initiative brought the League back into the centre of peace-searching activities. The League Commission was despatched to the Chaco. The Military Commission (composed of Britain, France, Italy, Spain, and Mexico) apparently enjoyed the goodwill of the American states. At their Seventh International Conference in December 1933, they extended 'a cordial greeting to the Commission whose high purposes made it worthy of the recognition of the nations of America.'[83] The League Commission's Report was rejected by Paraguay, and the prospect of an early termination of conflict and settlement of the dispute faded.

Undaunted in its peace-promoting efforts, the Committee of Three, without invoking any specific provision of the Covenant, considered the possibility of imposing an arms embargo on Bolivia and Paraguay as a means of weakening their capacity to wage war. The League Council did not make any recommendation concerning the imposition of an economic sanction. Of the League members, twenty-eight prohibited the sale of arms to the belligerents on their own initiative, hoping that their action would help to bring about an early termination of hostilities. The Chaco arms embargo was a lesson in the inefficacy of economic sanctions as a means of terminating conflict or of inducing changed behaviour from states which the international community considers as threatening world peace. Chile refused to prohibit transit of arms across its territory; Uruguay to impose the embargo. Some states made their co-operation conditional on the action of other states, while others excepted contracts made before the embargo went into effect. Consequently, the Chaco arms embargo, as a form of economic pressure, proved ineffective.[84] In fact, the subsequent use of economic coercion by international organizations in the search for world peace has hardly been more successful than the Chaco experiment.[85]

The extremely slow progress towards the settlement of the Chaco conflict was partly due to disagreements and political rivalry between the states of the Inter-American System, especially between the United States

83 J.B. Scott, ed., *The International Conferences of American States: First Supplement, 1933-1940* (Washington, 1940), 84
84 M.O. Hudson, 'The Chaco Arms Embargo,' *International Conciliation*, no. 320 (1936); RIIA., *International Sanctions* (London, 1938), chap. iv
85 Albert Highley, 'The First Sanctions Experiment,' *Geneva Studies* IX (1938); R. St J. Macdonald, 'The Resort to Economic Coercion by International Political Organizations,' *University of Toronto Law Journal* XVII (1967), 86-169; Margaret Doxey, *Economic Sanctions and International Enforcement* (London, 1971)

and Argentina.[86] Cordell Hull confessed in December 1934 that 'the time has not yet come when efficient Machinery is functioning nor have the peace machinery created by common agreement between the American nations so far acquired sufficient prestige to prove their usefulness at this juncture. Frequently, the peace efforts of the American nations during the years of the continuation of the Chaco dispute have broken down as a result of disagreement between the American mediating nations.'[87] Besides the political squabbles among the American states, the lack of confidence of the belligerents in the political neutrality of some of the neighbouring states partly accounted for the prolonged failure of Inter-American peace efforts. Surprisingly perhaps, the Buenos Aires Peace Conference which brought the conflict to an end was organized by the Latin American nations themselves.[88] But the remarks of the Portuguese member of the League Council may be regarded as an appropriate epitaph on the role the League had played in the adjustment of the dispute. According to de Vasconcelles, the Buenos Aires Peace Conference brought to a happy conclusion 'a conflict which has often led to unjust attacks against the League of Nations, without the latter ever having been discouraged in its action, pursued with perseverance, zeal and wisdom.'[89]

The Leticia conflict

The League of Nations was the central third party in the adjustment of the boundary dispute between Colombia and Peru. The Treaty of 1922, fixing the boundary between both countries, awarded Leticia to Colombia. In September 1932, some Peruvians attacked Leticia on their own authority. When the Colombian Government retaliated by force of arms, the Peruvian authorities felt bound to support the initially unauthorized action of the Peruvian citizens of Loreto. The result was a military conflict between two Latin American members of the League.[90]

The precise character of the relationship between the Inter-American System and the League of Nations in the settlement of the Leticia conflict was determined by a fortunate convergence of interests of both the United

86 Garner, *The Chaco Dispute, passim*; H. Peterson, *Argentina and the United States, 1810-1960* (New York, 1964), 385-9
87 *FRUS* iv (1934), 115
88 L.R. Rout, Jr, *The Politics of the Chaco Peace Conference, 1935-1939* (Austin, 1969)
89 *LNOJ* (February 1936), 87-8
90 Russell M. Cooper, *American Consultation in World Affairs* (New York, 1934), 285ff; Wood, *The United States and Latin American Wars, 1932-1942*, 169ff; Walters, *A History of the League of Nations*, 536-40

States and the world organization. In a dispatch to the US Ambassador in Peru on 5 September 1932, the American Secretary of State gave the following instruction which formed the basis of Washington's policy: 'The orderly procedure to follow in this case would seem to be to disavow the [Peruvian] occupation of Leticia and to assist in restoring Colombian authority there or at the very least to do nothing to thwart the re-establishment by Colombia of its jurisdiction ... To endeavour to negotiate on the basis of the occupation of Leticia by Peru is in effect to consider the boundary treaty a scrap of paper.'[91] Two days later, Stimson added: 'We are willing to do what we can to assist in a friendly manner to keep the question within proper bounds, but we have no responsibility to act as sole guardian of peace of Latin America nor do we desire to assume such responsibility.'[92] Unlike the Panama-Costa Rica boundary conflict of 1921 when the United States secured a settlement by threatening Panama with sanctions, the United States from the beginning seemed to have ruled out any unilateral intervention aimed at terminating the Leticia conflict. Washington committed herself to the maintenance of the territorial status quo ante bellum, that is, to a solution based strictly on respect for the Treaty of 1922 which Colombia and Peru had both ratified.

Peru externalized the dispute in October 1932 when she urged the Inter-American Permanent Commission in Washington – one of the two Commissions set up by the Gondra Treaty of 1923 – to institute an inquiry with a view to promoting a peaceful settlement. Colombia curiously enough objected to an external intervention claiming that the situation in Leticia fell within her domestic jurisdiction. In an effort to keep the situation within the American family of nations, Brazil formulated a set of proposals calling for the neutralization and demilitarization of Leticia, the administration of the disputed region by Brazil for a short period, followed by the return of Leticia to Colombia which would then administer it until such a time as Colombia and Peru were able to reach a mutually agreeable settlement by direct negotiation. The Brazilian proposals, though endorsed by the United States, were flatly rejected by Peru.[93]

Meanwhile, the Colombian Government had asked the League to intervene under Article 15 of the Covenant. The League's role should be examined in the light of the meeting which took place between Stimson and the Ambassadors of Britain, France, Italy, Germany, and Japan in Washington in January 1933.[94] Stimson discussed the Leticia dispute in the context of

91 *FRUS* v (1932), 278
92 *Ibid.*, 280
93 *LNOJ* (April 1933), 557
94 *FRUS* iv (1933), 421-2

the Kellogg-Briand Pact of 1928 which prohibited recourse to war as an instrument of national policy[95] and made no reference whatsoever to the role the League could play and indeed had been playing in promoting a peaceful settlement. At that meeting, Stimson informed the senior League members that the United States preferred and would support a solution along the lines of the Brazilian proposals. The fact that the League Council convened at all to consider the Colombian request may be interpreted as a clear assertion of competence to take cognizance of a dispute between two of its members in the Western Hemisphere. It was also a gentle rebuff to the United States which preferred to see the dispute resolved within the framework of the Kellogg-Briand Pact. However, one should not lose sight of the strong probability that the similarity between the League's proposed solution and the Brazilian formula endorsed by the United States might have been the measure of Washington's influence on the League of Nations.

The high-water mark of collaboration between the world organization, the Latin American nations, and the United States was the creation of a League of Nations Commission composed of Brazil, the United States, and Spain and empowered to administer Leticia for one year 'in the name of the Government of Colombia.'[96] A Memorandum prepared by White, the US Assistant Secretary of State, following a discussion with the Colombian Foreign Minister in March 1933, summarized the relationship between the US Government and the League of Nations in regard to the Leticia conflict:

The League, on its part, took action on a dispute between two of its members without any consultation with us whatsoever and after taking this action, had advised us thereof . . . Later on, the League presented a definite plan to Colombia and Peru. This plan was drawn up without any consultation with us and without our prior knowledge. We were asked to support the plan and we did so because we felt that the plan offered a satisfactory solution to the matter.[97]

Although the proposals of the League's Committee of Three providing the framework for the League policy were formulated without the knowledge of the United States, Washington was informed about them and indeed gave its approval before the proposals were submitted to the League Council for formal endorsement.[98] Thus, while rightly emphasizing the vigorous assertion of competence by the League of Nations, White underesti-

---

95 J.T. Shotwell, *War as an Instrument of National Policy* (New York, 1929); Edwin Berchard, 'The Multilateral Treaty for the Renunciation of War,' *AJIL* XXIII (1929), 116-20
96 *LNMS* XIII (1933), 105
97 *FRUS* IV (1933), 500
98 Cooper, *American Consultation in World Affairs*, 340-1

mated the political significance of US consultation with the senior members of the League. It was not merely accidental that the solution proposed by the League was closely tied to the status quo ante bellum, a policy goal to which the United States had been committed from the beginning. Similarly, it could hardly have been purely accidental that two of the three members of the League of Nations Commission for the administration of Leticia were from the United States and Brazil. The inclusion of Spain which had extremely close ties with Latin America was in all likelihood part of the Geneva strategy designed to emphasize the fact that the League had vital interest in matters affecting world peace.

The League set a precedent in trying to supervise the adjustment of a dispute in the traditional backyard of the United States. Cordell Hull later recalled that the decision to accept the League's invitation to participate in the work of the League Commission for the administration of Leticia was a 'delicate' one in as much as it involved acquiescence in the League's assumption of jurisdiction over a dispute in the heart of the Western Hemisphere without of course infringing in any way the Monroe Doctrine.[99] Credit for the resolution of the Leticia dispute belongs to the League of Nations which succeeded because of, and not in spite of, the convergence of the interests of the United States and Brazil with those of the League. Although the peace machinery of the Inter-American System was not directly involved in the final adjustment of the dispute, it is probable that Brazil acted unofficially on behalf of and in the interest of the members of the American family of nations.

Regional organizations were not the dominant agencies in the promotion of world order between the two World Wars but this is not quite the same as saying that the League of Nations proved to be an effective universal international peace machinery. The dynamics of international relations between the two World Wars cannot be adequately explained in terms of conflict and collaboration between the universal and the regional organizations or even between international regional systems of public order. The politics of universal-regional relationship became more important after 1945, because the world of the UN Charter differed significantly from that of the League Covenant.[100]

The 'failure' of the League, especially in the 1930s, arose mainly from the inability of the Great Powers to deal with those individual big powers who

---

99 Cordell Hull, *The Memoirs of Cordell Hull* 1 (New York, 1948), 310-11
100 C.W. Jenks, *The World Beyond the Charter* (London, 1969)

disregarded with impunity the law of the Covenant: the Japanese by occupying Manchuria, the Italians by annexing Albania and conquering Ethiopia, the Germans by annexing Austria and Czechoslovakia, and the Russians by occupying Finland.[101] The behaviour of the Great Powers between the World Wars can be explained with only a passing reference to their membership in the Locarno security system. The lack of cohesion in the Locarno group, the divergent conception of the value of the League among the Locarno members, and the political difference between Britain and France on the German question make it unrealistic to hypothesize the pattern of political conflict between 1920 and 1939 as one between the universal system of the League and the regional arrangement of Locarno. A predisposition to maintain at all cost the integrity of the Locarno at the expense of, and as a counterweight to, the League was not part of the policy of the members of the Locarno Pact. In contrast, the weakening of the influence and effectiveness of the United Nations has resulted partly from the increasing reliance being placed on regional organizations, especially by the big powers in both the Eastern and Western camps.

The relationship between the League and the Little Entente was complementary. The collective international behaviour of Rumania, Czechoslovakia, and Yugoslavia was as much dictated by the considerations of national interest as by the conception of the League as a superior international peace machinery. There is no doubt that the leaders of the three Little Entente powers linked the continued existence of their states as sovereign entities with the preservation of the integrity and authority of the League as the dominant international instrument for peace. Consequently, they tailored their foreign policy towards ensuring the effectiveness of the League.[102] In fact, it was Czechoslovakia probably acting on behalf of and with the support of the Little Entente powers which sought in 1921 to amend Article 21 so that all agreements between two or more members of the League would either be subject to the express approval of the League or negotiated under the direct auspices of the world organizations.[103]

Early in the 1920s, there were ominous signs that the United States, having refused to join the League, would oppose any possible extension of the jurisdiction of the League into the Western Hemisphere. Influential Americans like Henry Taft and Elihu Root captured the mood of the us Senate

101 Sir Albert Zimmern, *The League of Nations and the Rule of Law 1918-1935* (London, 1936)
102 Stefan Osusky, 'The Little Entente and the League of Nations,' *International Affairs* (London) XIII (1934), 373-93
103 *LNOJ* (May 1921) 252

when they urged Washington to regard even the most peaceful interventions of the League as 'contrary to the Monroe Doctrine.'[104] The leaders of the Geneva organization could not completely ignore the mood of the US Government, especially in the 1920s when the 'unofficial observer' of the United States in the League-sponsored meetings was 'something between a guest and a spy in a gathering called and financed by an organization which his Government considered too dangerous to approach except with the most extreme caution.'[105] But, beginning from 1928, and contrary to expectation, the Monroe Doctrine and the Inter-American System did not threaten the superior position of the League. Confrontation based upon a claim by either of exclusive jurisdiction was notably absent and mutual deference did exist. The League's hesitancy and caution reflected the hard political reality that disputes among its Latin American members were taking place in the backyard of a powerful non-League member. Washington's subsequent co-operation, even if not overtly enthusiastically given, reflected the increasing recognition among policy makers in Washington that the settlement of intra-Western Hemisphere disputes by the League need not be incompatible with the tenet of the Monroe Doctrine. The disputes the League attempted to settle in Latin America were connected with international boundaries which created intolerable situations in the Americas, but hardly interfered with the interests of the United States. Another possible explanation for flexibility in US behaviour is that the senior members of the League showed themselves politically sensitive to the American views without, of course abdicating the responsibility of the League. It is thus hardly surprising that the United States placed no serious obstacle in the way of League intervention, even though Washington indicated a definite preference for using regional machinery in the settlement of Western Hemisphere disputes.

The experience of the League and the Inter-American System in promoting peace in Latin America drew attention to the need for improving relations between the world and regional peace machinery. Colombia, in a letter to the President of the League Assembly in 1934, called for the establishment of a formal link between the League and the Pan-American Union and in particular for the appointment of official observers by both organizations to follow the work of the other.[106] The League Assembly postponed consideration on the proposal pending the publication of a similar study al-

104 Henry W. Taft, 'The Monroe Doctrine,' *League of Nations* II (1919), 154; C [Elihu Root?], 'The Monroe Doctrine,' *Foreign Affairs* II (1923-24), 387
105 Fleming, *The United States and World Organization*, 220
106 *LNOJ*, Special Suppl., no. 139 (1935), 93-4; *LNMS* (September 1934), 209

ready commissioned by the Pan-American Conference in 1933.[107] However, it authorized the Secretary-General of the League 'to maintain such relations for mutual information with the Director-General of the Pan-American Union as may prove desirable.'[108] Concern with the need to improve collaboration with the League also led the Inter-American Conference for the Maintenance of Peace in 1936 to urge American states which were not members of the League to co-operate with the world organization in the measures which it might adopt to prevent war or to settle disputes peaceably.[109]

107 Scott, ed., *International Conference of American States, First Supplement, 1933-1940*, 18
108 *LNOJ*, Special Suppl., no. 139, 95
109 Scott, ed., *International Conference of American States, First Supplement, 1933-1940*, 162

3

Constitutional relationships between the United Nations and regional organizations

The League of Nations was not altogether unsuccessful in establishing a harmonious working relationship with regional organizations in the promotion of peace in Europe and Latin America, and perhaps for that reason regional organization had a strong political appeal in the middle of the Second World War. Up to the spring of 1943, Churchill and Roosevelt were strongly in favour of the organization of a post-war international system on a regional basis.[1] According to Churchill, 'the central idea of the structure was that of a three-legged stool – the World Council resting on three Regional Councils.'[2] However, by October 1943 both leaders, along with their Soviet and Chinese counterparts, had accepted the 'necessity of establishing at the earliest practicable date a general international organization, based on the principle of sovereign equality of all peace-loving states, and open to membership by all such states, large and small, for the maintenance of international peace and security.'[3] This Moscow Declaration was conspicuously silent on the question of regional organization. As if to emphasize this fact, Cordell Hull, in a statement reminiscent of President Wilson's public utterances earlier in the century, told the joint session of the US Congress that when the provisions of the Moscow Declaration were implemented 'there will no longer be need for spheres of influence, for alliances, for balance of power, or any other of the special arrangements through which, in

1 Winston Churchill, *The Second World War*, 4: *The Hinge of Fate* (Boston, 1950), 802-5; Cordell Hull, *The Memoirs of Cordell Hull* 2 (New York, 1948), 1640
2 Churchill, *The Hinge of Fate*, 804
3 RIIA, *United Nations Documents 1941-45* (London, 1946), 13

the unhappy past, the nations strove to safeguard their security or to promote their interests.'[4]

The Dumbarton Oaks Proposals which embodied the results of the four-nation discussion on a general international organization accorded regional organizations a relatively minor and dependent existence. Russell recalls that 'at the beginning of the talks, Great Britain declared that all regional organizations should be auxiliary to, consistent with, and under the supervision of the world body when matters of world security were involved; hence the general character of the global organization should be decided before the regional aspects were discussed. The United States and the Soviet Union agreed.'[5] The section on regional arrangements in the Dumbarton Oaks Proposals states:

Nothing in the Charter should preclude the existence of regional arrangements or agencies for dealing with such matters relating to the maintenance of international peace and security as are appropriate for regional action, provided such arrangements or agencies and their activities are consistent with the purposes and principles of the Organization. The Security Council should encourage settlement of local disputes through such regional arrangements or by such regional agencies either on the initiative of the States concerned or by reference from the Security Council.

The Security Council should, where appropriate, utilize such arrangements or agencies for enforcement action under its authority but no enforcement action should be undertaken by regional arrangements or by regional agencies without the authorization of the Security Council.

The Security Council should at all times be kept fully informed of activities undertaken or in contemplation under regional arrangements or by regional agencies for the maintenance of international peace and security.[6]

The formulation of the Charter law of universal-regional relationship in Articles 51-54 was one of the most tedious assignments tackled by the draftsmen of the UN Charter. The fundamental problem then, as now, was how to devise a formula under which regional arrangements could legitimately exist without destroying the over-all responsibility of the universal organization to maintain global peace.

4 Hull, *Memoirs*, 1314-15
5 Ruth Russell, *A History of the United Nations Charter* (Washington, 1958), 472
6 Cmd 6560 (London, 1944)

The political forces shaping the formulation of the legal foundation of regional organizations in the UN Charter were clearly reflected in the various amendments to the provisions of the Dumbarton Oaks Proposals. The Canadian delegation to the San Francisco Conference summarized the three major categories of amendments:

> Australia, Belgium and Venezuela wanted to limit the right of a Great Power to veto regional enforcement action. Other delegations, chiefly those of Latin American Republics and of the League of Arab States, wanted to increase the autonomy of regional arrangements. The purpose of the third group of amendments was to ensure that the Charter did not interfere with the operation of pacts of mutual assistance directed against enemy states.[7]

The explicit declaration of the right of collective self-defence in the form of Article 51 pacified the political demands articulated by the sponsors of the first and second groups of amendments. The authors of the Charter bowed to the wishes of the Great Powers proposing the third group of amendments by permitting an exception to the general rule prohibiting regional enforcement action without the authorization of the Security Council. Resort to regional agencies or arrangements was added to the list of methods of peaceful settlement of disputes in Article 33(1). Under another amendment, members of the United Nations who are parties to regional organizations undertake to settle their disputes through regional agencies before referring such disputes to the world organization.[8]

FUNCTIONAL INTERPRETATION OF THE CHARTER LAW OF UNIVERSAL-REGIONAL RELATIONSHIP

As Bowett has pointed out, a proper interpretation of Articles 51-54 demands recognition and appreciation of the fact that the UN Charter differentiates regional organizations and determines their relationship to the United Nations on the basis of the particular function they are performing at a given time.[9] For each of the functions posited under Articles 51-54 (self-defence, pacific settlement, enforcement action by regional organizations

---

7 *Report of the United Nations Conference on International Organization* (Ottawa, 1945), 41

8 Yuen-li Liang, 'Regional Arrangements and International Security,' *TGS* XXXI (1945), 227

9 D.W. Bowett, *Self-Defence in International Law* (Manchester, 1958), 215-23. See also Michael Akehurst, 'Enforcement Action by Regional Agencies, With Special Reference to the Organization of American States,' *BYBIL* XLII (1967), 180

acting as agents of the Security Council, and enforcement action by the big powers against the enemy states of World War II), the Charter prescribes some essential rules of behaviour for regional organizations. A functional analysis helps to define and specify obligations the Charter imposes or the rights it bestows on UN members by ascertaining whether regional organizations are taking enforcement action previously authorized by the Security Council, exercising their right of collective and individual self-defence, taking enforcement action against 'enemy' states, or simply settling international disputes. This method avoids the Beckett-Kelsen controversy about whether a collective defence organization like NATO is a regional organization within the meaning of Articles 52-54 of the UN Charter.

The logic of functional interpretation demands the assumption that the authorization principle of Article 53 be read in the light of Article 51. The legal effect of Article 51 is that it overrides or at least restricts Article 53 which prohibits regional arrangements from taking enforcement action independently of prior Security Council authorization.[10] It has been argued that such an interpretation reduces the authorization principle of Article 53 to futility. One scholar observed that 'it would seem to be a technical fine point to say that a group of states can act independently of the Security Council under Article 51 (until the Council acts) and that the same group cannot act without authorization of the Council if they constitute a regional arrangement; but it could also be said that Article 53 has little meaning without such an interpretation.'[11] In 1945 it was assumed that should an aggression take place, the might of the Great Powers acting together would be more than sufficient to deal with it, and that all military action would be sponsored by the Security Council making use of regional facilities whenever possible, thus subordinating regional organizations to the UN. At the same time, it was understood that if a state were attacked, it could not be expected to await United Nations authorization before responding in self-defence.

A functional interpretation of Articles 51-54 makes it superfluous for any regional organization to define its relationship to the United Nations expressly in terms of specific constitutional provisions of the UN Charter. As long as the regional organization adheres strictly to the rules of behaviour defined by the Charter for the performance of specific functions, it can be said to be operating compatibly with the world organization.

10 Julius Stone, *Legal Controls of International Conflict* (New York, 1959), 262; Hans Kelsen, *The Law of the United Nations* (New York, 1950), 328
11 Clyde Eagleton, 'The North Atlantic Defence Pact,' *CJIA* III (1949), 29

The various provisions of the UN Charter dealing with the relationship between universal and regional organizations may be divided into two major categories: those concerned with the function of pacific settlement of local disputes and those relating to the permissible use of force by a regional organization either in self-defence against an armed attack or against an enemy state of the Second World War. This study deals primarily with the role of regional organizations in the functional areas of pacific settlement of disputes and collective self-defence against attack, but the two enemy state clauses of the Charter nevertheless require some comment.

The use of force against 'enemy' states
Articles 53 and 107 envisage the possibility of establishing regional organizations to deal with the renewal of aggression on the part of any enemy state of World War II. The drafting history of these Articles shows that the regional organizations contemplated were those of 'the Governments having responsibility for such action,' which were understood to be the Great Powers. At San Francisco, Britain, the United States, and the Soviet Union, desirous of implementing their mutual defence pacts directed against enemy states of the 1939-45 war, particularly against Germany, proposed amendments which sought to free enforcement action initiated under such defence treaties from the requirement of the Security Council's prior approval.[12] These amendments became the exception to the authorization principle of Article 53, in addition to Article 107 which also deals with the right of the Great Powers to use force against an enemy state. The New Zealand commentary on the Charter recorded the general feeling in 1945 about these enemy states clauses: 'It cannot perhaps be suggested that this is an ideal arrangement, but it was generally conceded that it was the best that could be made in the circumstances as they exist, and it was accepted accordingly.'[13] Thus, under Article 53, an action of a Great Power directed against the renewal of aggressive military policy on the part of any enemy state has been given a status similar to the action of a collective defence organization under Article 51. There is, however, an important difference. As the Commission to Study the Organization of Peace pointed out in its Eighth Report, 'the exception in Article 53 seems to have been retained

12 UNCIO, *Documents* III, 575, 598-599, 601
13 *Report on the Conference at San Francisco* (Wellington, NZ, 1945), 96

even after Article 51 was drafted because an action authorized by these arrangements might in some instances have gone beyond "collective self-defence if an armed attack occurs against a member of the United Nations" and also because the parties to the World War II alliances may have wished to escape the ultimate control of the Security Council provided for collective self-defence arrangements under Article 51.'[14] Thus, whereas the self-defensive measures taken under Article 51 can theoretically be terminated by the Security Council on its own initiative at any time, under Article 53 action taken by a regional organization of the Great Powers against the renewal of aggression by an enemy state cannot be terminated by the United Nations until a request has been received from 'the Governments having responsibility for such action.' In fact, on a strict interpretation of Article 107, the Security Council has no possible function.

Concerning the legal validity and applicability of the clauses against ex-enemy states Kelsen writes: 'The ex-enemy states are, in principle, outside of the law of the Charter. This outlawry is permanent; for according to the wording of Article 107, it is not terminated by the admission of an ex-enemy state to the Organization. The definition of the term "enemy state" in Article 53, paragraph 2, applies also to the states after they have become Members of the United Nations.'[15] Under Article 2(1), members of the United Nations are sovereign legal equals. If Article 107 remains valid against an ex-enemy state which has signed a peace treaty and has become a UN member, a new element of inequality would have been introduced among UN members in addition to the political inequality already expressly recognized and accepted under Articles 27(3) and 108. In 1968 when the Soviet Union threatened to invoke the enemy state clauses against the Bonn Republic, she was told bluntly by the British and US Governments that the enemy state clauses have become irrelevant today. As West Germany is a member of the Western Alliance, the British and American response can be understood only in the context of the balance of power between East and West. It has no support in law. It is, however, doubtful if the enemy state clauses are still legally valid against ex-enemy states like Italy, Germany, and Japan which have signed peace treaties and/or have been admitted into the world body. The British commentary on the Charter noted: 'It might. . .be assumed that, if any such [enemy] state were to be admitted to

14 *Regional Arrangements for Security and the United Nations* (New York, 1953), 23
15 Kelsen, *The Law of the United Nations*, 813-14

the Organization, the necessity of making special arrangements to prevent aggression on its part would disappear, since it could only be admitted if all the Permanent members of the Security Council and two-thirds of the members of the General Assembly were convinced that it qualified under Article 4.'[16] Although there is general support for this interpretation among international legal scholars,[17] there are some who would prefer to clarify the issue by means of technical amendments to the enemy state clauses.[18]

Collective self-defence and enforcement action
The Dumbarton Oaks Proposals prohibited regional enforcement action not authorized by the Security Council, thus symbolizing the subordination of regional organizations to the United Nations. It was viewed by many delegates at San Francisco in relation to and in the context of the Yalta Voting Formula positing unanimity among the Great Powers as the rule of decision on substantive matters in the Security Council.[19] Under the Dumbarton Oaks Proposals, the exercise of the veto power by a permanent Security Council member would make regional organizations useless as enforcement agencies. A number of proposals sought to emancipate regional organizations from the consequences of such potential political paralysis of the Security Council. The Belgian delegate recommended that the following words be added to Chapter VIII, Section c Paragraph 2 of the Dumbarton Oaks Proposals: 'Dissentient votes of the permanent Members of the [Security] Council which are parties to such [regional] arrangements or agencies will not impair the validity of a decision of the [Security] Council in this respect.'[20] The Australian proposal urged the creation of a separate section containing the following provision: 'If the Security Council does not itself take measures, and does not authorize action to be taken under a regional arrangement or agency for the maintaining or restoring of international peace, nothing in this Charter shall be deemed to abrogate the right of the parties to any arrangement which is consistent with the Charter to adopt such measures as they deem just and necessary for maintaining or re-

16 Cmd 6666 (London, 1945), par. 41
17 Stone, *Legal Controls of International Conflict*, 254; N. Bentwich and A. Martin, *A Commentary on the Charter of the United Nations* (London, 1968), 114, 186
18 See generally, the Cheng-Green Memorandum in ILA, *Report of the 46th Conference* (Edinburgh, 1954), 160-3. Tabata of Japan proposed in 1958 that the discriminating provisions of Articles 53 and 107 be deleted altogether (see *ILA, Report of the 48th Conference*, New York, 1958, 528-9).
19 UNCIO, *Documents* XI, 711-14
20 UNCIO, *Documents* XII, 767. See also L'Institut Royal des Relations Internationales, *La Belgique et les Nations Unies* (New York, 1958), 62-3, 160-1

storing international peace and security in accordance with that arrangement.'[21] The Latin American Republics, anxious to protect the autonomy of the Inter-American System, sought changes which went beyond what the United States and other Great Powers were prepared to accept.[22] The net result of these amendments was the Vandenberg formula known in the Charter as Article 51 (see Appendix C), which a leading participant at the San Francisco Conference called 'the most important contribution to the Charter made at San Francisco.'[23]

The question of when a collective self-defence organization may resort to the use of force is an integral part of the whole problem of the relationship between the United Nations and regional organizations performing the function of self-defence. The scope of autonomy enjoyed by a regional organization carrying out the function of legitimate self-defence depends in the final analysis on the ability of the Security Council to take measures necessary to restore peace and the interpretation that one places on the right declared in Article 51. Unfortunately, international legal scholars speak with discordant voices on this issue.[24] The controversy over Article 51 centres on whether the Article involves a restriction of the right of self-defence possessed by states under customary international law. Scholars who give an affirmative answer draw attention to the use of the phrase 'armed attack' in the formulation of Article 51 and contend that the Charter outlaws anticipatory or preventive self-defence.[25] Accordingly, until a member of the United Nations has become a victim of an armed attack, it will be illegal under the UN Charter to exercise the right of self-defence. This view essentially amounts to the proposition that the customary right of self-defence which permits anticipatory self-defence (subject of course to the restraint of proportionality and necessity) has been overriden by the law of the United Nations.

The UN Charter itself does not lend unequivocal support to such a claim.

21 UNCIO, *Documents* XII, 766. See also Harper and Sissons, *Australia and the United Nations* (New York, 1959), 49ff
22 J.A. Houston, *Latin America in the United Nations* (New York, 1956), 46-90; Russell, *A History of the United Nations Charter*, 693-703
23 Sir Charles Webster, 'The Making of the Charter of the United Nations,' in his *The Art and Practice of Diplomacy* (London, 1961), 90
24 M. Whiteman, *Digest of International Law* 5 (Washington, 1956), 971ff
25 Josef Kunz, 'Individual and Collective Self-Defence in Article 51 of the Charter of the United Nations,' *AJIL* XLI (1947), 877; Kelsen, *The Law of the United Nations*, 791ff; Ian Brownlie, *International Law and the Use of Force by States* (Oxford, 1963), 275-80; Quincy Wright, *International Law and the United Nations* (New Delhi, 1960), 100; Judge Krylov, in ILA, *Report of the 48th Conference* (New York, 1958), 512

It refers to the 'inherent' nature of the right of self-defence. As one authority has pointed out, this is an admission that 'the right is an existing right, independent of the Charter and not the subject of an express grant.'[26] Under international law, each state defines for itself whether circumstances justifying the exercise of the right of self-defence have arisen. Neither the League Covenant nor the Kellogg-Briand Pact of 1928 affected the nature of this right[27] and there is no persuasive reason to suppose that the UN Charter restricts it. According to Green, 'the right of self-defence was inherent before the Charter was written; it has remained inherent, and as such it covers preventive self-defence as well as self-defence resorted to after you have already been exterminated.'[28] In addition, a restrictive interpretation of Article 51 tends not only to ignore developments in military weapons system and the contemporary relevance and potency of non-military forms of attack, but also the fact that in practice states do not accept the 'sitting duck' conception of the right of self-defence.

The UN Charter imposes certain obligations on individual states or organizations of states exercising the inherent right of individual and collective self-defence. Members of a regional organization resorting to forceful action in collective self-defence are under obligation to report immediately to the Security Council the measures they have taken. The UN Charter reserves for the Security Council the right to take any action at any time that is deemed necessary in order to maintain or restore international peace and security. Theoretically, the Security Council can order collective self-defence measures to stop if the technicalities of Article 27(3) can be overcome. However, as each of the major regional organizations – NATO, SEATO, ANZUS Treaty Alliance, Rio Treaty, and the Warsaw Pact – established primarily to perform the function of collective self-defence contains at least one of the permanent members of the Security Council, it may be expected that a veto will almost certainly be used to prevent the Security Council from condemning unlawful regional collective action and from taking actions necessary for the maintenance of peace. Thus, in practice, regional or-

26 Bowett, *Self-Defence*, 187
27 L.C. Green, 'Armed Conflict, War and Self-Defence,' *Archiv des Völkerrechts* VI (1956-57), 410; Bowett, *Self-Defence*, 124, 125; C.H.M. Waldock, 'The Regulation of the Use of Force by Individual States in International Law,' *Recueil des Cours* LXXXI (1952), part II, 455-514. According to Waldock, when a state is under an imminent threat of attack, 'it would be a travesty of the purposes of the Charter to compel a defending State to allow its assailant to deliver the first and perhaps the fatal blow ... To read Article 51 otherwise is to protect the aggressor's right to the first stroke' (p. 498).
28 Green in ILA, *Report of the 48th Conference*, 581, cited in Whiteman, *Digest of International Law* 5, 982

ganizations of which the Great Powers are members can escape control and subsequent review of their action by the Security Council when they are allegedly performing the function of self-defence.

The terms 'enforcement action' and 'enforcement measures' have been used interchangeably in the UN Charter. In regard to the scope and content of the term 'enforcement action' as employed in the formulation of Article 53, it can be argued that the term embraces all measures contemplated in Articles 41 and 42 of the UN Charter.

There are two kinds of such measures: measures not involving the use of armed force, and measures involving the use of armed force. Both are "enforcement measures" or "enforcement actions" as they are sometimes called in the Charter . . . although only the measures determined in Articles 42 to 47 involve the use of "armed" force. The measures determined in Article 41 are especially: "complete or partial interruption of economic relations and of rail, sea, air, postal, telegraphic, radio, and other means of communication, and the severance of diplomatic relations." This purpose is defined in Article 41 as follows: "to give effect to its [the Security Council's] decisions"; that means to enforce the decision upon a recalcitrant state. Hence these measures, too, may be considered to be "enforcement measures" or "enforcement actions" referred to in various Articles of the Charter.[29]

A second interpretation, more restrictive than the first, is that the term 'enforcement action' as used in Article 53 includes *only* those measures contemplated under Article 42. Under this interpretation, regional organizations are obligated to seek prior approval of the Security Council *only* when they plan to take 'such action by air, sea, or land forces as may be necessary to maintain or restore international peace and security.' In support of this more restrictive interpretation, it is sometimes argued that, under Article 52(1), the principal limitation to the activities of regional organizations is the impermissible use of force, and that the authorization principle in Article 53, being a relative and not an absolute limitation on regional action, cannot be interpreted without considerations for the relational interest between the desire to preserve regional autonomy and the determination to uphold the dominant position of the Security Council.[30] Consistent with this reasoning, Garcia-Amador asked the following questions: 'If the expression "enforcement action" were understood to apply to all measures contem-

29 Kelsen, *The Law of the United Nations*, 724
30 Marvin G. Goldman, 'Action by the Organization of American States: When is Security Council Authorization Required under Article 53 of the United Nations Charter?' *UCLA Law Review* x (1962-63), 837-69

plated in the UN Charter, in what would regional action consist? In other words, why authorize regional arrangements or agencies to take up matters relative to the maintenance of international peace and security susceptible of regional action, if that action must be authorized by the Security Council?'[31]

Supported by the procès verbaux of the San Francisco Conference,[32] the first interpretation is the more persuasive of the two. The authors of the Charter, for good reason, considered it superfluous to define what enforcement action means under Article 53 when the term has already been amply illustrated in Articles 41 and 42 of the immediately preceeding Chapter of the Charter. It is reasonable to suggest that if a restrictive interpretation was intended for the term 'enforcement action' in the context of Article 53, the UN Charter would have said so. Apart from Article 51 which permits regional organizations to use force in self-defence on their own initiative until the Security Council is in a position to act, and the provision allowing actions against World War II enemy states by the big powers without the authorization of the Security Council, collective sanction against the will of a state was considered to be the prerogative of the Security Council. Any contrary interpretation is an ex post facto rationalization of the changes which have subsequently taken place in the world community and which have affected the proper working of the United Nations. Seen in this light, an interpretation limiting the meaning of the term 'enforcement action' as used in Article 53 to only those measures contemplated in Article 42 is a political and practical response to the acute problem of promoting peace in an international system in which the effectiveness of the world organization has been declining.

Pacific settlement of disputes
The Charter requires members of regional arrangements to make every effort to achieve pacific settlement of local disputes through regional arrangements before referring them to the Security Council. It also places on the Security Council an obligation to encourage the development of pacific settlement of such disputes through regional arrangements, either on the initiatives of the states concerned or by reference from the Security Council. Article 31(1) enumerates methods of peaceful settlement of disputes in regard to the role of regional organizations. There is nothing to suggest that resort to regional organizations takes precedence over resort to other me-

31 F.V. Garcia-Amador, *The Inter-American System* (New York, 1966), 191
32 UNCIO, *Documents* X, 507-8

thods of pacific settlement mentioned in Article 33(1), although it is often argued by legal scholars from the Soviet bloc that the list in Article 33(1) is hierarchic.[33]

The provisions of Article 52 do not constitute limitations on the authority of the United Nations to make recommendations in the functional field of pacific settlement of disputes. The Charter, under Article 35, grants UN members a constitutional right to bring any disputes to the attention of the Security Council or of the General Assembly. In addition, it declares the Security Council competent to investigate whether the continuance of a dispute or situation is likely to endanger world peace and security. It was the understanding in 1945 that 'no State, great or small, whether party to a dispute or not, can prevent the Security Council from taking cognizance of such [a] dispute and examining it and discussing it.'[34] Article 52(4) rescues Articles 34 and 35 from the implications of Article 52, paragraphs 1, 2, and 3. As the Stettinius Report on the San Francisco Conference rightly stated, Article 52(4) was inserted into the Charter 'to insure the paramount authority of the [Security] Council and its right to concern itself if necessary with disputes of this [local] character.'[35] The contention that peaceful solution of disputes between states which are members of a regional organization is the *exclusive* responsibility of members of that organization[36] has no basis in the Charter.

The nature of the power and competence of the Security Council in the field of pacific settlement of disputes has been very much debated. In support of the claim that the power of the Security Council is rather limited, attention is often drawn to the fact that while the Security Council can recommend a settlement procedure, parties to a dispute may or may not accept it, and that while the Security Council may propose terms of settlement, these are not binding on the parties. The claim that the authority of the Security Council is not so limited is based on two interrelated propositions: first, that the Council has primary responsibility for the maintenance of international

---

33 See the 1964 and 1966 Reports of the Special Committee on the Principles of International Law concerning Friendly Relations and Co-operation among States, UN Doc. A/5746 (16 November 1964), UN Doc. A/6230 (27 June 1966). See also Bogdanov in ILA, *Report of the 53rd Conference* (Buenos Aires, 1968), p. 4, who said: 'Negotiations occupy the first place among such means [of pacific settlement], and the Charter of the United Nations is very clear on this.'

34 Cmd 6666 (London, 1945), par. 86

35 *Report to the President on the Results of the San Francisco Conference* (1945), 105

36 J.M. Yepes, 'Les Accords Régionaux et le Droit International,' *Recueil des Cours* LXXI (1947), part II, 279

peace and security, and second, that the procedures for both pacific settlement and determination of threats to peace under Article 39 are in fact part and parcel of the same sequence of events. The provisions of Chapter VI of the Charter make it abundantly clear that the power of the Security Council in the field of pacific settlement cannot be enforced. But can the Security Council consider failure to accept its recommendation under Chapter VI as constituting a threat to international peace, and consequently invoke Article 39? The fundamental issue is whether the procedures for pacific settlement and those for determining threats to peace are necessarily logically connected in the same sequence of events. The formulation used in the Dumbarton Oaks Proposals would have made it mandatory for the Security Council to decide whether or not failure to settle a dispute constitutes a threat to international peace and to act accordingly in the event of an affirmative answer. Under the UN Charter, the two sets of procedures appear separate and independent. As one commentator pointed out

There is no specific reference in the Charter to the fact that a failure to settle a dispute according to the Council's recommendations may constitute a threat to peace. The Charter does not place the Security Council in a position of having to determine whether there has been a failure to settle a dispute according to its recommendations. It is only required to determine the existence of a threat to peace. The objective existence of this fact is not connected with any previous recommendations on any dispute or situation.[37]

A decision of the Security Council which, in fact, amounts to regarding failure to settle a dispute as constituting a threat to peace is at best only implied by the wording of Article 39. Strictly speaking, the power that Article 39 confers on the Security Council is not in the field of pacific settlement but in that of enforcement.

The constitutional relationship between the United Nations and regional organizations is complicated by the provision of Article 52(4) which raises the possibility of concurrent consideration of a dispute by both universal and regional agencies. At San Francisco, Peru's delegate expressed fear that Article 52(4) might result in practice in the simultaneous handling of disputes by a regional organization and the Security Council or in the failure of the Security Council to rely upon action being taken by the regional

37 E.J. de Arechaga, *Voting and the Handling of Disputes in the Security Council* (New York, 1950), 41. See also Wellington Koo, *Voting Procedures in International Political Organizations* (New York, 1947), 180

organization.[38] He was not taken seriously. Camargo, chairman of Committee III/4 which dealt with the problem of regional organization, attempted, unsuccessfully it seems, to allay this fear by offering the following interpretation:

If a dispute arises between two states which are members of a regional organization, such controversy should be settled by peaceful means established within the said organization. The obligation exists for all States which are members of a regional organization to make every effort to settle the controversy through this agency, and at the same time, the obligation exists for the Security Council to promote these regional peaceful settlements. But the Security Council has the right to investigate in order to determine whether the controversy may constitute a threat to international peace and security . . . [T]he Council has jurisdiction only to investigate, and the nations, whether or not they are members of the [UN] organization, have the right only to ask for an investigation . . . It is evident that if the regional systems for peaceful settlement fail, the Council can intervene . . . for the purpose of promoting formulas for settlement.[39]

If, as is the case, the Charter places no obligation on UN members to exhaust all the alternative procedures for pacific settlement enumerated under Article 33(1) before having recourse to the Security Council, if the Council may investigate any dispute *at any time*, and if any UN member or the Secretary-General may bring any dispute to the attention of the world body, then the possibility of simultaneous consideration of a dispute at the regional and the universal venues does exist. A strict legal interpretation of the Charter leads to the conclusion that the jurisdiction of both the Security Council and regional organization in the field of pacific settlement of disputes is concurrent but independent.

The San Francisco formula for dominance by the UN was clearly based upon the conception of regional organization as 'one of the cogs, and a very essential one, of the general mechanism for the establishment and defense of universal peace.'[40] The constitutional relationship between universal and

38 UNCIO, *Documents* XII, 685
39 *Ibid.*, 686-7. See also J.M. Yepes who writes: 'La solution pacifique des conflits entre les Etats membres d'un organisme régional est l'exclusive compétence de ce dernier . . . L'intervention due Conseil de sécurité, s'il y a lieu, ne viendra qu'après, le seulement si l'organisme régional a échoué' in 'Les Accords Régionaux et le Droit International,' *Recueil des Cours* LXXI (1947), part II, 279
40 UNCIO, *Documents* XI, 56

regional organizations was more systematically worked out in the UN Charter than in the League Covenant. The balance struck in 1945 theoretically preserved the over-all control and supervision of efforts geared towards the maintenance and promotion of peace under the ultimate authority of the United Nations. Senator Vandenberg, who played a leading role in the drafting of the Charter, expressed the general feelings of the delegates when he said:

We have found a sound and practical formula for putting regional organizations into effective gear with the global institution which we here erect on behalf of the world's peace and security . . . [W]e have infinitely strengthened the world organization by thus enlisting, within its overall supervision, the dynamic resources of these regional affinities. We do not thus substract from global unity on behalf of the world's peace and security; on the contrary, we weld these regional king-links into the global chain.[41]

Amidst the deafening chorus of praise for the San Francisco formula, there were a few voices counselling a more restrained and sober judgment. Yuen-li Liang, Technical Adviser to the Chinese Delegation to the San Francisco Conference, regretting that it had been necessary to introduce the concept of collective self-defence in order to mediate the competing claims of universalism and regionalism, warned:

The provisions of the United Nations Charter regarding regional arrangements cannot be said to have solved, even in a preliminary way, the problem of regionalism versus universalism. The most that can be said at this moment is that this part of the Charter, as indeed many other parts, is preeminently a compromise of conflicting political forces. And in this disillusioned world, so soon after the termination of the holocaust, it is but natural that on this question, the pendulum should swing somewhat towards the conception of individual and collective self-help than toward the ideal of organized society enforcing law on a global basis. If international lawyers would judge of the Charter in the political context, as statesmen and politicians are bound to do, then they would find that the solution of the question of regional arrangements and international security could not be expected until the emergence of a system which has its being in a world that has demonstrated its political and economic stability. And nothing short of complete confidence in the overriding authority of the World Organization, a confidence inspired by the ability and experience of

41 UNCIO, *Documents* XI, 52; Arthur Vandenberg, Jr, ed., *The Private Papers of Senator Vandenberg* (Boston, 1952), 198

the Organization to deal swiftly and effectively with situations in any part of the world, can persuade the regional groups to entrust their fate to a central regime of law, and to weld the various segments of the efforts to maintain peace into a comprehensive and indivisible whole in the interest of international community.[42]

42 Liang, 'Regional Arrangements and International Security', 230-1

4
Regional treaties and the UN Charter

If the principle of regionalism is to be deemed consonant with universality, it is essential that the legal framework of regional organizations reflect those common legal values, principles, processes, and institutions which form the core of the United Nations system. A legal analysis provides a necessary perspective to the problem of complementary coexistence between the United Nations and regional organizations by focusing attention on the legal question: Are regional treaties for the maintenance of peace compatible with the UN Charter?

THE UN CHARTER AS THE 'HIGHER LAW'

The paramountcy of UN Charter obligations over all other obligations whenever both lead to inconsistent duties was accepted in 1945, establishing the UN Charter as a higher law vis-à-vis the law of regional organizations, a conception which derives from the presumed theoretical superiority of the principle of universality over regionalism in international law and organization. The constitutional provision declaring this paramountcy (and therefore duties of UN membership) was formulated in Article 103 which differs in important respects from the language employed in Article 20 of the League Covenant. The authors of the Charter deliberately used the word 'supersede' instead of 'abrogate' which was used in Article 20 of the Covenant. According to the Report of the Rapporteur of Committee IV/2, '[a] few delegations have observed that the adoption of the terms of Article 20 of the Covenant of the League of Nations would be likely to produce uncertainty regarding the meaning of a great many treaties and to create many practical difficulties concerning the designation of the organ or organs which would be competent to determine a question of inconsistency.'[1]

With Article 103 of the UN Charter in mind, it has been common practice to include in the preamble or in the operative part of regional treaties statements declaring that none of the provisions of the particular treaty are to be construed as impairing the rights and obligations of UN membership, and reaffirming the commitment of members to the purposes and principles of the UN Charter.[2] Such deferential references to the UN Charter are quite unnecessary and certainly superfluous in so far as they do not add legal validity to the paramountcy rule of Article 103 already accepted by members of the United Nations. Yet, there is some symbolic value in having the superiority of the obligations of UN membership expressly declared in regional treaties.

In addition to a general tendency to make a formal acknowledgment of the UN Charter as the higher law, some regional treaties define their relationship to the UN Charter in specific terms. NATO, SEATO, ANZUS Treaty, and the Warsaw Pact justify their existence expressly or implicitly under Article 51 of the UN Charter. The authors of the OAS Charter and the Arab League Pact placed their respective regional organizations in the context of both Articles 51 and 52-54 of the Charter. However, relations of a regional organization to the United Nations are determined and defined not by the character of the regional organization, but by the function it is performing at a particular time.

MEMBERSHIP AND THE CONCEPT OF STATEHOOD

The search for solutions to constitutional problems of international organization naturally takes place against a background defined by international legal principles. This in part reflects the interdependent relationship which has developed between international law and international organization, and more important, the conviction that complementarity among legal regimes established at both the universal and regional levels can be achieved if those diverse legal regimes embody common principles of general international law.

The criteria of statehood, as laid down by the 1933 Montevideo Conven-

1 UNCIO, *Documents* XIII, 707
2 See for example, Statue of the Council of Europe, Art. 1(c); Manila Treaty, Art. 6; North Atlantic Treaty, Art. 7; OAS Charter, Art. 173; OAU Charter, Art. 2(1) (e); Warsaw Pact, Art. 1; ANZUS Treaty, Art. 6

tion on the Rights and Duties of States, are a permanent population, a defined territory, a stable and effective government, and capacity to enter into relations with other states.[3] As it has not always been possible to determine these criteria objectively, recognition of states in international law and the admission policy of international organizations have usually been based on the political interests of the recognizing state or of the admitting organization. The question is whether, in so doing, decision-makers have also usually disregarded the traditional criteria of statehood.

Article 4(1) of the UN Charter opens membership to peace-loving states. As interpreted in the *Conditions of Admission* case, '[t]he requisite conditions are five in number: to be admitted to membership in the United Nations, an applicant must 1/ be a state; 2/ be peace-loving; 3/ accept the obligations of the Charter; 4/ be able to carry out these obligations; and 5/ be willing to do so.'[4] Whether an applicant state satisfies these conditions depends on the judgment of both the General Assembly and the Security Council.[5] UN members have undoubtedly allowed non-legal factors to influence their voting behaviour in the admission of new members,[6] but as Higgins has rightly pointed out, 'variations in the United Nations practice concerning claims of statehood are a result not of an abandonment of traditional legal criteria of statehood but of the proper use of flexibility in interpreting these criteria in relation to the claim in which they are presented.'[7]

The provisions of regional treaties dealing with admission of new members into regional organizations have generally been based upon the principle of selectivity, and reflect the interest and goals of particular organizations. As a rule, membership has been attracted only from among those politically organized communities which are states in the international law sense.[8] For instance, the OAS Charter posits the following conditions of admission: 1/ an applicant state must be an independent American state

---

3 *LNTS* CLXV, 19; M.O. Hudson, *International Legislation* 6, 620
4 *Conditions of Admission* case: *ICJ Reports* (1947-48), 57 at p. 62
5 *Competence of the General Assembly for the Admission of a State to the United Nations, Advisory Opinion of March 3, 1950*: *ICJ Reports* (1950), 4 at p. 9
6 See generally, L.C. Green, 'Membership in the United Nations,' *CLP* II (1949), 258-82; A.W. Rudzinski 'Admission of New Members: The United Nations and the League of Nations,' *International Conciliation*, no. 480, (April 1952); Leo Gross, 'Progress Towards Universality of Membership in the United Nations,' *AJIL* L (1956), 791-827; Nathan Feinberg, 'L'Admission de Nouveaux Membres à la Société des Nations et à l'Organisation des Nations Unies,' *Recueil des Cours* LXXX (1952), part I, 279-389; Rosalyn Higgins, *The Development of International Law Through the Political Organs of the United Nations* (London, 1963), 11ff
7 Higgins, *The Development of International Law*, 54
8 D.W. Bowett, *The Law of International Institutions* (New York, 1963), 312

and 2/ must be willing to sign and ratify the OAS Charter.[9] In view of the series of anti-communist declarations since 1954,[10] it would seem that an independent *communist* American state cannot become a member of the OAS. The Punta del Este Declaration of 1962, which excluded the Castro Government of Cuba from participation in the OAS because Cuba officially adopted Marxist-Leninist ideology,[11] demonstrates that there is an underlying ideological foundation for the OAS, although 'no firm legal obligations backed by adequate sanctions have been agreed upon to assure the growth of [liberal] democracy throughout the [Western Hemisphere] region.'[12] It is difficult to accept the view advanced during Security Council debate on Cuba's protest against economic and diplomatic measures taken against her by the OAS at Punta del Este that the Government of Cuba was excluded from the OAS not because of her social and economic system but because of her violation of the Charter of the OAS.[13] The criterion of democratic capitalist ideology appears to have been added to the traditional legal criteria in defining the concept of statehood for the purposes of the OAS. In any case, the Punta del Este action against Cuba has been officially defended as 'implicit in the essential purposes of the Organization.'[14]

A similar conclusion seems valid for the Council of Europe. Membership is open to any European state which is willing and capable of accepting the principles of rule of law, fundamental freedoms, and human rights.[15] Commitment to this ideological requirement of membership led the Council to ask Greece, following the coup d'etat in Athens, to withdraw from the continental organization or face expulsion because the government had violated these principles.[16] With the restoration of constitutional democracy, Greece was subsequently readmitted into the European organization in 1974.

The Addis Ababa Charter makes membership in the OAU available only to independent African states which are also politically and ideologically

9 See The Act of Washington (Admission of New States to OAS), text in *ILM* IV (1965), 194; L.R. Scheman, 'Admission of States to the Organization of American States,' *AJIL* LVIII (1964), 968-74

10 The Caracas Declaration; see US Dept of State, *Bulletin* XXX (1954), 638

11 *Eighth Meeting of Consultation of Ministers of Foreign Affairs, 1962* (Washington, 1962), 6.

12 A van W. Thomas and A.J. Thomas, 'Democracy and the Organization of American States,' *Minnesota Law Review* XLVI (1961-62), 374

13 UN Doc. S/PV, 992-8

14 *Annual Report of the Secretary-General, 1962* (Washington, 1962), ii

15 A.H. Robertson, *The Council of Europe* (London, 1961), 12, 15-21; A. Kiss, 'L'Admission des Etats Comme Membres du Conseil de l'Europe,' *AFDI* IX (1963), 695-708

16 *ILM* VIII (1969), 890, 892; J.E.S. Fawcett, 'Council of Europe Action on Greece,' *World Today*, (November 1969), 464-5

acceptable. The question whether an independent state not under black African rule should qualify for OAU membership was much debated at the time the Addis Ababa Charter was being drafted. 'Some members contended that there would be nothing wrong in an independent state in Africa, with a non-African, possibly European Prime Minister, becoming a member of the Organization. Most members, however, preferred an independent state under an African Prime Minister as a candidate for membership.'[17] Boutros-Ghali has observed that

All African governments do not . . . have an equal right to adhere to the Organization . . . The African concept of legitimacy must be borne in mind: the government of a state that wishes to join the Organization must not only be in effective control of an African territory, but must also meet the ideological requirements laid down by the OAU – the requirements of African ethics, which recognize the right of all peoples to self-determination and call for the complete eradication of colonialism.[18]

African statesmen thus interpret the conditions of membership in a manner consistent with the ideological purposes and aspirations of the OAU, without denuding the concept of statehood of the meaning associated with it in traditional international law.

The Pact of the League of Arab States makes membership open to any independent Arab State. The fact that the Arab League accepted Trans-Jordan as a founding member at a time when the latter was still a mandated territory is not sufficient to cast doubt on the integrity of the requirement of independence as a condition of full membership in the regional organization. Perhaps to emphasize the principle of independence, but desirous of involving the Palestine Arabs in the work of the League, provision was made for a representative of Palestine, selected by the League itself, to participate in the work of the League 'until that country can effectively exercise its independence.'[19]

The admission policy of the North Atlantic Treaty Organization, Southeast Asia Treaty Organization, and ANZUS Treaty Alliance is restrictive and selective but is not based upon the abandonment of the traditional criteria of statehood.

Under the Warsaw Pact, membership is open to states, 'irrespective of

17 T.O. Elias, 'The Charter of the Organization of African Unity,' *AJIL* XLIX (1965), 251
18 B. Boutros-Ghali, 'The Addis Ababa Charter,' *International Conciliation*, no. 546 (January 1964), 38-9
19 Annex Regarding Palestine; see R.W. Macdonald, *The League of Arab States* (Princeton, 1965), 325

their social and political structure, which express their readiness . . . to help in combining the efforts of peace-loving States to ensure the peace and security of the peoples' (Article 9). In so far as it is claimed by the Soviet leaders and scholars that relations among socialist states are qualitatively different from and superior to those among capitalist states or to those between socialist and capitalist states,[20] there would seem to be no room for a non-socialist state in the Warsaw Treaty Organization. Admission of non-socialist states into the Warsaw Treaty Organization will certainly radically transform the character of that organization.

No international organization need be obliged to admit to its membership states which do not share its sense of common purpose or retain members which persistently violate the obligations of membership. Regional treaties have been guided by this rationality. At the same time, in formulating their 'functional' qualifications for membership, they (like the UN Charter) have not, as a rule, violated the generally accepted criteria of statehood in international law.

PRINCIPLES OF INTERNATIONAL LAW IN
REGIONAL TREATIES

Since the law of international institutions is nothing but a specialized branch of general (customary) international law upon which it rests, it is not surprising that principles of international law like sovereign equality, self-defence, non-interference in the domestic affairs of any state, good faith, and peaceful settlement of disputes are as much enshrined in the UN Charter as they are in regional treaties.[21] What is of interest are those obligations and principles which have come to be associated with some regional treaties and which appear either to be potentially incompatible with, or alter substantially, the generally accepted norms of international law.

The Warsaw Pact members are under obligation to 'act in the spirit of friendship and cooperation . . . in accordance with the principles of respect for each other's independence and sovereignty and of non-interference in each other's domestic affairs' (Article 8). This pledge has been reiterated in many declarations of communist bloc conferences.[22] But the Brezhnev Doc-

20 K. Grzybowski, *The Socialist Commonwealth of Nations* (New Haven, 1964), 256ff; G.I. Tunkin, *Droit International Public* (Paris, 1965), chap. 12
21 See, for instance, Arab League Pact, Art. 2, 5, 8; Statute of the Council of Europe, Art. 1(c); North Atlantic Treaty, Preamble; OAU Charter, Art. 3; OAS Charter, Art. 3, 9, 18, 21, 23-6
22 Grzybowski, *The Socialist Commonwealth of Nations*, chap. 7

trine, first explicitly formulated in the wake of the Warsaw Pact invasion of Czechoslovakia in 1968, amounts to a repudiation of the principle of sovereignty of any socialist state accessible to the Soviet Union. This Soviet doctrine, which deals with 'the question of the correlation and interdependence of the national interests of the socialist countries and their international duties,' establishes two basic propositions: 1/ 'each Communist party is responsible not only to its own people, but also to all the socialist countries, to the entire Communist movement. Whoever forgets this, in stressing only the independence of the Communist party, becomes one sided. He deviates from his international duty,' and 2/ in so far as one or another socialist state, staying in a system of other states composing the socialist community, cannot be free from the common interest of that community, '[t]he sovereignty of each socialist country cannot be opposed to the interest of world socialism.'[23] To the extent that the common interest of the socialist commonwealth of Eastern Europe is usually defined by the Soviet Union, the Brezhnev Doctrine of limited sovereignty amounts to a claim by the Kremlin of the right of intervention in the domestic affairs of the socialist states of Eastern Europe. It has long been recognized that

[I]n the final analysis, the question of the legal nature of the communist bloc is reduced to relationship of those powers that claim to watch over the purity of communist ideology and in the observance of party discipline. This peculiar union of communist bloc countries does not lend itself to analysis in terms of general international law, which traditionally regulates only relations between states and not relations between [political] parties. And the rules governing inter-party relations leave no room for application of the principle of co-existence between states-sovereignty, equality, and non-intervention.[24]

The OAU Charter no doubt represents, on the whole, the most classical form of international law.[25] However, the principle of 'absolute dedication to the total emancipation of African territories which are still dependent' (Article 3(2)) raises doubt about the possibility of harmonious relations between African states and colonial regimes and seems to have priority over

23 Text of the Brezhnev Doctrine may be found in *ILM* VII (1968), 1323; D.W. Bowett, *The Search for Peace* (London 1972), 136-43 See R.J. Mitchell, 'The Brezhnev Doctrine and Communist Ideology,' *Review of Politics* XXXIV (1972), 190-209; Charles T. Baroch, 'The Soviet Doctrine of Sovereignty,' *Bulletin* (Institute for the Study of the USSR) XVIII (1971), 7-25
24 D.A. Loeber, 'The Legal Structure of the Communist Bloc,' *Social Research* XXVII (1960), 200-1
25 B. Boutros-Ghali, 'The Addis Ababa Charter,' *International Conciliation*, no. 546 (1964)

those obligations of the UN Charter which enjoin members to co-operate with one another within the United Nations.[26]

MODES OF DECISION MAKING

Another area in which comparable developments have taken place in the constitutional prescriptions and political practice of the United Nations and regional organizations is decisionmaking, which is integrally tied to the legal doctrine of equality of states. Traditionally, sovereign equality of states has been interpreted as implying the principle of unanimity in decisionmaking at the international level.[27] The League Covenant permitted exceptions to the general rule of unanimity which it endorsed, and which was more respected in theory than in practice.[28] Although a remnant of the unanimity principle is found in a special and limited form in Article 27(3), the UN Charter reflects the triumph of the principle of majority over that of unanimity.[29] Even in the Security Council, it has been the practice to regard intentional abstention and absence of a veto-wielding big power as compatible with the requirement of Article 27(3).[30]

A transformation in the mode of decisionmaking from the traditional one of unanimity to the majority principle has also taken place in some regional organizations. The Pact of the League of Arab States prescribes different voting rules for various situations, an example which has been adopted by the Council of Europe and the Organization of African Unity

26 C.J.R. Dugard, 'The Organization of African Unity and Colonialism,' *ICLQ* XVI (1967), 157ff; V.M. Krishnan, 'African State Practice Relating to Certain Issues of International Law,' *IYBIA* XIV (1965); L.C. Green, 'New States, Regionalism and International Law,' *CYbIL* V (1967), 118-41

27 P.S. Reinsch, *Public International Unions* (Boston, 1911); F.S. Dunn, *The Practice and Procedure of International Conferences* (Baltimore, 1929); Normal Hill, *The Public International Conferences* (Stanford, 1929)

28 C.A. Riches, *The Unanimity Rule and the League of Nations* (Baltimore, 1933)

29 C.W. Jenks, 'Unanimity, the Veto, Weighted Voting, Special and Simple Majorities and Consensus as Modes of Decisions in International Organizations,' in R.Y. Jennings, ed., *Cambridge Essays in International Law: Essays in Honour of Lord McNair* (London, 1965), 48-63

30 Leo Gross, 'Voting in the Security Council: Abstention from Voting and Absence from Meeting,' *Yale Law Journal* LX (1951), 209-57; Yuen-li Liang, 'Abstention and Absence of a Permanent Member in Relation to the Voting Procedure in the Security Council,' *AJIL* XLIV (1950), 694-700; C.A. Stravropoulos, 'The Practice of Voluntary Abstentions by Permanent Members of the Security Council under Article 27, Paragraph 3, of the Charter of the United Nations,' *AJIL* LXI (1967), 737-55; S.D. Bailey, 'New Light on Abstentions in the Security Council', *International Affairs* L (London 1974), 554-73

and the Organization of American States. In each of these organizations, decisions are made by a simple or a special majority.[31] The Southeast Asia Treaty, the North Atlantic Treaty, the Warsaw Pact and the ANZUS Treaty Alliance are all silent on rules governing decisionmaking. In practice, however, the SEATO Council has been operating on the basis of unanimity.[32] In making decisions, no formal voting takes place in the ANZUS Council; discussion continues until a consensus reflecting a unanimity of opinion emerges.[33] The search for consensus is also the distinctive characteristic of decisionmaking in both the NATO Council and the Political Consultative Committee of the Warsaw Treaty Organization.[34] In all of these organizations, no state is bound by a resolution which it opposes, a fact which reflects the decentralized character of international society.

It is worth asking whether the majority principle as a rule of decisionmaking in international organizations composed of sovereign states subverts the principle of the sovereign equality of states. When a state, by an act of free will, accepts membership in an international organization where unanimity is not the basis of decisionmaking, that state may be regarded as having consented to some limitation on its sovereignty. There is nothing incompatible with sovereignty in freely agreeing to some limitation on its exercise.[35] The major element in decisionmaking is not so much whether resolutions are passed (important as these are gradually becoming in terms of the collective political legitimization they provide for particular positions), as whether such resolutions constitute binding obligations and can be enforced against a state which wants no part of them. With a few exceptions, resolutions of most international organizations are as a rule recommendations which have legal effects but do not per se create legal obligations.[36]

31 Macdonald, *The League of Arab States*, 56ff; Robertson, *The Council of Europe*, 35ff; Cervenka, *The Organization of African Unity* (New York, 1969), 45-6, 51

32 RIIA, *Collective Defence of South Asia* (London, 1956), 119, 191

33 J.G. Starke, *The ANZUS Treaty Alliance* (Melbourne, 1965), 168

34 RIIA, *Atlantic Alliance* (London, 1952), 42; Grzybowsi, *The Socialist Commonwealth of Nations*

35 Hans Kelsen, 'The Principle of Sovereign Equality of States as a Basis for International Organization,' *Yale Law Journal* LIII (1944), 207-20; Boutros-Ghali, 'Le Principe d'Egalité des Etats et les Organisations Internationales,' *Recueil des Cours* C (1960), part II, 1-73

36 Higgins, *The Development of International Law*, p. 5; G.I. Tunkin, *Droit International Public* (Paris, 1965), 101ff; Obed Y. Asamoah, *The Legal Significance of the Declaration of the General Assembly of the United Nations* (The Hague, 1966), 6; Jorge Castaneda, *The Legal Effects of the United Nations Resolutions* (New York, 1969)

PACIFIC SETTLEMENT OF DISPUTES: PRINCIPLES, PROCEDURES AND MACHINERY

In its approach to the task of maintaining international peace, the UN Charter, like the Covenant before it, proceeded on the basis of a clear distinction between permissible and impermissible resort to war, together with a clear awareness that the obligation not to resort to illegal war and the obligation to submit disputes to pacific settlement procedures were complementary factors. Under the UN Charter, Article 31(1), a more specific formulation of Article 2(3), enumerates various procedures for the peaceful settlement of disputes. Among them are negotiation, enquiry, mediation, conciliation, arbitration, and judicial settlement. The Charter appears to limit the obligation of members to settle their disputes peaceably to only those disputes 'the continuation of which is likely to endanger the maintenance of international peace and security.' Choice of procedure has been left to the discretion of the parties to the dispute. However, the Security Council can itself recommend both the method and the terms of settlement considered appropriate. The UN Charter, without proclaiming the superiority of judicial method over all other procedures for peaceful settlement, appears to have given this method special emphasis by designating the International Court of Justice as its principal judicial organ. The Court is empowered to deal with cases referred to it and with all matters specially provided for in the Charter or in treaties and conventions in force in accordance with international law. If a party fails to comply with the decision of the Court, the Security Council, on appeal from the other party, may recommend or decide on measures to give effect to the judgment (Article 94).

Regional treaties from the Pact of the Arab League drawn up in 1945 to the Charter of the Organization of African Unity drafted at Addis Ababa in 1963 have similarly imposed on their members obligations to settle their disputes in a peaceful manner. Some of the treaties set out with precision detailed procedures which designated organs are to follow in discharging functions assigned to them in these matters. The Pact of the Arab League prohibits the use of force to resolve disputes arising between contracting members and authorizes the Arab League Council to 'mediate in all differences which threaten to lead to war between two member states or a member state and a third state, with a view to bringing about their reconciliation' (Article 5). For the Arab League Council to mediate in a dispute between a member state and a third party, the latter must of course accept the League's jurisdiction and consent to have its dispute brought before the

Arab League Council.[37] It is doubtful, however, whether the Arab League Council can mediate impartially in a dispute between a member of the regional organization and a non-member. The Arab League Pact recognizes arbitration as a method of pacific settlement, but excludes disputes involving a state's independence, sovereignty, and territorial integrity from the type of disputes which members may bring before the Arab League Council. This is not unusual in treaties of arbitration.[38] But it is significant that the Pact designated the Arab League Council, a political body, as the arbitral 'court' pending the establishment of an Arab Tribunal of Arbitration, and further, that the Arab League members deliberately rejected judicial settlement as a proper method of peaceful adjustment of disputes among themselves.[39]

The Organization of American States provides the most comprehensive set of rules and procedure governing the pacific settlement of disputes among its members. Mediation, conciliation, arbitration, good offices, and judicial process are recognized by the OAS Charter (and by the Pact of Bogota, signed only by a few states) as appropriate methods of peaceful settlement. Great care has been taken to establish elaborate guidelines and machinery for effecting settlement through these methods. While accepting judicial method, members of the OAS have refrained from creating a regional court. On the contrary, the signatories to the Pact of Bogota accepted 'the jurisdiction of the [World] Court as compulsory ipso facto, without the necessity of any special agreement so long as the present Treaty is in force, in all disputes of judicial nature that arise among them' (Article 31). The International Court of Justice has been empowered to decide whether a particular dispute falls within the domestic jurisdiction of a state. (Peru and the United States of course made reservations to the effect that they alone are competent to determine what matters fall within their domestic jurisdiction.) Compulsory arbitration is recognized in cases where the International Court of Justice rules that it has no jurisdiction to adjudicate a dispute. The obligation undertaken by OAS members to submit their disputes first to the pacific settlement procedures of the regional organization before having re-

---

37 Status of Eastern Carelia, Advisory Opinion of 23 July 1923; see Hudson, *World Court Reports* 1, 190
38 J.L. Simpson and H. Fox, *International Arbitration* (London, 1959), 15ff; Hudson, *International Tribunals* (Washington, 1944), chap. 6; L.B. Sohn, 'The Function of International Arbitration Today,' *Recueil des Cours* CVIII (1963), part I, 9-113
39 Anabtawi, *Arab Unity in Terms of Law*, (The Hague, 1963), 82ff, E. Foda, *The Projected Arab Court of Justice* (The Hague, 1957)

course to the Security Council of the United Nations[40] involves a limitation to their right under Article 35(1) of the UN Charter. However, as this Article sets forth a constitutional right to be exercised at the discretion of members rather than a legal duty, members of a regional organization may agree among themselves to limit their right under the Article so long as by so doing they do not interfere with the rights of other UN members.

Established primarily to defend member states from unprovoked attack from non-members, NATO, ANZUS Treaty Alliance, SEATO, and the Warsaw Treaty Organization made no provision for rules, procedure and machinery for the pacific settlement of disputes arising among their members, although the treaties under which those regional organizations have been organized impose upon members the obligation to refrain from the use of force in the settlement of their international disputes. It is technically possible for these regional defence systems to be turned into ad hoc pacific settlement agencies. In 1957, for example, the NATO Council passed a resolution on Pacific Settlement urging members to use each other's 'good offices' to settle their disputes before resorting to any other international organization.[41]

The European Convention for the Pacific Settlement of Disputes drawn up by the Council of Europe in 1957 lists methods of peaceful settlement in the following order: judicial settlement, conciliation, and arbitration.[42] The order is not hierarchic. The High Contracting Parties undertake to submit to the judgment of the International Court of Justice all international disputes which arise among them,[43] and to comply with the decision of the World Court (Article 39).

Although the Addis Ababa Charter of the OAU envisages the necessity of non-peaceful relations with the white racist regimes in Africa which deny the right of self-determination to the black majority of their population,[44] it affirms the principle of pacific settlement of disputes among its signatories by negotiation, mediation, conciliation, or arbitration (Article 3). Following the example of members of the Arab League, OAU members rejected judi-

---

40 Charter of Bogota, Art. 23; Pact of Bogota, Art. 50; Rio Treaty, Art. 2
41 Text of the Resolution in *NATO: Facts About the North Atlantic Treaty Organization* (Paris, 1962), 277-8
42 Jean Salmon, 'La Convention Européenne pour le Règlement Pacifique des Différends,' *RGDIP* xxx (1959), 21-54
43 Art. 35(4). A contracting state which already accepted the compulsory jurisdiction of the International Court of Justice under Article 36(2) with reservation is permitted to make the same reservation to the Convention.
44 Boutros-Ghali, 'The Addis Ababa Charter,' *International Conciliation*, no. 546 (January 1964)

cial method of pacific settlement. In accordance with the pledge contained in Article 19 of the OAU Charter, a separate Protocol, approved by the Assembly of Heads of State and Government, established a Commission of Mediation, Conciliation, and Arbitration with an elaborate system of rules of procedure for the settlement of disputes by peaceful means.[45]

The dominant feature of regional peace treaties is the great extent to which they have endeavoured to capture the spirit of the UN Charter with regard to principles, processes, and machinery for peaceful adjustment of disputes.

LEGAL REGULATION OF THE USE OF FORCE

A similar conclusion seems valid for the manner in which regional treaties have dealt with the problem of legal regulation of the use of force. Traditional pre-twentieth-century international law sought neither to define limits nor to stipulate conditions for the use of force in international relations, but to regulate the conduct of hostilities when war existed with a view to mitigating its evils.[46] Twentieth-century law has sought to restrict the use of force as a method of political change. The Covenant of the League of Nations, the Kellogg-Briand Pact, and the UN Charter have all approached the issue of the use of force from a realistic attitude which recognizes the legitimacy of force only in some defined situations. The principle of self-defence has come to mark the dividing line between legal and illegal resort to war in defence of the national interest. In 1928, there seemed to be a general consensus behind the view that each state alone is competent to decide whether circumstances justifying recourse to war in self-defence have arisen.[47] The use of the word 'inherent' in Article 51 of the UN Charter is evidence of the customary nature of the right of self-defence. If this right includes the right of anticipatory self-defence, there is much to be said for the view that the liberty of states to resort to war is still substantial. It was envisaged by the authors of the San Francisco Charter that the propriety of the initial act of self-defence by an individual state or a regional organization would subsequently be subject to review by the Security Council, provided of course

---

45 T.O. Elias, 'The Commission of Mediation, Conciliation and Arbitration of the Organization of African Unity,' *BYBIL* xxxx (1964), 336-54; D.V. Degan, 'Commission of Mediation, Conciliation and Arbitration of the OAU,' *Revue Egyptienne de Droit International* xx (1964), 53-80

46 Georg Schwarzenberger, *International Law* 2 (London, 1968), 38ff; Stone, *Legal Controls of International Conflict* (New York, 1959), 297ff

47 Cmd 3109 (London, 1928), 25

that the voting technicalities of Article 27(3) were overcome. The Security Council can theoretically order the termination of measures already taken in the exercise of the right of self-defence against armed attack.

The use of force by the United Nations to maintain peace is deemed clearly in order by the UN Charter, which also contemplated the establishment of an international force contributed by members in accordance with special agreements. Owing to disagreements among the major powers in the Security Council, it has not been possible to establish a UN force of the type envisaged under Article 43. Equally important is the fact that, unlike the Covenant, the UN Charter, subject to Article 51, leaves the determination of what constitutes a threat to peace or a breach of the peace to the Security Council rather than to the individual state. In addition, UN members are obligated to accept and carry out decisions taken by the Security Council in accordance with the Charter. This obligation of course presupposes valid Security Council decisions made by an affirmative vote of nine out of fifteen members, including the concurring votes of the five permanent members of the Council. The founders of the world organization no doubt meant to ensure that resort to impermissible use of force by any state does not go unpunished by the organized international community.

The establishment of regional organizations to perform the function of self-defence against armed attack raises two general issues in regard to the use of force which have great bearing on the question of the compatibility of defence-oriented regional treaties with the UN Charter. The preliminary question is whether regional treaties which established collective self-defence organizations *in advance* of armed attack violate the UN Charter. The other issue is whether regional regulation of the use of force meets the minimum standards established under the UN Charter.

It has been claimed that Article 51 of the UN Charter does not permit the creation of regional defence systems prior to and in anticipation of an armed attack. This claim, advanced by the Soviet Union in 1949 as part of her argument that the North Atlantic Treaty is incompatible with the UN Charter,[48] has been given a scholar's stamp of approval by Castaneda, who contends that

The creation of permanent agencies of collective defence represented quite a deviation from the system established by the Charter. Self-defence under Article 51 of the Charter was thought of as a real exception to the essential principle of an orderly co-

---

48 UN *Bulletin* VI (1949), 410. See also M. Kukanov, *NATO – Threat to World Peace* (Moscow, 1971), 42

existence . . . Therefore, its scope was limited to a simple initial and provisional action against armed attack . . . Collective defence was never conceived of as a substitute for the collective security system of the United Nations, nor was it thought that a right granted to the states for emergency cases would become a duty through treaties.[49]

The claim should not be taken too seriously. Regional collective self-defence organizations have been established in preparation for, and not in the exercise of the right of, self-defence.[50] It is difficult to understand why, if article 51 permits self-defensive action by a state and expects it to prepare for the exercise of that right, it should be a 'deviation from the system established by the Charter' for the same state and its allies organized in a regional arrangement to prepare for self-defence.[51] Castaneda made a valid point in saying that what was a right of self-defence under Article 51 of the Charter has become a legal *duty* in regional treaties; but this development in no way constitutes a breach of the UN Charter.

Turning to the second issue, all the regional treaties examined employed the term 'armed attack' in consistency with the letter of Article 51 of the UN Charter. The only situation in which regional treaties expressly claim the right to a collective use of force is in the event of an armed attack. The extent of this self-imposed limitation will, of course, depend on whether or not signatory states accept the existence of the right of preventive self-defence, a right which tends to blur the fine line between permissible and impermissible use of force.

The processes, machinery, and responsibilities involved in the regulation of the use of force at the regional level are fairly elaborate. In the event of an armed attack against any of its signatories, each regional treaty generally demands two types of obligation from other parties, namely, the obligation to consult and the obligation to come to the assistance of the victim of armed attack.[53] The duty to consult generally arises if in the opinion of one of the signatories, a threat of armed attack or a threat to the integrity of the territory and political independence of the member state exists.[54] Consulta-

49 Jorge Castenada, *Mexico and the United Nations* (New York, 1958), 153. See also F.B. Schick, 'The North Atlantic Treaty and the Problem of Peace,' *Juridical Review* CLII (1950), 48, 50

50 Kelsen, *The Law of the United Nations* (New York, 1950), 915

51 Green, 'Armed Conflict, War, and Self-Defence,' *Archiv des Volkerrechts* VI (1956-57), 435

52 Bowett, *Self-Defence*, 225; Whiteman, *Digest of International Law*, 5, 1077ff

53 Boutros-Ghali, *Contribution à Une Théorie Générale des Alliances* (Paris, 1963), 34

54 Manila Treaty, Art. 2; North Atlantic Treaty, Art. 3; Warsaw Pact, Art. 3; ANZUS Treaty, Art. 3; Rio Treaty, Art. 7

tion is an aspect of preparation for possible self-defensive action which comes within the letter of Article 51 of the UN Charter. The precise nature of the obligation to assist a victim of armed attack varies from one treaty to the other.[55] Signatories of the Brussels Treaty, for instance, undertook to provide automatic 'military and other aid' to any of their members which becomes a victim of attack in Europe.[56] Under the Southeast Asian Treaty and the ANZUS Treaty, each party merely recognizes that an armed aggression against any one of them constitutes a danger to its own peace and security, and undertakes to act to meet the common danger in accordance with its constitutional processes. Both treaties permit each signatory to decide whether aggression has indeed occurred and what measures it will take.[57] Unlike the Warsaw Pact (Article 4) or the Rio Treaty (Article 3(2)), neither the Manila Treaty nor the ANZUS Treaty contemplates collective action to meet a common danger beyond and subsequent to the initial measures already taken individually. On the theory that an armed attack against one is an attack against all, the North Atlantic Treaty, the Rio Treaty, the Warsaw Pact, and the Collective Self-Defence Pact of the Arab League create a legal duty for their signatory states to go to the defence of a state which has been attacked and which has requested assistance. What is left for the individual state to determine is the nature of the assistance it is prepared to offer. Of the three treaties only the Rio Treaty explicitly contemplates the use of the regional defence system against an aggressor signatory to the treaty.[58] This of course does not necessarily mean that the Warsaw Treaty Organization or NATO cannot legally be used to assist a member which has been attacked by another signatory provided that members are willing to use the organization in such a situation.

Finally, and perhaps most important, in accordance with the requirement of Article 51 of the UN Charter, regional treaties expressly provide that measures taken in self-defence shall not only be reported to the Security Council but also be terminated as soon as the Security Council has been able to take the necessary action to restore peace.

The similarity in the legal regulation of the use of force by both the UN Charter and regional treaties should not be permitted to obscure the important difference in the scope of the right of the universal and regional organizations to employ force. As a collective security agency, the UN has been

55 Boutros-Ghali, *Contribution à Une Théorie Générale des Alliances*, 59ff
56 Sir Eric Beckett, *The North Atlantic Treaty, the Brussels Treaty and the Charter of the United Nations* (London, 1950), p. 23
57 RIIA, *Collective Self-Defence in South East Asia*, 13; Starke, *ANZUS Treaty Alliance*, 124
58 Boutros-Ghali, *Contribution à Une Théorie Générale des Alliances*, 64

empowered to maintain peace globally (Article 2(6)). The right of the UN to enforce peace when disturbed is not, strictly speaking, limited to the situation of an armed attack as is the case of regional organizations. To further emphasize the more stringent limitations imposed upon the right of regional organizations to the use of force, Article 53 prohibits regional enforcement measures except with the prior approval of the Security Council. Whatever current practice may be, the UN Charter definitely preserves a distinction between 'collective security' and 'collective self-defence.'

The conclusion emerging from the foregoing discussion is that the problem of mutual compatibility between the United Nations Charter and regional treaties for the maintenance of peace has not in fact been one of legal engineering. The international legal scholar whose preference is for the emergence of an effective and superior universal legal system need not, at least in one sense, despair at the proliferation of diverse systems of legal order. He could take partial consolation in the fact that regional treaties are generally similar to the UN Charter in so far as they have generally restated for local application those legal principles and practices of general international law which found their way into the UN Charter.[59] A hardheaded political realist would, of course, be inclined to pay more attention to how, in concrete cases, statesmen had interpreted the constitutional competences, legal obligations, and political roles of both the United Nations and regional organizations. He would regard the emerging trend as a more reliable indicator of which organization, universal or regional, has in practice more often commanded superior loyalty from the nation states, and under what circumstances.

59 For a similar conclusion, see 'Diverse Systems of World Order Today,' ASIL, *Proceedings* (1959), 21-45; Howard S. Levie, 'Some Constitutional Aspects of Selected Regional Organizations: A Comparative Study,' *CJTL* v (1966), 14-67, Starke, 'Regionalism as a Problem of International Law,' in G.A. Lipsky, ed., *Law and Politics in the World Community* (Berkeley, 1953), 126

5
Pacific settlement of disputes: jurisdiction and venue

The compatibility of a regional treaty with the UN Charter depends on the consistency of duties deriving from the two sets of obligations. The Report of the Rapporteur of Committee IV/2 stated *inter alia*: 'It has been deemed preferable to have the rule depend upon and linked with the case of a conflict between two categories of obligations. In such a case, the obligations of the Charter would be preeminent and would exclude any others.'[1] The extent to which the operational behaviour of regional organizations is consistent with the duties of UN membership is consequently a matter of empirical determination.

THE GUATEMALAN CASE: 1954

Faced with subversive intervention by insurgent forces crossing from the Honduran-Nicaraguan frontiers and aiming at the overthrow of his communist-dominated government, Colonel Arbenz, Head of the Guatemalan Government, appealed in June 1954 to both the Organization of American States and the United Nations to help put a stop to an open aggression allegedly sponsored by Honduras and Nicaragua.[2] The Arbenz request to the OAS was subsequently suspended and finally withdrawn. When the Security Council first convened on 20 June 1954, it considered a Brazilian-Colombian draft resolution urging the Security Council to refer the Guate-

1 UNCIO, *Documents* XIII, 707
2 Cmd 9277 (London, 1954); UN Doc. S/3232

malan complaint to the OAS for action.[3] The resolution was not adopted as a result of a Soviet veto. But a French sponsored resolution calling for cessation of the subversive intervention was unanimously passed. The Security Council met a second time on 25 June. It was unable to adopt an agenda and the Guatemalan complaint of aggression could not be further considered. The Arbenz government was left to face the possibility of dealing with a regional organization which, against the background of the anti-communist Caracas Declaration of March 1954, seemed determined to indict Arbenz as an agent of international communism in the Western Hemisphere instead of taking up the charge of aggression preferred against Honduras and Nicaragua. Meanwhile, Arbenz had been ousted, and with the formation in Guatemala of a new anti-communist government, the situation appeared to have passed the crisis point.

The simultaneous appeal by the Arbenz government to the UN and the OAS brought into sharp focus for the first time the problem which had agitated Peru at San Francisco,[4] – the concurrent consideration of a dispute or situation by both a regional organization and the United Nations. The problem in June 1954 was, however, fundamentally more serious than this in as much as it involved a determined attempt by a regional organization led by a most powerful state to deny United Nations competence to deal with the matter. The legal and political battle in the Security Council was over what Ambassador Lodge aptly described as 'the fundamental question of venue,'[5] involving, as it did, interpretation of the relevant provisions of the UN Charter. The Guatemalan affair was a confrontation between the principles of universality and regionalism in the search for peace, but also a confrontation between the United States and the Soviet Union concerning how the powers and authority of the United Nations should be exercised. Working out an acceptable relationship between the world and regional organization should therefore be placed in the context of the developing relations between the East and the West.

In terms of the UN Charter, Security Council debate centred on the competing claims of Articles 31(1) and 52(2) on the one hand, and of Articles 34, 35, and 39 on the other. Some members, principally the United States, Brazil, and Colombia, argued that in accordance with Articles 33(1) and 52(2) of the UN Charter, Article 23 of the revised OAS Charter, and Article 2 of the Pact of Bogota, Guatemala was under obligation to seek redress first

3 UN Doc. s/3636 (1954)
4 UNCIO, *Documents* XII, 685
5 UN Doc. s/pv. 675, par. 1 (1954)

with the OAS.[6] They defended the regional priority argument on both legal and practical grounds. Another group of members, notably Britain, New Zealand, and France accepted the regional priority argument on these grounds, but defended the responsibility and competence of the United Nations.[7] According to the British representative, 'there is a state of affairs to which the Security Council certainly cannot remain indifferent since it raises a problem concerning the maintenance of peace and security.'[8] However, by not voting in support of the adoption of the agenda on 25 June, Britain and France demonstrated that political loyalty to the United States overrides loyalty to the UN Charter. Commenting on the way the British delegate voted, Sir Anthony Eden later wrote: 'If allies are to act in concert only when their views are identical, alliances have no meaning.'[9] A third policy, 'keeping OAS out,' was adopted by Guatemala and the Soviet Union. Treating the Arbenz complaint as one involving an act of aggression against Guatemala rather than simply a dispute between Guatemala and her neighbours, the Soviet and Guatemalan representatives called for Security Council action on the basis of Articles 24, 25, 39, and 42 of the UN Charter. The Soviet Union considered the OAS legally incompetent to deal with a complaint of aggression and defended both the unchallengeable constitutional right of Guatemala to appeal to the Security Council and the duty of the world body to stand up to its responsibility.

A possible way of dealing with the complaint most consistent with the UN Charter would have been to accept the amendment proposed by the Lebanese delegate to the Brazilian-Colombian draft resolution. Malik urged the Security Council to accept and face the fact that the OAS was already seized of the matter, but to refrain from explicitly referring it to the regional organization. This would ensure that the jurisdiction of the Security Council was maintained[10] and would have discouraged the impression that the Council was abandoning its responsibility to a 'lesser' body. If the complaint was a dispute between Guatemala and her neighbours, Article 52(3) would clearly have provided legal support for the referral of the dispute to the OAS, especially as Guatemala had herself appealed to the OAS. Furthermore, there is nothing in Article 36(1) to suggest that the Security Council cannot recommend that a dispute be referred to a regional organization. If

---

6 UN Doc. S/PV. 675, par. 63, 65, 156, 157 (1954); UN Doc. S/PV. 676, par. 19, 27 (1954)

7 UN Doc. S/PV. 675, par. 75, 92 (1954)

8 *Ibid.*, par. 86

9 Sir Anthony Eden, *Full Circle* (London, 1960), 138

10 UN Doc. S/PV. 675, par. 130 (1954)

the matter was indeed one of aggression, the decision or recommendation which the Security Council is competent to make under Article 39 does not exclude the referral of the complaint to the OAS, although such a procedure might not have been intended by the authors of the San Francisco Charter.[11]

In terms of the jungle law of international behaviour under which considerations of legal niceties are very often subordinated to calculations of political advantages, the main issue at stake for the United States in the Security Council debate was whether the Soviet Union should be permitted to meddle in the affairs of the Western Hemisphere through permanent membership in the Security Council. Addressing the Soviet delegate, Lodge of the United States said: 'Stay out of this hemisphere and do not try to start your plans and conspiracies over here.'[12] At the time of the Soviet armed intervention in Hungary in 1956 and of the Soviet-sponsored invasion of Czechoslovakia in 1968, the Soviet representative likewise took the position that it was no business of the Security Council of which the United States is a permanent member to interfere in the affairs of the socialist commonwealth of Eastern Europe.[13] In the Guatemalan case, the Soviet Union was a vigorous defender and champion of an effective universal organization. But there is no doubt that this position was motivated by a desire to deny the United States the opportunity of using the OAS to indict Guatemala as an agent of communism. The Guatemalan case represents a victory for the view that a member of a regional organization should first go to that organization before appealing to the Security Council. By closing its door to a UN member, the Security Council established a precedent based on a distorted interpretation of the Charter law of universal-regional relationship.

THE CUBAN CASE: 1960

In July 1960, Cuba lodged before the Security Council a complaint of repeated threats, harrassment, intrigues, and aggression allegedly directed against her by the United States.[14] According to the Cuban Minister for Foreign Affairs, Raul Roa, the international behaviour of the United States

11 J.E.S. Fawcett, 'Intervention in International Law: A Study of Some Recent Cases,'
   Recueil des Cours CIII (1961), part II, 382
12 UN Doc. S/PV. 675, par. 172 (1954)
13 See Thomas M. Franck and Edward Weisband, *World Politics: Verbal Strategy Among the Super Powers* (London, 1971)
14 UN Doc. S/4378 (1960)

towards Cuba 'constitutes political intervention and economic aggression, which are expressly condemned in Articles 15 and 16 of the Charter of the Organization of American States.'[15]

The concept of 'economic aggression' deserves some preliminary comments. The authors of the UN Charter deliberately avoided placing any definition on the term 'aggression,'[16] but the use of the term in the Charter cannot be construed as necessarily excluding forms of intervention other than the use of armed force. Although Latin American and Afro-Asian states have characterized economic pressure and coercion as forms of aggression within the context of the UN Charter, consensus has yet to emerge among UN members on the meaning of economic aggression and specifically on whether economic pressure constitutes a form of aggression.[17] Largely at the instigation of the Latin American Republics, the OAS Charter, in contrast, states specifically that 'No State may use or encourage the use of coercive measures of an economic or political character in order to force the sovereign will of another State and obtain from it advantages of any kind' (Article 19).

The Security Council went into session on 18 July to consider the Cuban charge. Cuba argued before the Security Council that if Article 52(2) of the UN Charter was invoked to support the legal obligation on her part to have recourse to the OAS before going to the Security Council, such contention ignores the important reservation in Article 52(4). While acknowledging that the OAS Charter requires all international disputes between American states to be submitted to the pacific procedures of the OAS before they are referred to the Security Council (Article 23), the Cuban spokesman drew attention to the provisions of Article 137 of the OAS Charter which states that none of the provisions of the OAS Charter should be construed as impairing the rights and obligations of member states under the UN Charter.[18] The essence of the Cuban argument was that a regional organization like the OAS has no exclusive jurisdiction over a dispute that may arise among its members. While the OAS may be a proper forum for discussing any US-Cuban controversy, it is by no means the only forum. The Cuban representative

---

15 UN Doc. S/PV. 874, par. 69 (1960)
16 Julius Stone, *Aggression and World Order* (Berkeley, 1958), 41ff; Okon Udokang, 'The Role of the New States in International Law,' *Archiv des Völkerrechts* xv (1971), 154
17 See the 1964 and 1966 Reports of the UN Special Committee on Principles of International Law Concerning Friendly Relations and Co-operation among States, UN Doc. A/5746 (16 November 1964); UN Doc. A/6230 (17 June 1966)
18 UN Doc. S/PV. 874, par. 6-9 (1960)

was persuasive when he said: 'Were it otherwise, we would be obliged to reach the sad conclusion that the American States, upon forming a regional agency, suffered an impairment of their rights, that they renounce their rights under the United Nations Charter, whereas there can be no question that what they did was to supplement their rights under the United Nations Charter with those which they enjoy under the regional agency.'[19] Support for the Cuban position came from the Soviet Union and Poland. The Soviet bloc countries insisted that the Security Council had a clear obligation to discharge its constitutional responsibility by dealing with the complaint. The Soviet representative forcefully argued that, from the legal standpoint, the proposal to refer the complaint to the Organization of American States was 'contrary to the United Nations Charter.'[20] This is incorrect; but the Soviet representative was more convincing when he declared that, from the political standpoint, whether or not its sponsors so intended, 'the effective purpose of the proposal is to prevent the Security Council from taking the requisite effective measures to protect the national independence and political and territorial integrity of Cuba, a purpose that suits the convenience of the United States.'[21]

The argument invoked by the OAS members of the Security Council to use OAS first was based not so much on legal as on practical grounds. Lodge announced that the United States 'does not think that a theoretical and legal analysis of this question is indispensable.'[22] In support of the proposal urging the Security Council to desist from acting on the Cuban complaint, Lodge offered this explanation: 'If we look at the matter from a practical standpoint – and since it is generally recognized that no country can be denied access to organizations of which it is a member – we find one circumstance which cannot but affect our decision. That circumstance is that the situation with which we are dealing is already under consideration by the Organization of American States; and this is a fact we cannot overlook.'[23] The explanation is not persuasive since neither the constitutional right of UN members to have recourse to the Security Council nor the competence of the Security Council to investigate any complaint brought to its attention is in any way qualified by the condition that when a matter is already being examined by a regional organization, a party to the dispute can no longer exercise its right under Article 35(1) or that the Security Council must await

19 *Ibid.*, par. 8
20 UN Doc. S/PV. 876, par. 128 (1960)
21 *Ibid.*
22 UN Doc. S/PV. 874, par. 134 (1960)
23 *Ibid.*

the result of regional investigation and action before discharging its responsibility under the Charter.

The Security Council approved a draft resolution which requested the Council to take note of the fact that the complaint was being investigated by the OAS, to adjourn consideration of the matter pending receipt of an OAS report, and to invite the OAS to assist in promoting pacific settlement.[24] Earlier, the Security Council had rejected a Soviet amendment calling for the omission of all references to the OAS in the draft sponsored by Ecuador and Argentina. The way in which the Cuban complaint was dealt with leaves much to be desired in as much as the Security Council discharged its responsibility in a manner that reflected easy capitulation to the OAS. The Ceylonese representative pointed out that the proposal to adjourn amounted to 'only an interruption of the discussion that is now proceeding in this Council . . . It cannot be construed as an attempt to deny Cuba the right to have its case heard and decided here. It is not in any sense, therefore, a kind of manoeuvre to put off consideration.'[25]

It was generally agreed that the right of a UN member to bring its complaint to the Security Council cannot be denied, but there is the question of whether the United Nations can be said to be effectively discharging its functions by merely undertaking to review the work of a regional organization. The decision of the Security Council to refer the Cuban complaint to the OAS constituted a precedent.

THE DOMINICAN CRISIS: 1965

The outbreak of civil war in the Dominican Republic in April 1965 brought the United Nations and the OAS together, for the first time, in a concurrent but independent search for peace in the Western Hemisphere. The Dominican crisis also saw the creation of an Inter-American Peace Force and the specific assignment of political functions to the Secretary-General of the OAS.

President Johnson ordered the US Marines into Santo Domingo, ostensibly to protect the life of American citizens. He later increased the strength of the American troops in order to forestall an alleged communist take-over of the Dominican government.[26] At the request of Chile, the Tenth Meeting of Consultation of the OAS met on 30 April to consider the situation. The

24 UN Doc. S/4395 (19 July 1960)
25 UN Doc. S/PV. 875, par. 32 (1960)
26 US Dept of State, *Bulletin* LII (May 1965), 738

OAS grappled with the crisis first by despatching its Secretary-General on a peace mission to Santo Domingo. Later, it established a five-man Special Committee with a broad political mandate to help establish peace in the strife-torn Republic. The mandate of the Special Committee was at one stage transferred to the Secretary-General and, subsequently, to a three-man Ad hoc Committee through which peace in the Republic was finally achieved.[27]

From the beginning, the OAS did not treat US intervention as a case of aggression in violation of Article 18 of the amended OAS Charter. The Tenth Meeting of Consultation of the OAS was neither convened under Article 6 of the Rio Treaty which deals with aggression which is not armed attack, nor under Article 3 concerning armed aggression, but under Article 59 of the OAS Charter 'in order to consider problems of an urgent nature and of common interest to the American States.' The Tenth Meeting of Consultation, after a heated debate in which Uruguay, Mexico, Ecuador, Chile, and Peru opposed unilateral intervention by the United States in the Dominican Republic, adopted on 6 May one of the most significant resolutions bearing on the Dominican crisis. The Resolution provided the basis for the creation of the Inter-American Peace Force,[28] made up of contingents from several member states with a unified command under the authority of the OAS, and empowered to supervise the cessation of hostilities and to maintain law and order. The Force was deployed without the consent of the Government of the Dominican Republic, but this is not quite the same thing as saying that the Peace Force was deployed *against* its will. There was no central authority in Santo Domingo at that time. One of the two provisions in the temporary cease-fire agreement negotiated by the Papal Nuncio on 30 April was the undertaking by the OAS to serve as arbitrator in the conflict.[29] The Constitutionalist Government under Colonel Caamano promised 'to accept the mediation of the [OAS] Special Committee,'[30] and, under the Act of Domingo, both General Imbert and Colonel Caamano declared that they accepted and recognized 'the full competence of the Special Committee . . . for the purposes of the faithful observance of what is agreed to in the

27 Pan American Union, *Annual Report of the Secretary-General* (Washington, 1965); John Carey, ed., *The Dominican Republic Crisis 1965* (New York, 1967), 36-8
28 *ILM* IV (1965), 594; James R. Jose, *An Inter-American Peace Force within the Framework of the Organization of American States: Advantages, Impediments, Implications* (Metuchen, 1970)
29 UN Doc. S/6364, Report of the OAS to the UN Secretary-General (1965)
30 *Ibid.*

[Santo Domingo] Agreement.'[31] Neither faction asked why and by whose authority the OAS Peace Force was in Santo Domingo, but merely complained about how the Force was being used. As the Inter-American Peace Force was, in conception and practice, peace-keeping and not an enforcement force, its establishment does not require the prior approval of the Security Council.

The Security Council was called into session to consider the question of the armed interference by the United States in the internal affairs of the Dominican Republic.[32] The representative of Jordan cast the problem faced by the Security Council in this pertinent question: 'Are we, in the world today, trying to establish a strong international system for world peace and order, or are we tending to substitute for it a regional system for the same objectives? On the answer to that question depends the course of action we should adopt.'[33] The decision of the Security Council, while making some concession to the first, leans more heavily on the second alternative. After a protracted debate, the Council decided to send a special Representative to Santo Domingo with a restricted mandate to secure a cease-fire, observe, and report to the Security Council.[34] This decision represents a minimalist interpretation of the competence of the United Nations. For all practical purposes, the United Nations was completely overshadowed by the US-led Organization of American States,[35] but it is significant that for the first time in the history of the United Nations, both the world organization and the OAS operated concurrently at the scene of action in the resolution of a crisis.

The issue of the respective competences of the United Nations and the OAS in the search for peace in the Dominican Republic was viewed by the Soviet Union primarily in the context of the military intervention of the United States in the domestic affairs of a sovereign member of the United Nations. Such an intervention would constitute a violation of the fundamental principle of the UN Charter and of the universally recognized rule of customary international law, unless a request for foreign assistance had ac-

31 *Ibid.*
32 UN Doc. S/6316 (1965)
33 UN Doc. S/PV. 1215, par. 12 (1965)
34 UN Doc. S/6355 (1965)
35 Dona Baron, 'The Dominican Crisis of 1965: A Case-Study of the Regional vs. the Global Approach to International Peace and Security,' in Andrew Cordier, ed., *Columbia Essays in International Affairs*, III: *The Dean's Paper, 1967* (New York, 1968), 1-31; L.B. Miller, *World Order and Local Disorder: The United Nations in Internal Conflicts* (Princeton, 1967), 149ff

tually been made by the legitimate constitutional authority in Santo Domingo. In the Dominican situation, as in the Hungarian crisis almost a decade before, the authenticity of the request for assistance purported to have been made is highly questionable.[36] Thus, as a case of armed intervention without an authentic request, it was correctly urged by Fedorenko, the Soviet representative, that '[t]he Security Council is . . . not only within its rights, but is in duty bound to give urgent consideration to the question.'[37] The legal competence of the Security Council, it was urged, rested firmly on the provisions of Articles 24, 25, and 39 of the UN Charter.

The main argument advanced by the United States and her supporters was that 'the purposes of the United Nations Charter will hardly be served if two international organizations are seeking to do things in the same place with the same people at the same time.'[38] The coalition in support of the thesis of OAS supremacy did not so much deny the competence of the Security Council as assert the practical common sense in allowing the regional organization to continue with the search for peace. In obvious reference to the Guatemalan and Cuban cases, Ambassador Stevenson of the United States declared that 'it would be constructive and in keeping with precedents established by this Council to permit the regional organization to deal with this regional problem.'[39] Stevenson was suggesting that, as the Security Council had abdicated its role in the previous cases and hence set a precedent, there was no reason why such precedent could not be followed in the Dominican case. Discountenancing the charge of aggression against the United States, Stevenson continued to refer to Articles 33(1) and 52(2) of the UN Charter as providing the necessary support for the effort to make the matter the primary responsibility of the OAS. In fact, supporters of the OAS priority argument would concede the appropriateness of UN intervention only when it could be demonstrated that the OAS was acting improperly and deficiently. They denied that this position would in any way 'deprive the Security Council . . . of the possibility of action in other situations at earlier stages, or of resuming its activities in this case if it became necessary to do so.'[40]

Preference shown by the United States in favour of the settlement of the Dominican crisis and the preservation of peace in Western Hemisphere un-

36 Theodore Draper, *The Dominican Revolt: A Case Study in American Policy* (New York, 1968), 121
37 UN Doc. S/PV. 1198, par. 143 (1965)
38 UN Doc. S/PV. 1217, 21 (1965)
39 UN Doc. S/PV. 1196, par. 88 (1965)
40 UN Doc. S/PV. 1204, par. 91-2 (1965); UN Doc. S/PV. 1217, par. 26-32 (1965)

der the auspices of the OAS instead of the United Nations clearly reflected American determination to prevent the Soviet Union from meddling in the affairs of the New World. So determined was the United States to influence outcome and stage-manage the promotion of peace in the Dominican Republic that she considered it necessary to sponsor unilaterally an American presidential mission under McGeorge Bundy to seek peaceful settlement independently of the efforts of the Organization of American States.[41]

The attempt to reduce the essence of universal-regional relationship in the peaceful adjustment of disputes to the provision of Article 54, which requires regional organizations to keep the Security Council informed of their activities, leaves much to be desired. In a situation where charges of unauthorized armed intervention have been made, merely keeping the Security Council informed of the activities of a regional organization is, as the Cuban representative pointed out, a very poor substitute for the direct cognizance of the situation by the Security Council.[42]

THE LEBANESE CRISIS: 1958

In May 1958, the Republic of Lebanon faced a major constitutional crisis arising from the attempt by President Chamoun to amend the nation's constitution so that he might again be a presidential candidate in the forthcoming elections. The crisis led to disturbances organized by forces hostile to the Chamoun Government. Accusing the United Arab Republic of supplying arms to subversive elements in Lebanon and inciting them to overthrow his legitimate government in Beirut, President Chamoun appealed to the League of Arab States and the Security Council to condemn and put an end to foreign intervention in the domestic affairs of his country.[43]

The Security Council convened immediately on 25 May to examine the Lebanese complaint against the UAR. It was urged before the world body that as Lebanon herself had appealed to the Arab League, the Security Council had a duty to allow the regional organization to promote peace in the Middle East. Consequently, the Security Council unanimously voted to suspend consideration of the complaint when it was learned that the Arab League was about to deal with the same matter. Lebanon, which had called the Security Council into session, did not object to deferment of Security

---

41 R.J. Dupuy, 'Les Etats-Unies, L'O.E.A. et L'O.N.U. à Saint Dominque,' *AFDI* XI (1965), 71-110; Jerome Slater, *Intervention and Negotiation: The United States and the Dominican Revolution* (New York, 1970)
42 UN Doc. S/PV. 1198, par. 68 (1965)
43 UN Doc. S/4007 (23 May 1958)

Council consideration, but reserved her right to request the world body to take up the complaint at any time.[44] Thus, at the early stages in the search for peace in the Middle East, the simultaneous consideration of a complaint by both the universal and the regional organization appeared to have been deliberately avoided.

The Lebanese complaint was taken up by the Arab League Council at its extraordinary session held at Benghazi. The Lebanese delegation reiterated its accusation against the UAR and asked the regional organization to censure the UAR for fomenting disorder in Lebanon in violation of Article 8 of the Pact of the League of Arab States which prohibits interference by one state in the domestic affairs of another. Emphatically denying the charge of armed intervention in the internal affairs of Lebanon, the UAR delegation contended that the crisis was precipitated by domestic political differences between the governing party and the National Front. A burning desire to keep the promotion of peace under the auspices of the Arab League was particularly evident in the deliberations of the Arab League Council. To this end, Saudi Arabia, Iraq, Jordan, Yemen, Libya, and the Sudan sponsored a resolution which, among other things, urged Lebanon to withdraw the complaint it had placed before the Security Council, called upon the various groups in Lebanon to settle their domestic problems by peaceful and constitutional means 'in accordance with the letter and the spirit of the Pact of the League of Arab States,' and authorized the Arab League Council to despatch a committee to Lebanon to help to promote peace.[45] The resolution was apparently acceptable to both the Lebanese and the UAR delegations; but the Lebanese Government, in a surprise announcement, rejected the resolution on 5 June 1958. This led to speculation that the Chamoun government was not sincerely interested in having the crisis resolved at the regional level as it lacked confidence in the impartiality of a regional organization dominated by the very state against which a charge of unprovoked intervention had been laid. After the failure of the Arab League to take a decision acceptable to Lebanon, the Chamoun government requested the Security Council to resume consideration of the complaint.

The fundamental question of venue was in the minds of members of the Security Council when the world body went into session in June 1958. Accordingly, the Lebanese representative, Malik, thought it necessary to remind the Security Council of the following facts:

44 *SCOR*, 13th Yr., 818th Mtg (25 May 1958)
45 Text of the resolution in *SCOR*, 13th Yr. 823rd Mtg (6 June 1958)

Lebanon placed its present complaint first before the League of Arab States. We are a member of that regional organization and we wanted its machinery to deal first, with our issue. Then we brought it to the attention of the Security Council . . . The Arab League has been in session for six days on this question. It has taken no decision on it. Consequently, the Government of Lebanon is now bound, much to its regret, to press this issue before the Security Council.[46]

Faced with the question of whether the disturbances in Lebanon were caused by internal antagonism or were provoked by foreign armed support for the anti-government forces, the Security Council, with only the Soviet Union abstaining, adopted a Swedish draft resolution calling for the establishment of an observer group 'to proceed to Lebanon so as to ensure that there is no illegal infiltration of personnel or supply of arms or other material across the Lebanese borders.'[47] Neither Lebanon nor the UAR objected to the resolution. The Secretary-General proceeded to set up the United Nations Observation Group in Lebanon (UNOGIL) and the Security Council thus successfully seized political initiative from the League of Arab States. With the aggravation of the situation in the Middle East brought about by the overthrow of the Iraqi government in July 1958 and the landing of American troops in Lebanon at the request of the Chamoun government,[48] the claim that the League of Arab States should be the primary agency for bringing about peace between Lebanon and its neighbours receded further into the background. If the Security Council had not been involved in the search for peace in the Middle East, the logic of the new situation created by the presence of American forces in Lebanon would certainly have made UN involvement absolutely imperative.

Those who condemned US intervention as either politically unwise or as a violation of the UN Charter were all in agreement with the view of the representative of Japan that 'a solution to the Lebanese question should be sought only through the machinery of the United Nations . . . [I]t is not desirable that one country should take on its own judgment specific measures without waiting for . . . the United Nations.'[49] The Security Council was unable to pass any resolution on the basis of which the new problem created

46 *Ibid.*
47 Security Council Resolution s/4023 (1958)
48 Dupuy, 'Aggression indirecte et intervention solicitée: A propos de l'affaire libanaise,' *AFDI* v (1959), 451-67; Quincy Wright, 'United States Intervention in the Lebanon,' *AJIL* LIII (1959), 112-25
49 *SCOR*, 13th Yr., 833rd Mtg (18 July 1958), cited in L.B. Sohn, *The United Nations in Action* (Brooklyn, 1968), 209

by American intervention could be solved, and an emergency meeting of the UN General Assembly was called in August 1958.

Having failed to keep the Lebanese complaint exclusively within their regional organization, the Arab states were determined to act in concert to ensure the early withdrawal of US forces from Lebanon. Coincidentally, in a letter to the President of the General Assembly, the US Secretary of State gave assurance that American forces would be withdrawn from Lebanon 'whenever this is requested by the duly constituted Government of Lebanon or whenever, as a result of the further action of the United Nations or otherwise, their presence is no longer required. The United States will in any event abide by a determination of the United Nations General Assembly that action taken or assurance furnished by the United Nations makes the continued presence of United States forces in Lebanon unnecessary for the maintenance of international peace and security.'[50] On the basis of a proposal sponsored by ten Arab States, including Lebanon and the UAR, the General Assembly adopted unanimously a resolution calling upon the Secretary-General to make practical arrangements, in consultation with the Governments concerned, for an early withdrawal of foreign troops from Lebanon and Jordan, and upon UN members to refrain from interfering in the domestic affairs of other states.[51] The United States completed the evacuation of her forces in October 1958 and after the new government of General Chehab had established its control over the entire Lebanese territory, the expanded UNOGIL was dismissed in December 1958.[52]

CYPRUS CRISIS: 1963-64 AND 1974

The Cyprus problem has been a divisive issue within the North Atlantic Alliance since the 1950s.[53] The island of Cyprus is composed of two ethnic groups, the Greek Cypriots, who constitute about eighty per cent of the total population, and the Turkish Cypriots. Two NATO members, Greece and Turkey, have been specially interested in protecting the rights of their respective groups. Greece has always urged a political solution based on the principle of self-determination, majority rule, and internationally guaran-

50 UN Doc. A/3876 (18 August 1958)
51 General Assembly Resolution 1237 (ES-III) 21 August 1958
52 D.W. Wainhouse et al., *International Peace Observation* (Baltimore, 1966), 374-86
53 Stephen Xydis, *Cyprus: Conflict and Conciliation, 1954-1958* (Columbus, 1967); Thomas Ehrlich, 'Cyprus, the "Warlike Isle": Origins and Elements of the Current Crisis,' *Stanford Law Review* XVIII (1965-66), 1021-98

teed minority rights.[54] Turkey seems to prefer partition of the island along ethnic lines and would have intervened militarily in 1964 but for the restraining influence of the United States.[55] Britain was especially interested in preserving her strategic military bases on the island, while the NATO concern arose from the fear that a conflict between Turkey and Greece over Cyprus might impair the co-operation of both members within the North Atlantic Alliance.[56] In late 1963, a civil war broke out between the Greek and the Turkish communities in Cyprus despite protracted efforts to evolve an acceptable solution under the auspices of the North Atlantic Alliance.[57]

The Anglo-American strategy aimed at keeping the promotion of peace between the two Cypriot communities within the NATO framework. Thus, for instance, Britain, supported by the United States, proposed the creation of a NATO peace-keeping force of ten thousand men to separate the two warring communities. It was calculated that effective policing of a cease-fire by a NATO force would make a UN intervention less justifiable. The British plan was of course rejected by the Archbishop Makarios, who insisted that the United Nations was the most appropriate organization to deal with the situation.[58] Even if Cyprus were a NATO member, it would still have been within its constitutional right to have direct access to the world body. Archbishop Makarios' preference for the United Nations as a venue for the search for settlement did not provoke open challenge from the NATO powers which had hoped to prevent Soviet participation in the evolution of a settlement through the Security Council.

The Security Council responded to the 1963-64 crisis in Cyprus by agreeing unanimously to create a UN peace-keeping force to be stationed in Cyprus with the consent of the Cyprus government, and to appoint a mediator mandated to promote peaceful settlement of the problem of coexistence between the two communities.[59] For the past ten years the UN has helped to maintain a semblance of political order between the two Cypriot communi-

---

54 Theodore Couloumbis, *Greek Political Reaction to American and NATO Influences* (New Haven, 1966), 176ff; Calogeropoulos-Stratis, *La Grèce et les Nations Unies* (New York, 1957), 147-56
55 University of Ankara, *Turkey and the United Nations* (New York, 1961), 195-6
56 Philip Windsor, 'NATO and the Cyprus Crisis,' *Adelphi Papers*, no. 14 (November 1964)
57 Cmd 566 (London, 1958)
58 Linda B. Miller, *Cyprus: The Law and Politics of Civil Strife* (Cambridge, Mass., 1968), 27ff, Windsor, 'NATO and the Cyprus Crisis,' 13
59 Security Council Resolution s/5735, 4 March 1964; James A. Stegenga, *The United Nations Force in Cyprus* (Columbus, 1968)

ties by periodically renewing the mandate of the UN Peace-keeping Force (UNFICYP) stationed on the strife-torn island.

The Greek-Turkish cleavage over the political future of Cyprus surfaced dramatically again in July 1974 when the Greek officers seconded to the Cypriot National Guard engineered a coup against the government of Makarios and installed the former EOKA terrorist, Nikos Sampson, as President of the Republic. The coup achieved for Athens de facto *enosis* (union between Greece and Cyprus) unacceptable to Ankara, thus precipitating the Turkish invasion of Cyprus on 20 July 1974.

In the ensuing search for peace, no serious consideration was at any time publicly given to NATO as a venue for the resolution of the crisis. There was, however, broad support for Security Council initiative. The Council discussed the threat to peace in the eastern Mediterranean in full awareness that the 1960 Treaty of Guarantee, which assigned special responsibilities to Greece, Turkey, and the United Kingdom and under which Cyprus became independent, provides a political framework for resolution of conflicts. Thus, while calling for an immediate cease-fire, an end to foreign military intervention, and a prompt withdrawal of unauthorized foreign military personnel from Cyprus, Security Council resolution 353 of 20 July expressly urged the three guarantors of the 1960 London-Zurich treaty to enter into negotiations for the restoration of peace and constitutional government in Cyprus. Pursuant to this resolution and in keeping with the Treaty of Guarantee, negotiations for peaceful settlement proceeded in Geneva, only to be subsequently interrupted by the resumption of fighting in Cyprus. The Council's efforts have since been to arrange resumption of negotiations in Geneva, to ensure all-party co-operation with UNFICYP in maintaining peace, and to achieve compliance with the resolution of 20 July.[60]

THE ALGERIA-MOROCCO BORDER DISPUTE: 1963

The UN and the OAU have had to grapple with two types of disputes in Africa: inter-state disputes arising out of the colonial legacy of artificial boundaries, and intra-state political crises leading to civil war and secession. The Organization of African Unity, without expounding a rigid thesis of exclusive regional jurisdiction, has usually indicated its preference for solutions within the framework of the principles and institutions established under the Addis Ababa Charter. The UN has also tended to encourage the

60 For texts of relevant Security Council resolutions, see US Dept of State, *Bulletin* LXXI (12 August 1974), 266 and (9 September 1974), 368-9

OAU to promote peace not only between African States but also between warring factions within African states.

The boundary dispute between Algeria and Morocco which erupted into open military hostilities in late 1963 provided the first opportunity for observing the implementation of the UN Charter law of universal-regional relationship in the promotion of peace in Africa. The fundamental question of the appropriate venue for the resolution of the dispute was not raised in an acute manner.[61] King Hassan II of Morocco, reluctant to seek OAU mediation, brought the dispute to the attention of U Thant, the UN Secretary-General; but he did not request a meeting of the Security Council. The Moroccan government reasoned that its case was unlikely to be impartially considered by a regional organization which is unequivocally committed to the preservation of the territorial status quo in Africa. President Ben Bella of Algeria, on the contrary, by calling for OAU intervention sought recourse to a forum where he believed Algeria enjoyed comparative diplomatic advantage of sympathetic support over the boundary issue. Predictably, OAU members were themselves in favour of the dispute being considered by their regional organization rather than by the United Nations. But at no time was the constitutional right of Morocco to go before the United Nations challenged. The major Western powers, anxious to avert a possible competitive involvement of the big powers in Africa, persuaded King Hassan to seek regional solution under the auspices of the OAU.[62] There was clearly a general consensus that the dispute should be left for African leaders to settle. At first, Emperor Haile Selassie of Ethiopia and President Modibo Keita of Mali brought President Ben Bella and King Hassan together at Bamako in October 1964. When Algeria and Morocco agreed at the Four-Power Conference there to request the OAU Council of Ministers to create a Committee of Arbitration mandated to effect a definitive solution to the dispute, the jurisdictional issue regarding the respective competences of both the OAU and the UN was averted.

At its First Extra-Ordinary Session held in Addis Ababa in November 1963 to discuss the Algerian-Moroccan dispute, the OAU Council of Ministers adopted the Bamako Agreement as a basis of action and created an Ad

---

61 P.B. Wild, 'The Organization of African Unity and the Algerian-Moroccan Border Conflict: A Case Study of New Machinery for Peaceful Settlement of Disputes,' *International Organization* XX (1966), 18-36; Samuel Chime, 'The Organization of African Unity and African Boundaries,' in C.G. Widstrand, ed., *African Boundary Problems* (Uppsala, 1969), 65-79

62 Hazel Fox, 'The Settlement of Disputes by Peaceful Means and the Observation of International Law – African Attitudes,' *International Relations* (London) III (1968), 389-440, 443

Hoc Commission of Seven authorized to promote peace between Algeria and Morocco. In addition, the Council of Ministers in its final resolution re-iterated the imperative necessity to settle inter-state disputes in Africa by peaceful means and within a strictly African framework.[63] Even though the OAU Ad Hoc Commission failed to secure a settlement of the border dis-pute, it was a constructive influence to the extent that it kept reminding Al-geria and Morocco of the necessity to negotiate and to avoid the use of force.[64] When the dispute was finally resolved in June 1972, it was on the basis of the OAU Charter.

THE ETHIOPIAN- SOMALI- KENYAN BORDER DISPUTES: 1964-73

In 1964, the OAU was again called upon to promote peace between Ethiopia and Somalia and between Kenya and Somalia.[65] At the Addis Ababa Con-ference of the African Heads of State and Government in May 1963, the Somali President, Aden Abdullah Osman, had accused Ethiopia of taking possession of a large portion of Somali territory without the consent and against the wishes of the inhabitants. President Osman also laid claims to the Northern Frontier District of Kenya. Both Ethiopia and Kenya repeat-edly complained of the intrusion of armed bands allegedly sponsored by the Somali government with the aim of annexing the Ethiopian province of Ogaden and the Northern Frontier District of Kenya. In February 1964, fighting broke out between Ethiopia and Somalia. President Osman, like King Hassan in 1963, initially bypassed the OAU believing that the OAU could not be counted upon to give sympathetic hearing to the Somali case because the principle of boundary revision was anathema to many African states. Somali asked the Security Council to consider her charge of armed aggression against Ethiopia.[66] African leaders in general viewed with disfav-our the Somali call for UN intervention and persuaded President Osman to withdraw his request to the world body. Consequently, Somalia notified the Security Council that she no longer wished to raise the Ethiopian-Somali

---

63 ECM/Res. 1 (I) of 18 November 1963; text in *Resolutions, Recommendations and Statements adopted by the Ordinary and Extra-Ordinary Sessions of the Council of Ministers 1963-1967* I (Addis Ababa: OAU Secretariat, 1973), 11-12

64 B. Boutros-Ghali, *L'Organisation de L'Unité Africaine* (Paris, 1969), 53-5

65 For relevant documents, see Catherine Hoskyns, ed., *The Ethiopia-Somali-Kenya Dispute, 1960-67* (Dar-es-Salaam, 1969)

66 UN Doc. s/5536

dispute before that body 'while the problem is in the hands of the OAU.'[67] This second note appeared to have been interpreted by the Somali government as calling for a suspension of Security Council action rather than a withdrawal of the original request. Yet, in her subsequent communication with the President of the Security Council, Somalia continued to emphasize that the world body was 'virtually seized with the Somalia-Ethiopia question,'[68] a claim which has no basis since the request of 10 February 1964 was not even put on the agenda of the Security Council, let alone debated by that organ.

The OAU launched its campaign for peaceful settlement of the Ethiopian-Somali and Kenyan-Somali dispute at the Second Extra-ordinary Session of the Council of Ministers held in Dar-es-Salaam in February 1964. Reiterating its familiar thesis that the unity of Africa requires the solution to all disputes between member states to be sought first within the Organization of African Unity, the Council of Ministers called upon Ethiopia and Somalia to order an immediate cease-fire and enter into direct negotiations for peaceful settlement.[69] Kenya and Somalia were similarly urged to settle their dispute in the spirit of the OAU Charter. The Second Ordinary Session of the Council of Ministers, which met in Lagos shortly after, continued to encourage peaceful settlement through bilateral negotiations in the context of the Dar-es-Salaam Resolution.[70] Pursuant to the resolutions of the OAU, Ethiopia and Somalia met in Khartoum (March 1964), Addis Ababa (September 1967), Mogadishu (February 1968), and again in Addis Ababa (September 1968). The principal decision at Khartoum was agreement to appoint a Joint Commission composed of the representatives of the two Governments to supervise the complete withdrawal of military forces to a distance of ten to fifteen kilometres from either side of the border. At Addis Ababa in September 1967, agreement was reached to set up a Joint Commission to examine complaints of violation of the Khartoum Agreement. The main decision of the Mogadishu talk was to reactivate the Joint Commission set up in March 1964. By September 1968, the situation was sufficiently improved that Ethiopia and Somalia agreed to establish a Joint Ministerial Consultative Committee which was to meet periodically to dis-

---

67 UN Doc. s/5542
68 UN Docs s/5557 and s/5558
69 Hoskyns, *The Ethiopia-Somali-Kenya Dispute 1960-67*, 60
70 CM/Res. 16 (II) of February 1964; text in *Resolutions, Recommendations and Statements adopted by the Ordinary and Extra-Ordinary Sessions of the Council of Ministers, 1963-1967* I, 25

cuss common problems between the two countries.[71] The surfacing of the dispute in a rather dramatic manner in mid 1973 signalled the failure of the Joint Ministerial Consultative Committee. An OAU Committee under General Gowon of Nigeria is presently involved in the promotion of a peaceful settlement of the boundary dispute.

The search for pacific settlement of the Kenyan-Somali dispute was also vigorously pursued in the context of both the Dar-es-Salaam and Lagos resolutions of the OAU Council of Ministers. At the instigation of President Nyerere, the respresentatives of Kenya and Somalia met at Arusha, Tanzania, in December 1965 to discuss the normalization of relations between their two countries. The meeting was deadlocked as Somalia refused to renounce her claims to Kenya's Northern Frontier District. But at the Kinshasa Summit of the OAU Heads of State and Government in September 1967, Kenya and Somalia agreed to accept invitation from President Kaunda of Zambia to work out ways of settling their differences.[72] In fact, the Kinshasa Conference requested Kenya, Somalia, and Zambia to submit a progress report on the outcome of the proposed meeting to the Secretary-General of the OAU. At the Arusha Conference convened by President Kaunda in October 1967, Kenya and Somalia agreed to resume diplomatic relations, to maintain peace on both sides of the border, and to appoint a Working Committee of three states – Kenya, Somalia, and Zambia – not only to review periodically the implementation of the agreement reached at Arusha, but also to promote peaceful relations between Kenya and Somalia.[73]

Preference shown by members of the OAU for the view that inter-state disputes in Africa should be resolved through and by African agencies has been successfully maintained partly because no African state has adamantly insisted on ignoring the OAU and on having direct access to the world body. In addition, the acceptability of this claim has been aided by the obvious reluctance of members of the UN at large, especially the big powers, to be drawn into African disputes which were not perceived as raising fundamentally critical issues of global strategic significance.

THE CONGO CRISIS: 1960-64

The UN Charter law of universal-regional relationship which defines the respective competences of both the United Nations and regional organiza-

71 *Africa Contemporary Record* (1968-69), 623-4
72 *Africa Research Bulletin* IV (1967), 856
73 *Africa Contemporary Record* (1968-69), 624-5

tions performing the function of pacific settlement is not strictly applicable to situations of civil strife. Unless such situations threaten international peace, they fall within the domestic jurisdiction of the state concerned. The involvement of the UN and the OAU in the Congo and Nigeria is a special case. The UN was in the Congo at the invitation of the Lumumba Government, while the Nigerian Federal Military Government tacitly accepted OAU intervention as soon as it became clear that the regional organization would support the campaign for the maintenance of the territorial integrity and political unity of Nigeria in its internal conflict.[74]

Shortly after the Belgians granted independence to the Congo (now Zaire) Republic in June 1960, some sections of the national army mutinied. Faced with the intervention of Belgian forces and the secession of Katanga announced by Moise Tsombe in July 1960, the Congolese Government requested the United Nations for military assistance to protect the Congo Republic from the Belgian aggression.[75] In response to the request, the United Nations authorized Dag Hammerskjold, its Secretary-General, to furnish the necessary assistance to the Lumumba Government.

The search for peace in the Congo under the auspices of the UN was a complicated political and military exercise. The world body was able to set up an international peace-keeping force within a remarkably short period of time to supervise the cessation of hostilities and its competence to promote peace in the Republic was at no time challenged. Nevertheless, difficulties arose which militated against an early solution to the problem of domestic peace, stability, and unity in the Congo. Among these were the unspecific character of the UN mandate being implemented by the Secretary-General, the refusal of the Belgians to withdraw their troops, the competitive intervention by the big powers, and the deep division among African states on the crisis.[76] The UN did not concern itself merely with maintaining law and order, but also sought to promote national reconciliation. It sponsored a Reconciliation Commission empowered to devise a constitutional formula under which the diverse Congolese elements could live as a nation. In an attempt to insulate the crisis from the ever present threat of big power intervention and, at the same time, to emphasize its African character without of course abdicating legitimate UN responsibility, participation of African

74 Z. Cervenka, *The Organization of African Unity and Its Charter* (New York, 1969), chap. 9; *Report on the OAU Consultative Mission to Nigeria* (Lagos, 1967), 1-2

75 UN Doc. s/4381

76 L.B. Miller, *World Order and Local Disorder: The United Nations and Internal Conflicts* (Princeton, 1967), 66-116; Stanley Hoffmann, 'In Search of a Thread: The UN in the Congo Labyrinth,' *International Organization* XVI (1962), 331-61

forces in the UN peace-keeping activities and African membership in the UN Reconciliation Commission on the Congo was deliberately encouraged. The explanation for the prolonged failure of the United Nations to bring peace into the Congo should ultimately be sought in the competitive diplomatic activities of the Soviet Union and the Western powers, particularly the United States, which were based more on the cold calculation of national advantages than on unquestionable support for the UN.

African countries individually had been involved with the UN in seeking solutions to the Congo crisis since 1960. The formation of the OAU in 1963 introduced another agent into the scene. Unfortunately, the effectiveness of the OAU as a peace-promoting agency was compromised by the divergent views held by many of its members on the situation in the Congo. The regional organization's main goal was to prevent the intervention of foreign powers in Africa. It was believed this result could be achieved by Africanizing the peace-promotion exercise as much as possible.[77] OAU's strategy of Africanization neither carried with it a restrictive interpretation of the competence of the United Nations nor a loss of confidence in the ability of the world organization. Some individual African states, however, were critical of the role played by the United Nations. In fact, it was alleged by radical African states that the world organization was being used by the Western powers to keep their puppets in power in Leopoldville (Kinshasa).[78] The dependence of the Tshombe regime on Western military assistance and its heavy reliance on mercenaries recruited from Belgium, Rhodesia, and South Africa did much to encourage radical African support for the National Liberation Council led by Christopher Gbenye.

The role played by the OAU in the Congo crisis should be examined in the context of the resolution passed by the Council of Ministers in its Third Extra-Ordinary Session held at Addis Ababa in September 1964. The resolution, which expressly asserted 'the responsibilities and . . . competence of the Organization of African Unity to find a peaceful solution to all the problems and differences which affect peace and security in the African continent', created an Ad Hoc Commission of ten members under the chairmanship of Jomo Kenyatta with the mandate to help promote national

---

77 See R.C. Pradhan, 'The OAU and the Congo Crisis,' *Africa Quarterly* v (1965), 30-42; Yashpal Tandon, 'The Organization of African Unity as an Instrument and Forum of Protest,' in Robert I. Rotberg and Ali A. Mazrui, eds, *Protest and Power in Black Africa* (New York, 1970), 1153-83

78 See for example, Jitendra Mohan, 'Ghana, the Congo and the United Nations,' *JMAS* VII (1969), 369-406

reconciliation in the Congo as well as the normalization of relations between the Democratic Republic of the Congo and her neighbours.[79]

Even though Tshombe was disappointed that his call for the formation of an African force to be placed at the disposal of his central government fell on deaf ears at the Addis Ababa meeting of the OAU Council of Ministers, he pledged to implement the OAU resolution 'in the light of our sovereignty, our territorial integrity and our inalienable right to national independence.'[80] As it turned out, Tshombe never really placed any trust on the impartiality of the OAU as a promoter of peace between his central government and Gbenye's National Liberation Council. Tshombe's distrust seemed to have been reinforced by two decisions made by the Kenyatta Commission. The first was to invite representatives of the National Liberation Council to present the 'rebel' case before it; the second was to despatch a delegation to urge the US government to suspend military assistance to the regime in Leopoldville.

The search for peace by the OAU Ad Hoc Commission already prejudiced by the hostile posture adopted by the Tshombe government, was suddenly interrupted by the notorious Belgian-American intervention in Stanleyville in November 1964 – ostensibly to rescue foreign nationals being held as hostages by the rebel forces of the National Liberation Council. Undoubtedly, the Stanleyville operation shattered the fragile shell of unity within the OAU and exposed the inability of the regional organization to promote peace in a situation too much dominated by conflicts of big power interest. At its Fourth Extra-Ordinary Session held in New York in December 1964, the OAU Council of Ministers expressed the view that the American-Belgian intervention 'compromised the efforts being made by the OAU to secure national reconciliation in the Congo' and called upon the Security Council to recommend an African solution to the Congo problem.[81]

Intervention by the United States and Belgium in the Congo provided a good opportunity for a consideration of the Congo situation by the Security Council in December 1964. The OAU joined in calling for a meeting of the Security Council specifically to condemn the foreign military intervention. At the end of a most bitter debate featuring charges of aggression against the Western powers, accusations of deliberate activities calculated to frus-

79 Hoskyns, ed., *The Organization of African Unity and the Congo Crisis, 1964-1965* (Dar-es-Salaam, 1969), 20
80 *West Africa* (29 September 1964)
81 ECM/Res. 7 (IV) of 21 December 1964; text in Ian Brownlie, ed., *Basic Documents on African Affairs* (Oxford, 1971), 537-8

trate the work of the Kenyatta Commission against the United States and Belgium, and vigorous denials of those charges,[82] the Security Council was able to pass a resolution which clearly placed the problem of peace promotion in the lap of the OAU, at the same time urging all states to assist the regional organization in its search for peace.[83]

The deep division among OAU members, coupled with the danger that the centre of the cold war might be shifted, at least temporarily, to Africa, created a situation in which, if the UN involvement had not existed, it would have been necessary to invent it. It has neither been claimed that the OAU undermined the capacity of the UN to find a solution to the Congo problem, nor that the world organization abdicated its responsibility by excessively deferring to the OAU.

THE NIGERIAN CRISIS: 1967-70

Nigeria is a polyethnic society with a strong sense of regional consciousness. It became independent in 1960 under a federal constitutional arrangement. The process of federal integration which formally began in 1954 was accompanied by a host of political crises arising from the excesses of ethnic chauvinism and ruthless struggle for power among rival elites. In January 1966, the Balewa Government was overthrown in a military coup d'etat. The solid domination of the first Military Government under General Aguiyi-Ironsi by the Ibos of the Eastern Region called into question the national character of the January coup. When General Ironsi abolished the federal system and replaced it with a unitary one, he aroused the fear of the numerically preponderant northerners who quickly planned and successfully executed the second coup d'etat in July 1966. The situation deteriorated quickly. Against the background of the extensive massacre of the Ibos in the North, and the non-implementation or apparent repudiation of the Aburi settlement of January 1967 by the Federal Government, Colonel Odumegwu Ojukwu took the Eastern Region out of the Nigerian Federation on 30 May 1967, as the Republic of Biafra.

Biafran secession and the resulting protracted conflict between the military forces of the federal government and those of the rebel authority brought about a lively debate on the permissible and impermissible role of third parties in the adjudication of intra-state disputes. At the outset, the Gowon government in Lagos predictably took the strictly legal view that

82 *UN Yearbook* (1964), 95-100
83 UN Doc. s/6128

the situation fell within the domestic jurisdiction of Nigeria. Respect for this legal position marked the response and determined attitudes of both the OAU and the UN Security Council to the crisis in Nigeria.[84]

The United Nations, for reasons more political than legal, excluded itself from the search for peace in Nigeria. To lament the failure of the Security Council to take direct cognizance of the crisis is to assume that, though the crisis appeared to be a domestic one, it constituted a threat to international peace. But as the determination of whether a situation is a threat to international peace is the responsibility of the Security Council, the non-intervention of the Security Council is a clear evidence that the world body did not accept the view that the Nigerian civil war was a threat to world peace. The history of the United Nations hardly encourages reliance on Article 2(7) of the Charter (see Appendix C) as inhibiting in any absolute way UN 'action' in the domestic affairs of member states.[85] The posture of non-involvement maintained by the Security Council in the Nigerian crisis has therefore been criticized as based upon a restrictive interpretation of the competence of the United Nations in the promotion of peace. The United Nations confined itself to the humanitarian aspects of the civil war not so much because Article 2(7) prohibits UN intervention as because the world organization was willing to defer to a majority of African states which not only supported the Lagos government but warned the world body not to intervene politically in Nigeria.[86] The big powers, seeking to win over the new states to their side against their ideological adversaries, were not likely to ignore the fact that thirty-nine African states did not want a United Nations intervention. U Thant reflected the view of a vast majority of UN members when he declared on many occasions that the OAU was the appropriate agency for the promotion of peace in Nigeria.[87] It may be questioned whether the anti-UN intervention warning of the OAU did not in fact amount to a subtle attempt to prevent the world organization from participating in the search for peace in Nigeria. By maintaining a controversial posture of non-intervention, the United Nations appeared to have given

---

84 Cervenka, *The Organization of African Unity and Its Charter*, chap. 9; D.A. Ijalaye, 'Some Legal Implications of the Nigerian Civil War,' in NSIL, *Proceedings* (1969), 70-99; T.O. Elias, 'The Nigerian Crisis in International Law,' *NLJ* v (1971), 1-18

85 M.S. Rajan, *The United Nations and Domestic Jurisdiction* (London, 1961); Rosalyn Higgins, *The Development of International Law through the Political Organs of the United Nations* (London, 1963), 58-130; Miller, *World Order and Internal Disorder, passim*

86 *Report of the OAU Consultative Mission to Nigeria*, 1-2; K. Whiteman, 'The OAU and the Nigerian Issue,' *World Today* (November 1968), 449-53

87 *UN Monthly Chronicle* v (1968), 98-9; vi (1969), 56

support to, or at least acquiesced in, the claim by African states that the so-lution to African problems should be found within the framework of the principles and machinery of the OAU.

The role of the OAU in the promotion of peace in Nigeria is best under-stood against the background of the perceived implications of and issues raised by the 'biafran' secession. Since practically every African state is po-tentially vulnerable to disintegrating forces of ethnic secession and since African leaders believe that balkanization can serve only the interest of the neocolonial powers, the political commitment of a vast majority of the OAU members to the preservation of the territorial integrity of Nigeria is not difficult to understand and indeed seems quite logical. African leaders rec-ognize the relevance of the principle of self-determination only in the con-text of decolonization.[88] This is consistent with the OAU view that the bor-ders of African states 'constitute a tangible reality.'[89]

The attitude of the OAU on the Nigerian crisis was defined at the Kinshasa Summit of the African Heads of State and Government in Sep-tember 1967. The Kinshasa Resolution condemned the 'biafran' act of se-cession, recognized that the crisis was an internal matter to be solved by the Nigerians themselves, expressed confidence in the Lagos government, and decided to dispatch to the Head of the Federal Government a Consultative Mission of six Heads of States in order to assure General Gowon of OAU's desire for the territorial integrity, unity, and peace of Nigeria.[90] The OAU subsequently dealt with the Nigerian civil war through its ad hoc Consulta-tive Committee made up of Cameroun, Ethiopia, Ghana, Liberia, Congo (Kinshasa) – now Zaire – and Niger.

The search for peace in Nigeria was not complicated by any jurisdic-tional dispute over the respective competences of the United Nations and the OAU. But the premature recognition accorded to the rebel government by four members of the OAU,[91] the half-hearted support given by some Afri-can states to Nigeria, and foreign intervention on the side of the rebels ap-

88 Rupert Emerson, *Self-Determination Revisited in the Era of Decolonization* (Cambridge, Mass., 1964), 35-6; H.S. Johnson, *Self-Determination Within the Community of Nations* (Leyden, 1967), 53; Ali A. Mazrui, *Towards a Pax Africana* (London, 1967), 23

89 OAU Resolution on Border Disputes, 1964; see Brownlie, ed., *Basic Documents on African Affairs*, 360-1

90 AHG/Res. 51 (IV) of September 1967; text in *Resolutions and Statements adopted by the Meetings of the Assembly of Heads of State and Government, 1963-1972* (Addis Ababa: OAU Secretariat, 1973), 70

91 D.A. Ijalaye, 'Was "Biafra" at Any Time a State in International Law?' *AJIL* LXV (1971), 551, 553-4; Douglas Anglin, 'Zambia and the Recognition of Biafra,' *African Review* I (1971), 102-36

peared to have strengthened the 'biafran' will to resist solution on the basis of the OAU resolutions. Efforts of the OAU Consultative Committee in Nigeria to promote agreement in Niamey and at Addis Ababa in 1968 proved abortive. When the OAU Summit at Algiers (September 1968) called on the rebel authority to co-operate with the Lagos government in order to restore peace and unity in Nigeria, the secessionist leaders lost all faith in the impartiality and usefulness of the OAU.

In retrospect, it is not surprising that the search for peace under the auspices of the OAU yielded little result as the rebel government, while it survived military onslaught, never accepted the premise of the OAU mandate, which was to promote solution on the basis of a united Nigeria.[92] It is doubtful whether the OAU, which stands for the status quo with respect to international boundaries, could reasonably be expected to act as an impartial conciliator between the Lagos government which was determined to preserve the territorial integrity of Nigeria and the rebel government bent on breaking up the Federation.

Three issues are at the heart of the relationship between the United Nations and regional organizations in the settlement of disputes. The first is the question of the priority of the use of one organization before resort to the other. The issue of priority of the use of regional organizations has been raised most frequently in cases involving the Organization of American States. This is partly because the OAS is the only regional organization which expressly obligates its members to use the regional machinery to settle their disputes before taking them to the UN Security Council, and partly because the United States, the dominant regional power, has found it politically expedient to favour the use of an agency which does not give the Soviet Union the opportunity of participating in the promotion of peace in the Western Hemisphere. The second issue concerns the constitutional right of a member of a regional organization to have recourse to the Security Council. It is essential that this right be preserved. At the same time, it should be recognized that under normal circumstances, the regional forum is an appropriate place to seek solutions to disputes between two members of a regional organization. The third issue focuses on the response of the Security Council to disputes between parties to a regional treaty or between factions within a member state of a regional organization. Security Council response has been determined largely by political considerations. This is hardly surprising considering that the United Nations is 'a political body, charged

92 C. Odumegwu Ojukwu, *Biafra* 2 (New York, 1969), 183-90

with political tasks'[93] and that the Security Council is alone competent to interprete its own authority.[94]

The issue of jurisdiction concerning the respective competences of the United Nations and regional organizations in the settlement of local disputes and the resulting fundamental question of venue may be prevented from arising or from being raised in an acute form if parties to a dispute agree to go before the regional organization and waive their right of appeal to the Security Council. The simultaneous consideration of a dispute by both the world and the regional bodies may similarly be avoided if a member of a regional organization having appealed to the world body agrees to ask the Security Council to defer consideration of the matter while the regional organization is seized of it. It is essential, however, that preference for regional organizations in the settlement of disputes should be allowed neither to cast doubt on the competence and authority of the Security Council nor to pre-empt the right of a member state to have its dispute with another state brought before the world body.

93 Reparations for Injuries case: *ICJ Reports* (1948), 121 at p. 179
94 UNCIO, *Documents* XIII, 703, 709; Pollux (Edvard Hambro?), 'The Interpretation of the Charter,' *BYBIL* XXIII (1946), 56

6

Regional enforcement action and collective self-defence

OAS MEASURES AGAINST THE DOMINICAN REPUBLIC: 1960

Members of the Organization of American States decided collectively in August 1960 to sever diplomatic relations with, and to apply partial economic sanctions on, the Dominican Republic on the grounds of complicity of the Dominican Government in the attempted assassination of the President of Venezuela.[1] In January 1962, similar measures were authorized by the OAS against Cuba for allegedly introducing international communism into the Western Hemisphere and thus violating the fundamental ideological principle of the Inter-American System,[2] embodied in the famous 1954 Caracas Declaration which states that domination or control of the political institutions of any American state by international communism constitutes a threat to the sovereignty and political independence of the American states. Under Article 20 of the Rio Treaty, OAS resolutions imposing economic sanctions constitute a binding obligation on all members. Later in October 1962, the OAS, in a famous resolution, urged its members to take 'all measures, individually and collectively, including the use of armed force, which they may deem necessary to ensure that the Government of Cuba cannot continue to receive from the Sino-Soviet powers military material and related supplies which may threaten the peace and security of the [American] Continent and to prevent the missiles in Cuba with offensive ca-

1 US Dept of State, *Bulletin* XLIII (1960), 358
2 *Ibid.*, XLVI (1962), 282

pability from ever becoming an active threat to the peace and security of the Continent.'[3] In each of these three cases, the OAS considered it unnecessary to secure the prior approval for the measures from the Security Council, but merely kept the world body informed about them pursuant to Article 54 of the UN Charter.

At the request of the Soviet Union, the Security Council was summoned into session in September 1960 in connection with matters arising from the measures collectively imposed on the Dominican Republic by the OAS. The Soviet Union urged the Security Council to 'approve the decision of the Organization of American States, so as to give it legal force and render it more effective.'[4] In so far as Article 53 of the UN Charter speaks of prior rather than subsequent approval of regional enforcement measures by the Security Council, the Soviet attempt to have the Security Council give ex post facto legitimization to the enforcement measures already applied by the OAS is rather strange. The Soviet motive was probably best explained by Claude:

The legal implication was clear: the Council would be asserting its authority to disapprove as well as to approve, and the Soviet Union would enjoy the right to veto Council decisions in such matters. Moreover, the political meaning of the move was apparent: Soviet initiative in promoting Council approval of OAS sanctions in the Dominican case was designed to lay the groundwork for Soviet obstruction of Council approval – that is, for Council *disapproval* of possible OAS enforcement measures against Cuba.[5]

During the Security Council debate, the Soviet Union, Poland, and Ceylon contended that the collective economic measures imposed by OAS members against the Dominican Republic were enforcement measures within the meaning of Article 53 in as much as the term 'enforcement action' in Article 53 embraces measures enumerated in Article 42 as well as those in Article 41.[6] Furthermore, as the Security Council alone is empowered by the UN Charter to authorize the application of regional enforcement measures, the approval of the world body was necessary to legalize the collective OAS measures against the Dominican Republic.

An opposing view, which seems excessively generous to the autonomy of regional organizations, was vigorously defended by the United States, the

3 *Ibid.* XLVII (1962), 722-3; L.M. Tondel, Jr, ed., *The Inter-American Security System and the Cuban Crisis* (Dobbs Ferry, 1964), 27
4 UN Doc. S/PV. 893, par. 24
5 Inis L. Claude, Jr, 'The OAS, the UN, and the United States,' *International Conciliation*, no. 547 (March 1964), 48-9
6 UN Doc. S/PV. 894, par. 14, 16, and 17 (1960)

United Kingdom, Argentina, and Ecuador. Rejecting Kelsen's interpretation, the representatives of these states asserted that enforcement measures imposed by a regional organization require prior Security Council authorization *only if* those measures called for the use of armed force.[7] According to the representative of the United Kingdom

[I]t is common sense to interpret the use of this term [enforcement action] in Article 53 as covering only such actions as would not normally be legitimate except on the basis of a Security Council resolution. There is nothing in international law, in principle, to prevent any State, if it so desires, from breaking off diplomatic relations or instituting a partial interruption of economic relations with any other State. These steps, which are the measures decided upon by the Organization of American States with regard to the Dominican Republic, are acts of policy perfectly within the competence of the members of the Organization of American States acting collectively.[8]

The proposition that a regional organization, whose relationship to the United Nations is carefully defined by a set of behavioural rules, can do collectively what each member of the organization can do singly is excessively logical. While the lawfulness of an act of diplomatic rupture or of partial interruption of economic relations on the part of one state vis-à-vis another does not depend upon the authorization of the Security Council, the lawfulness of the same measures applied to a collective decision of a regional organization has to be viewed in the context of the UN Charter law of universal-regional relationship. The argument of the United Kingdom representative ignores the importance of drawing a line between what the Ceylonese delegate called 'the individual rights of each State which is a member of the regional organization and the rights of States as members of the organization.'[9] Under the UN Charter and subject to Articles 51 and 107, collective punitive action on the part of a regional organization against any state has the character of enforcement action, and, thus requires the prior approval of the Security Council.

In the end, the Security Council adopted a three-power draft resolution urging the Council to merely 'take note' of the OAS action and especially its resolution of 20 August 1960.[10] This meant that the term 'enforcement action' as used in Article 53 was interpreted as not encompassing measures enumerated in Article 41. Therefore, regional enforcement action which does not involve the employment of armed forces does not require the prior

7 UN Doc. S/PV. 893, par. 32, 66, and 96 (1960)
8 UN Doc. S/PV. 893, par. 16 (1960)
9 UN Doc. S/PV. 894, par. 14 (1960)
10 UN Doc. S/4491 (1960)

approval of the Security Council. A precedent was clearly established. Schachter has pointed out that 'once a decision is rendered by an authoritative body, it has entered into the stream of decisions that will normally be looked to as a source of law. Considerations of equity and equal treatment will tend to favor its application in "equivalent" situations; moreover, the reasons which impelled its adoption in the one case are likely to have some influence in other cases.'[11]

OAS MEASURES AGAINST CUBA: 1962

The Dominican precedent was invoked in February 1962 when Cuba asked the Security Council to condemn the measures taken against her at the Punta del Este meeting of the OAS as a violation of the UN Charter.[12] At the preliminary discussion on whether to entertain the Cuban complaint, it was urged that the legal question involved had already been decided in September 1960 during debate on the San Jose measures against the Dominican Republic. The Security Council failed to adopt an agenda and the Cuban complaint was not considered. Later in March 1962, Cuba requested the Security Council to ask the International Court of Justice for an advisory opinion on whether the economic measures imposed on her by the OAS amounted to enforcement action under Article 53.[13] The arguments advanced were the familiar ones of September 1960. The Security Council turned down the request for an advisory opinion and declared, at least by implication, that exclusion of a member from participation in the activities of a regional organization does not constitute an enforcement action.[14]

OAS QUARANTINE OF CUBA: 1962

In both the Dominican and Cuban cases the interpretation placed on the term 'enforcement action' was based largely on the *nature of the measures* imposed by the OAS. During the Cuban missile crisis, a new type of argument was employed by the United States to justify the imposition by the OAS of a naval 'quarantine' around Cuba. The proposition was advanced that whether or not regional measures require the prior approval of the Security Council depends also on the obligatory nature of the resolution authorizing the collective regional action. The United States argued that the

11 Oscar Schachter, 'The Quasi-Judicial Role of the Security Council and of the General Assembly,' *AJIL* LVIII (1964), 965
12 UN Doc. S/PV. 991 (1962)
13 UN Doc. S/5095 (1962)
14 UN Docs S/PV. 992-8 (1962)

non-obligatory nature of the OAS resolution of 23 October 1962 makes the authorization requirement of Article 53 inapplicable.

Claiming that the presence of 'offensive' weapons secretly introduced by the Soviet Union into Cuba 'constitutes an explicit threat to the peace and security of all the America, in flagrant and deliberate defiance of the Rio Pact of 1947,' and amounted to 'a deliberately provocative and unjustified change in the status quo which cannot be accepted,' President Kennedy ordered 'a strict quarantine of all offensive military equipment under shipment to Cuba.'[15] Analysis of the legal aspects of the Cuban missile crisis involves four relevant considerations. First, the naval quarantine was as much directed against Cuba as against the Soviet Union. Second, the implementation of a naval quarantine necessarily involves the use of armed force. Third, although President Kennedy's announcement did not exclude the defence of the measures imposed as an act of self-defence, the legal officers of the State Department made it clear that the President deliberately avoided invoking the inherent right of self-defence in defence of the legality of the limited naval quarantine.[16] And fourth, the naval quarantine, though unilaterally announced by the United States, was implemented by the OAS resolution which recommended individual and collective action, including the use of force, to prevent further delivery of 'offensive' weapons to Cuba. In other words, the quarantine measure was an act of the OAS.

The validity of two interrelated propositions advanced by the United States in defence of the legality of the naval quarantine deserves careful consideration. Concerning the first proposition that enforcement action under Article 53(1) does not include action of a regional organization which is only recommended to, but not made obligatory for, its members, Leonard Meeker, Deputy Legal Adviser to the US State Department, commented: 'As understood by the United States, "enforcement action" means obligatory action involving the use of armed force. Thus, "enforcement action," as the phrase appears in Article 53(1), should not be taken to comprehend action of a regional organization which is only recommendatory to the members of the organization.'[17] In the Dominican and earlier Cuban cases, the Security Council had 'accepted' the interpretation that enforcement action by a regional organization which does not entail the use of force could legitimately be undertaken without prior authorization by the Security Council. In the

15 US Dept of State, *Bulletin* XLVII (1962), 715; Tondel, ed., *The Inter-American System and the Cuban Crisis*, 26

16 Abram Chayes, 'The Legal Case for US Action on Cuba,' US Dept of State, *Bulletin* XLVII (1962), 764; Leonard C. Meeker, 'Defensive Quarantine and the Law,' *AJIL* LVII (1963), 515

17 Meeker, 'Defensive Quarantine and the Law,' 515

Cuban missile crisis, a more provocative claim was made to the effect that collective use of force on the initiative of a regional organization and independently of the right of self-defence falls within the legal competence of a regional organization as long as the resolution authorizing the regional action is merely recommendatory. If, as was the case, the naval quarantine was implemented in the context of the OAS resolution and indeed operated under a joint quarantine command,[18] then it was an act of the regional organization. The question of the nature of the enabling resolution seems irrelevant, more especially as no resolution creating an obligatory duty for OAS members to use force will itself be legal under the Rio Treaty (Article 20).

The second claim put forward by Meeker is that, under Article 52(1), a regional organization may legitimately employ force on its own initiative to remove threats to peace in its region of operation.

The quarantine was based on a collective judgment and recommendation of the American Republics made under the Rio Treaty. It was considered not to contravene Article 2, paragraph 4, because it was a measure adopted by a regional organization in conformity with the provisions of Chapter VIII of the Charter. The purposes of the Organization and its activities were considered to be consistent with the purposes and principles of the United Nations as provided in Article 52. This being the case, the quarantine would no more violate Article 2, paragraph 4, than measures voted by the [Security] Council under Chapter VII, by the General Assembly under Articles 10 and 11, or taken by the United Nations Members in conformity with Article 51.[19]

This statement asserts three interrelated hypotheses; 1/ that there is a legal right of collective forceful action possessed by regional organizations independent of and in addition to the right enjoyed under Article 51; 2/ that the legality of such regional collective action depends only on whether the action was taken in conformity with the procedures and processes laid down in the appropriate regional treaty; 3/ and that the prohibition in Article 2(4) is removed in favour of regional organizations seeking to preserve peace and security in their respective regions as long as the purposes of regional organization are consistent with those of the United Nations.

It was urged that under Article 52(1), regional organizations are competent to deal with 'matters relating to the maintenance of peace and security as are appropriate for regional action'; that actions by regional organiza-

---

18 Chayes in Tondel, ed., *The Inter-American Security System and the Cuban Crisis*, 40
19 Meeker, 'Defensive Quarantine and the Law,' 523-4

tions can take forms of activities which are neither of the nature of pacific settlement nor of the application of measures established under Article 53; and that in carrying out these other activities related to the maintenance of peace, the only obligation imposed on regional organizations by the UN Charter is that contained in Articles 52(4) and 54.[20] Dean Rusk, US Secretary of State at the time of the Cuban missile crisis, stated at the OAS Meeting of 23 October 1962 that, in so far as the missile threat was to the Western Hemisphere, the American Republics had 'primary responsibility and duty to act.'[21] It is certainly impossible to reconcile such an assertion with Article 24 of the UN Charter, but it is no doubt consistent with the expanded construction being placed on the authority and competence of regional organizations.

It was not intended that regional organizations operating on their own initiative under the provisions of Articles 52-54 should be anything other than pacific settlement agencies. The contention that a regional organization can act in breach of Article 2(4) if it is legitimately maintaining the peace and security of its region begs the question of the legitimacy of and legal basis for its use of force. It is not enough merely to say that the measures taken were permited by the Rio Treaty whose signatories have consented to its powers and procedures, or that the political processes and procedures by which the OAS made a decision to use force gave assurance that the decision had not been rashly taken. As U Thant pointed out in 1965, '[i]f a particular regional organization, under the terms of its own constitution, deems it fit to take certain enforcement action in its own region, it naturally follows that other regional organizations should be considered competent, because of the precedent, to take certain enforcement action in their own regions.'[22] The crux of the American argument is that the OAS occupies a position in the Western Hemisphere analoguous to the position envisaged by the UN Charter for the United Nations in the world at large. According to Abram Chayes, Legal Adviser to the US State Department, the OAS 'is [a] kind of junior grade U.N. in the sense that it exercises within its regional sphere all the kinds of activities that the U.N. engages in, world-wide,' and 'this was the conception of a regional organization that is in Chapter VIII of the U.N. Charter.'[23] Legally, unless the use of force is justified under Article 51, the naval quarantine sponsored by the OAS violates Article 2(4) in so far as the prohibition contained in Article 2(4) is not removed in favour of re-

20 Garcia-Amador, *The Inter-American System* (Dobbs Ferry, 1966), 181; also 'The Dominican Situation: The Jurisdiction of Regional Organization,' *Americas* XVII (1965), 1-3
21 US Dept of State, *Bulletin* XLVII (1962), 722
22 *UN Monthly Chronicle* II (1965), 69
23 Cited in Tondel, ed., *The Inter-American Security System and the Cuban Crisis*, 37

gional organizations seeking to preserve peace and security in their regions outside the context of self-defence.[24] The naval quarantine measure had the character of an enforcement action in the context of Article 53 and therefore required prior Security Council authorization to be a valid exercise of the use of force.

Politically, the argument in favour of increased autonomy for regional organizations seems to rest on the demonstrated ineffectiveness of the UN Security Council as a universal agent. In his defence of the naval quarantine, Chayes drew attention to the importance of coming to grips with political changes that had developed since 1945. 'The withering away of the Security Council has led to a search for alternative peacekeeping institutions. In the United Nations itself, the General Assembly and the Secretary-General have filled the void. Regional organizations are another obvious candidate.'[25] He further contended that because unexpected responsibility had devolved on regional organizations as peace-keeping agencies, Article 53 'cannot be left as a derelict adrift with no other function but to cause shipwrecks.'[26] The political argument for wanting to increase the autonomy of regional organizations is persuasive up to a point, but the expansive construction being placed on the authority and competence of regional organizations cannot be accommodated under the 1945 Charter of the United Nations.

The Cuban quarantine represented a high point in the jurisdictional dispute regarding the proper relationship between the United Nations and regional organizations.[27] The Security Council which met at the request of the United States did not take up the issue of the limits of regional authority defined in Articles 52-54 of the UN Charter. It is a matter of conjecture what position the Council would have taken on the thesis advanced by the

24 See G.I.A.D. Draper, 'Regional Arrangements and Enforcement Action,' *REDI* xx (1964), 1-44. For a contrary opinion, see C. Christol and C.R. Davis, 'Maritime Quarantine: The Naval Interdiction of Offensive Weapons and Associated Material, 1962,' *AJIL* LVII (1963), 537-9

25 Abram Chayes, 'The Legal Case for US Action on Cuba,' 765

26 Chayes in ASIL *Proceedings* (1963) 12. See also Tondel, ed., *The Inter-American System and the Cuban Crisis*, 46-7

27 Claude, 'The OAS, the UN and the United States,' 57; R. St J. Macdonald, 'The Developing Relationship between Superior and Subordinate Political Bodies at the International Level: A Note on the Experience of the United Nations and the Organization of American States,' *CYbIL* II (1964), 54; R. Simmonds, 'Peace-keeping by Regional Organizations : A Critique of the Experience of the Inter-relationships between the Organization of American States and the UN Organization Within the Context of Collective Security,' *University of Ghana Law Journal* XI (1974), 43-82

United States. But at least, Zorin, the Soviet representative, in the course of the debate in the Security Council, repeatedly made the point that the imposition of collective sanctions against Cuba by the OAS at the instigation of the United States was a usurpation of the prerogatives of the Security Council and, hence, a legally unjustifiable interpretation of the competence of regional organizations.[28]

THE WARSAW PACT INVASION OF CZECHOSLOVAKIA: 1968

The invasion of Czechoslovakia by the military forces of five of the Warsaw Pact members on 20 August 1968 is a good illustration of the inherent tension between the concept of international duty of socialist states and the principle of state sovereignty which has been the corner-stone of international law.[29] It also provides an example of the break-down of the UN Charter law of universal-regional relationship. Two propositions were advanced during the crisis by the Soviet Union. One asserts that the measure taken by the Warsaw Pact members was an act of self-defence, and the other that the Soviet-led invasion was a matter concerning only the Czechoslovak people and the states of the socialist community bound by appropriate mutual obligations. The second proposition is an implied limitation on the right of Warsaw Pact members under Article 35(1) of the UN Charter and on the territorial scope of the competence of the United Nations. Both propositions, in effect, place an expansive construction on the role and competence of a regional organization.

The Warsaw Pact invasion and the claims advanced during the Czechoslovak crisis are best viewed against the background of events in Eastern Europe since 1945. During his trip to Moscow in October 1944, Winston Churchill proposed to Marshal Stalin a division of the Balkans into spheres of influence. Under the Churchill-Stalin agreement, Rumania and Bulgaria were to be within Soviet spheres of influence; Greece within a British sphere (in conjunction with the United States); Yugoslavia and Hungary were to be shared between Britain and the Soviet Union. Churchill wrote in his memoirs:

Then he [Stalin] took his blue pencil and made a large tick upon it, and passed it back to us. It was all settled in no more time than it takes to set down . . . After this

28 L.B. Sohn, *The United Nations in Action* (Brooklyn, 1967), 338
29 G. Ginsburgs, 'Socialist Internationalism and State Sovereignty,' *YBWA* XXVI (1971), 35-55

there was a long silence. The penciled paper lay in the centre of the table. At length, I said: 'Might it not be thought rather cynical that it seemed we had disposed of these issues, so fateful to millions of people, in such an offhand manner? Let us burn the paper.' 'No, you keep it,' said Stalin.[30]

The Soviet Union took the Churchill-Stalin 'deal' of 9 October 1944 seriously and continued to regard Eastern Europe as her sphere of influence.[31] In 1955, the Soviet Union sponsored the formation of the Warsaw Treaty Organization as a means of consolidating her hegemonial control over the 'socialist commonwealth' of Eastern Europe.[32] But the Warsaw Pact, which represents the military face of Soviet-dominated Eastern Europe, is largely a political response to the changes in the political morphology of Europe anticipated by the accession of West Germany to the North Atlantic Treaty. The Soviet Union and her allies firmly believe in what may properly be called a Soviet Monroe Doctrine multilaterally formulated and applicable to Eastern Europe. The *Warsaw Letter* of 15 July 1968 formulated the Doctrine:

The frontiers of the socialist world have shifted to the center of Europe, to the Elbe and the Bohemian Forest. And never will we consent to allow these historical gains of socialism and the independence and security of all our peoples to be jeopardized. Never will we consent to allow imperialism, by peaceful or non-peaceful means from within or without, to make a breach in the socialist system and change the balance of power in Europe in its favor.[33]

The Soviet Union engineered the overthrow of Nagy when he declared his government's intention to withdraw Hungary from the Warsaw Pact in 1956; the socialist states which had defended the Soviet action could not be expected to take kindly to the possibility that Czechoslovakia, a key member of the Warsaw Pact, might become an untrustworthy ally. The geo-

30 Winston Churchill, *Triumph and Tragedy* (Boston, 1953), 227-8
31 For instance, in the Security Council debate over the distribution of non-permanent seats in the Security Council, the USSR has usually claimed the right to nominate the East European representative. See L.C. Green, 'Gentlemen's Agreements and the Security Council,' *CLP* XIII (1960), 225-75; and 'Representation in the Security Council: A Survey,' *IYBIA* XI (1962), 48-75; Andrew Boyd, *Fifteen Men on a Powder Keg* (London, 1971), 100-13
32 R.A. Remington, *The Warsaw Pact: Case Study in Conflict Resolution* (Cambridge, Mass., 1971); K. Grzybowski, *The Socialist Commonwealth of Nations: Organizations and Institutions* (New Haven, 1964); Andrzej Korbonski, 'The Warsaw Pact,' *International Conciliation*, no. 573 (May 1969)
33 *ILM* VII (1968), 1265

graphical position of Czechoslovakia is of acute strategic significance, being contiguous with West Germany.[34] Soviet leaders have traditionally been sensitive to the vulnerability of their western frontiers and have accordingly made the search for security the central theme of their foreign policy. It was therefore not likely that the Soviet Union would permit Czechoslovakia to became a 'security risk' if the Kremlin had reason to believe that was the case. But Czechoslovakia is a sovereign member of the United Nations entitled to enjoy the protection the UN Charter affords.

The *Tass* statement announcing the Warsaw Pact invasion made two important claims. The first is that the Warsaw Pact forces were requested by certain 'party and government leaders of the Czechoslovak Socialist Republic.'[35] The Soviet intervention in Hungary in 1956 was defended on similar grounds; but the UN Special Committee on the Problem of Hungary was unable to establish and confirm the claim.[36] The second claim in 1968 was that the decision to invade was 'fully in accord with the right of states to individual and collective self-defence envisaged in treaties of alliance concluded between the fraternal socialist countries.'[37] Both claims are closely related. With respect to the first, the Presidium of the Czechoslovak Communist Party Central Committee, in its first statement to the nation on 21 August 1968, declared that the invasion took place 'without the knowledge of the President of the Republic, the Chairman of the National Assembly, the Premier, or the First Secretary of the Czechoslovak Communist Party Central Committee.'[38] As the Warsaw Pact forces were not invited by the duly constituted legal authorities in Prague, the presence of those armed forces in Czechoslovakia was, in the very words of the Czechoslovak Presidium, 'contrary not only to the fundamental principles of relations between socialist states but also contrary to the principle of international law.'[39]

However, the second claim cannot easily be dismissed. As the legal authorities in Prague did not express fear that Czechoslovakia was under imminent threat of attack from the so-called counter-revolutionary forces, and consequently never considered asking for consultation with or assistance from their allies in accordance with Articles 3 and 4 of the Warsaw Pact, one can only assume that the Soviet Union and its allies in the regional or-

34 For a cogent analysis of legal, economic, and political interests resulting from geographical contiguity, see Quincy Wright, 'Territorial Propinquity,' *AJIL* XII (1919), 519-61
35 *ILM* VII (1968), 1283-84. See also D.W. Bowett, *The Search for Peace* (London, 1972), 135
36 *GAOR*, 11th Sess. Suppl. no. 18 (A/3592), par. 263
37 *ILM* VII (1968), 1283-84
38 *Ibid.*, 1285; see also UN Doc. S/8765
39 *ILM* VII (1968), 1285; Bowett, *The Search for Peace*, 143-4

ganization, by invading Czechoslovakia, were acting in their own self-defence and not in defence of Czechoslovakia. It may be objected that such a distinction is not warranted in view of the fact that the language of Articles 3 and 4 of the Warsaw Pact suggests that a threat of attack or actual attack on a signatory state justifies 'joint measures necessary to restore and maintain international peace and security.' It is doubtful whether the obligation to render assistance to a victim of attack under a treaty exists independently of an express request for assistance from the duly constituted leaders of the victim of attack.[40] That the Kremlin thought it necessary to emphasize the alleged invitation from the Prague Government is a clear recognition of the strength of this point. It is also difficult to understand why in the Czechoslovak case, the victim of an alleged collective self-defence action by the Warsaw Pact members should turn out to be the very state which was purportedly being protected from an imminent threat of attack by counter-revolutionary forces.

The right of states to a legitimate use of force in self-defence is preserved in the UN Charter. Under the Warsaw Pact, the Soviet Union, Hungary, Poland, East Germany, Rumania, Czechoslovakia, Bulgaria, and Albania have agreed to exercise that right collectively, and in preparation for the exercise of the right, have established an integrated high command. Like any member of the United Nations, signatories to the Warsaw Pact are each alone competent to judge whether circumstances justifying the exercise of the right of self-defence have arisen. Thus, there is room for the contention that counter-revolution instigated by Western Powers against 'socialist' gains in a strategic state of Czechoslovakia opens the Soviet Union and her allies to threats of aggression from the ideologically hostile and antagonistic 'capitalist' states of the West.[41] A similar argument was employed in defence of Soviet intervention in Hungary in 1956.[42] The self-defence argument may be objected to on the ground that the means used were not proportional to the alleged threat, or that the necessity for self-defensive action was not overwhelmingly imminent; it may not be objected to on the ground that an 'armed attack' had not yet occurred if only because the formulation of Article 51 does not exclude the exercise of the right of preventive self-defence. The self-defence argument may be objected to on the ground that

---

40 B. Boutros-Ghali, *Contribution à Une Théorie Général des Alliances* (Paris, 1963), 67ff; Daniel Vignes, 'La Place des Pactes de Défense dans la Société internationale actuelle,' *AFDI* C (1959), 64-5

41 R.M. Goodman, 'The Invasion of Czechoslovakia: 1968,' *International Lawyer* IV (1969), 42-79

42 UN Doc. S/PV. 754, par. 53 (1956)

it over-extends the concept of self-defence to cover threats of 'ideological' aggression in much the same manner as the new states of Africa and Asia are now arguing that the use of force to liquidate colonialism is an instance of legitimate self-defence, colonialism being regarded as a form of permanent aggression.[43] The argument based on self-defence may be considered inadmissible on the ground that a definite violation of the substantive legal right of the state or states acting in self-defence is a necessary condition for a legitimate exercise of that right.[44] But this view is itself open to criticism. The exercise of the right of self-defence is no doubt open to abuse, and when abused, the line between aggressive and self-defensive use of force tends to disappear altogether. The Warsaw Pact invasion of Czechoslovakia can be defended on the grounds of self-defence *only* because each state is alone competent to judge whether circumstances requiring recourse to forceful action in self-defence have arisen. But whether the circumstances were appropriate and compelling enough to justify resort to war in self-defence is another matter. The UN Charter itself contemplates a political and post mortem review of the propriety of the initial decision to resort to the use of force on the grounds of self-defence, provided of course that the technicalities of Article 27(3) can be overcome. The paramount legal issue is not so much whether the Soviet Union and her allies were acting in self-defence as whether the Soviet thesis that the United Nations was not the appropriate forum to deal with the situation in Czechoslovakia was a valid claim under the UN Charter. The inherent right of self-defence was intended to be available to states only on a temporary basis until the Security Council has taken measures necessary to maintain international peace.

The Council convened on 21 August 1968 at the request of the Western Powers.[45] In his letter to the Council President, Malik, the Soviet representative, vigorously opposed the consideration of the matter, because 'events in Czechoslovakia are a matter that concern the Czechoslovak people and the States of the socialist community, which are bound by appropriate mutual obligations.'[46] This view was repeated many more times in the course of the Security Council debate.[47] The message carried by the proposition is by no means new in the history and jurisprudence of the United Nations. The le-

43 Green, 'New States, Regionalism and International Law,' *CYbIL* v (1967), 118-41; C.J.R. Dugard, 'The Organization of African Unity and Colonialism,' *ICLQ* xvi, 4th Series (1967), 157-90

44 Bowett, *Self-Defence in International Law* (Manchester, 1958), 216

45 UN Doc. s/8758 (1968), *ILM* vii (1968), 1287; Boyd, *Fifteen Men on a Powder Keg*, 305

46 UN Doc. s/8759 (1968); *ILM* vii (1968), 1288-9

47 *UN Monthly Chronicle* v (1968), 35ff

gal competence of the United Nations to deal with the Czechoslovak situation was ignored by the Soviet Union because of political conveniences, to prevent western intervention within its sphere of influence. In 1954, as well as in 1960 and 1965, the Kremlin found it convenient to defend the right of the Security Council to deal with any acts of aggression and to take cognizance of any dispute wherever it may arise in the world and also condemned the OAS for usurping the Council's special responsibility.[48]

While the Soviet and the Hungarian negative votes could not prevent the adoption of the agenda, the Soviet veto effectively killed a draft resolution condemning the invasion and demanding the withdrawal of the Warsaw Pact forces. In an attempt to drive home the point that the Communist governments have no special immunity from the requirement of the Charter, the Western powers further tried to sponsor a UN presence in Prague. Malik saw this proposal as a trick 'to drag the Secretary-General of the United Nations into a dirty business of intervening in the affairs of a socialist state and in the common cause of fraternal socialist countries'[49] and declared that this would not succeed. In the language of Security Council diplomacy, this amounts to a warning that the Soviet Union would not hesitate to veto the proposal. Lodge and Stevenson had behaved in a similar manner in the Guatemalan and Dominican crises, although in the latter, the United States did reluctantly agreed to a UN presence in Santo Domingo.

In support of the thesis of exclusive competence of the regional organization, Malik, following the example of Sobolev during the Hungarian crisis,[50] used Article 2(7) for justification:

But what does all this have to do with the Security Council and with the United States representative here? What relation can the Council have to the internal affairs of Czechoslovakia, what interest in them? The answer to this is to be found in the Charter of the United Nations, Article 2, paragraph 7, and that answer, the only one, is that the Security Council has nothing to do with the internal affairs of Czechoslovakia and the processes going on there ... These problems can be settled by the Czechoslovak people and Party and the sound forces in that country, with the support of the fraternal socialist states, and without the participation of the Security Council.[51]

48 See Thomas M. Franck and Edward Weisband, *World Politics: Verbal Strategy Among the Super Powers* (London, 1971)
49 *UN Monthly Chronicle* v (1968), 64
50 UN Doc. S/PV. 746, par. 13 (1956)
51 Cited in *International Review Service* XIV (1968), 32

As Article 2(7) does not limit the competence of the Security Council if there is a possibility of action under Chapter VII of the UN Charter,[52] Lord Caradon's rebuttal is effective. He thought it 'the height of impudence for the representative of the Soviet Union, after the invasion for which his country was responsible, to lecture the Council about Article 2, Section 7 of the United Nations dealing with the right of any people to maintain their own sovereignty and to order their own life.'[53]

When a regional organization includes a permanent member of the Security Council, the problem of a proper interpretation of the UN Charter law of universal-regional relationship becomes dependent on the use to which the veto power is put. With the aid of the veto, the Soviet Union succeeded in preventing the Security Council from taking action to maintain peace in Eastern Europe. Equally important, the Soviet veto stopped the Council from declaring the Soviet-led Warsaw Pact invasion of a sovereign member of the United Nations as anything but an act of self-defence, which is a good example of how acts of aggression by states or regional organizations may commonly be represented.

OAU, COLONIALISM AND SELF-DEFENCE

The OAU Charter is a living symbol of African opposition to colonialism. When viewed from a historical perspective and in the context of the forces operating on the African political scene today, it may correctly be described as 'a charter of liberation.'[54] After committing themselves to the total emancipation of dependent African territories as well as the eradication of all forms of colonialism from Africa, OAU members, in their Resolution on Decolonization, established the Liberation Committee, empowered to coordinate assistance from African states to freedom fighters and a special fund in aid of various African national liberation movements.[55] The commitment to both the liquidation of colonialism and the struggle against racialism has come to be regarded as an underlying ideological requirement of OAU membership.[56] Although the resolution stops short of an explicit en-

52 Hans Kelsen, *The Law of the United Nations* (New York, 1950), 786; M.S. Rajan, *The United Nations and Domestic Jurisdiction* (London, 1961), 93-7
53 *UN Monthly Chronicle* v (1968), 48
54 Dugard, 'The Organization of African Unity and Colonialism,' 158
55 *Basic Documents of the Organization of African Unity* (Addis Ababa, 1963), 18
56 Boutros-Ghali, 'The Addis Ababa Charter,' *International Conciliation*, no. 546 (January 1964)

dorsement of the use of force, there is no doubt that such was contemplated. Spokesmen for many African states in the United Nations and in other forums have usually justified use of force as a lawful exercise of the right of collective self-defence. They argue that colonialism is, to paraphrase Krishna Menon of India, permanent aggression and that in defending the right of self-determination, they are defending a *legal* right under modern international law.[57] Three interrelated propositions often advanced by new states bear on the dominant question of the legality of the use of force by the OAU in aid of the campaign against colonialism.

The relatively new claim that self-determination has become a recognized legal right under modern international law[58] is being asserted with great intensity, even though tradition views it as a political and not a legal right.[59] Neither the League Covenant nor the UN Charter enshrined self-determination as a legal right.[60] The meaning of the term 'self-determination of peoples' in Article 1(2) of the UN Charter appears equivalent to 'sovereignty of states.'[61] Treaties, as a general rule, are usually drawn up in the light of the political interests of the participating parties. Colonial powers, who in 1945 as well as in 1919 were clearly reluctant to preside over the liquidation of their overseas colonial empires, could not have been expected then to recognize and· accept the existence of a legal right to decolonization.

57 U.O. Umozurike, 'International Law and Colonialism in Africa,' *East African Law Journal* III (1970)

58 M.K. Nawaz, 'The Meaning and Range of the Principle of Self-Determination,' *Duke Law Journal* v (1965), 82-101; Ian Brownlie, *Principles of Public International Law* (Oxford, 1966), 482-5; Rosalyn Higgins, *The Development of International Law Through the Political Organs of the United Nations* (London, 1963), 90-106; G. Osnitskaya, 'The Downfall of Colonialism and International Law,' *International Affairs* (Moscow, January 1961), 39; Edward McWhinney, 'The "New" Countries and the "New" International Law: The United Nations Special Conference on Friendly Relations and Cooperation Among States,' *AJIL* LX (1966), 1-33; Piet-Hein Houben, 'Principles of International Law Concerning Friendly Relations and Cooperation Among States,' *AJIL* LXI (1967), 703-36

59 M. Whiteman, *Digest of International Law* 5, 38-86. As Rupert Emerson pointed out, 'Where so substantial a body of doubt and opposition exists, including major Powers and those still possessed of colonies, the existence of a rule of international law cannot lightly be assumed.' See his 'Self-Determination,' *AJIL* LXV (1971), 462

60 Kelsen, 'Legal Technique in International Law: A Textual Critique of the League Covenant,' *Geneva Studies* x (1939), 157; and *The Law of the United Nations*, 50-3. G.I. Tunkin admits that while the UN Charter contains some 'progressive provisions' relating to the right of self-determination, 'it would be an exaggeration to assume that the Charter adequately reflected the historical law of decolonization' ('The Legal Nature of the United Nations,' *Recueil des Cours* CXIX 1966-III, 16)

61 Kelsen, *The Law of the United Nations*, 50-3

Disputing the thesis that 'the principle of self-determination is well established in the United Nations doctrine and practice, as the principle that the use of force is prohibited in the resolution of disputes between states,'[62] the Western world explains that while 'international interest demands that no juridical support, however indirect, be given to any such conception of the Resolutions of the General Assembly as being of no consequence,'[63] such resolutions, as a general rule and except in a few cases, have no legal binding force.[64] The view held by new African states that the various UN resolutions, declarations, and activities in the field of human rights and colonialism[65] have in effect created a legal obligation to decolonize, reflects the tendency of post-1945 international politics to take a strong anti-colonial direction. This point of view, while emphasizing the importance of United Nations practice, unfortunately either ignores or does not sufficiently appreciate the crucial importance of state practice and state acceptance of resolutions in the evolution of rules of international law. The extent to which resolutions and declarations of multinational organizations are in fact observed by states is clearly more important than the initial votes in support of a particular resolution or the phraseology of a specific declaration in determining whether a rule of international law has emerged. This is particularly the case because voting in the UN tends to be based not always on a sense of obligation but on opportunistic calculation of political advantages, on the issue of decolonization. For example, the major colonial powers abstained from voting on the celebrated Declaration on Colonialism in 1960.[66]

While one cannot deny that the principle of self-determination has become a very powerful political force in contemporary international politics, it is at best doubtful whether one can deduce from this the existence of a legal obligation to decolonize. Yet, to express such a doubt is not to accept the view that a member of the United Nations is entitled to simply ignore an overwhelmingly approved resolution of the General Assembly such as

62 The Ambassador, 'Future United Nations in the Maintenance of International Peace and Security,' in R.N. Swift, ed., *Annual Review of the United Nations Affairs, 1965-1966* (New York, 1967), 117-18

63 Judge Lauterpacht, *ICJ Reports* (1955), 122. See also Obed Y. Asamoah, *The Legal Significance of the Declaration of the General Assembly of the United Nations* (The Hague, 1966), 6

64 Higgins, *The Development of International Law*, 5; Tunkin, *Droit International Public* (Paris, 1961), 101ff

65 For a comprehensive account, see Whiteman, *Digest of International Law* 13, 679ff

66 For text of the Declaration, see Ian Brownlie, ed., *Basic Documents in International Law* (Oxford, 1967), 176-7

the UN Declaration on Colonialism. The 'good faith' provision of Article 2(2) of the UN Charter is intended to limit the discretion of members of the UN to refuse compliance with resolutions of the General Assembly, including the famous declaration on colonialism.

A major claim advanced to support the use of force by the OAU's Liberation Committee against colonial and minority racist regimes of Southern Africa is that colonialism is 'permanent aggression' and that there does exist a legitimate right of self-defence against colonial regimes in aid of the right of self-determination.

Traditional international law defends the colonial system not only by recognizing the legal claims of ownership of the colonies by the metropolitan powers,[67] but also by considering interference by another state in the affairs of the colony as a violation of the sovereignty of the imperial power. Thus, for a long time, the relationship between a colonial power and its colonies has been strictly a 'domestic' matter governed by the law of the metropolitan power and consequently, colonial wars always had the character of domestic strife. A metropolitan 'white' state resorting to the use of force against non-white majorities inhabiting its overseas colony was not considered as committing any act of aggression, although it may in the process have incurred world opprobrium for inhuman treatment of its subject peoples.

This view of colonial relations has come under heavy attack from Soviet[68] and especially from Afro-Asian leaders who have directly experienced the ordeal of colonialism.[69] At the Conference of the non-aligned

---

67 S. McCalmont Hill, 'The Growth and Development of International Law in Africa,' *Law Quarterly Review* XVI (1900), 249-68; C.H. Alexandrowicz, 'The Afro-Asian World and the Law of Nations (Historical Aspects),' *Recueil des Cours* CXXIII (1968), part I, 169ff

68 G. Osnitskaya, 'The Downfall of Colonialism and International Law,' *International Affairs* (Moscow, January 1961); George Ginsburgs, 'Wars of National Liberation and the Modern Law of Nations – The Soviet Thesis,' in Hans W. Baade, ed., *The Soviet Impact on International Law* (Dobbs Ferry, 1965), 66-98

69 See, for instance, the Joint proposal by Algeria, Burma, Cameroon, Dahomey, Ghana, India, Kenya, Lebanon, Madagascar, Nigeria, Syria, the UAR, and Yugoslavia presented to the UN Special Committee on the Principles of International Law concerning Friendly Relations and Co-operation among States (UN Doc. A/6230, 27 June 1966). It states in part: 'Territories under colonial domination do not constitute parts of the territories of states exercising colonial rule' (205); 'The use of force by a colonial Power against such territories should be regarded as an international and not domestic matter' (223). See also Green, 'The Impact of the New States on International Law,' *Israel Law Review* IV (1969), 48-53; V.M. Krishnan, 'African State Practice Relating to Certain Issues of International Law,' *IYBIA* XIV (1965), 196-241

states in Cairo in 1964, it was asserted that 'colonized peoples may legitimately resort to arms to secure the full exercise of their right to self-
determination and independence if the colonial powers persist in opposing
their natural aspirations.'[70] OAU members believed that the recalcitrance of
the Salazar and Caetano governments in opposing the natural aspirations of
the black majorities in Mozambique, Angola, and Portuguese-Guinea for
national independence provided ample justification for implementing the
substance of the 1964 Cairo resolution of the Afro-Asian Summit. However,
the OAU strategy of armed confrontation against Portugal has been abandoned in recent months as the new government in Lisbon publicly conceded the right of self-determination to its African territories and proceeded
to recognize the independence of Guinea-Bissau, to grant independence to
Mozambique in 1975, and to negotiate the formation of a provisional government for Angola, promising independence for November 1975.

The Security Council debate on the Portuguese indictment of India for a
'condemnable act of aggression' in Goa in 1961[71] exemplifies the relationship between colonialism, aggression, and self-defence as viewed by Afro-
Asian and Soviet-bloc members of the UN. India admitted using force, bas-
ing her defence on the legally controversial ground that use of force to put
an end to colonialism does not amount to aggression because the Portuguese colonialism which she sought to terminate was clearly a continuing
aggression and therefore illegal.[72] The Indian representative further
charged that Portugal had not fulfilled her obligation to decolonize under
the UN Declaration on Colonialism. While it is indeed true that any colonial
power which refuses to decolonize will not be acting in good faith under the
1960 General Assembly Declaration on Colonialism, this is not a breach of
a recognized rule of international law. Representatives of Liberia, Ceylon,
the United Arab Republic, and the Soviet Union claimed that if a case of
the use of force against a colonial regime which refuses to decolonize were
brought before the Security Council, the supreme question before the Council should not be one of aggression, but one of violation by the colonial regime of the 1960 Declaration on Colonialism.[73] The claim is not an irrebuta-

---

70 Indian Society of International Law, *Asian-African States: Texts of International Declarations* (New Delhi, 1965), 82
71 Wright, 'The Goa Incident,' *AJIL* LVI (1962), 617-32; T.R. Reddy, *India's Policy in the United Nations* (Rutherford, 1968), 82ff
72 UN Doc. S/PV 987, par. 61 (1961). See also Maurice Flory, 'Les implications juridiques de l'affaire de Goa,' *AFDI* VIII (1962), 479-91
73 UN Doc. S/PV. 987, par. 95-9, 105 (1961); UN Doc. S/5033 (1961)

ble one since the 1960 Declaration neither authorizes the use of force for its implementation nor claims to override the Charter injunctions against the use of force.

The OAU has not been formally charged with aggression; it is in any case unlikely to be successfully indicted by the UN. This is the subtle message of the Goa affair. But the high probability that a UN resolution condemning the forceful activities of the Liberation Committee is unlikely to be adopted should not be allowed to determine a priori the legal consistency of the activities of the OAU with the UN Charter.

As the military activities of OAU's Liberation Committee in giving both direct and indirect aid to armed bands operating against the colonial and apartheid regimes of Southern Africa have not been authorized by the Security Council, they can only be lawful under both the UN Charter and customary international law as acts of legitimate self-defence. The question then is whether it is indeed lawful to resort to the use of force as an act of self-defence against regimes whose only 'crime' is that they practise colonialism or accept apartheid as a basis of public policy. Only an over-extended interpretation of the word 'aggression' would tolerate the characterization of colonialism as 'permanent aggression.' Classical international law did defend the institution of colonialism; but while the new international morality calls it anachronistic and demands its termination, it falls short of equating it with aggression as this term is used in the UN Charter. The UN Charter prescribes sanctions against acts of aggression, but the 1960 Declaration on Colonialism nowhere authorizes the use of force against failure to decolonize. The African position cannot cogently be defended on the grounds that colonialism amounts to aggression within the meaning of the UN Charter.[74] Yet, it is quite possible to defend the military activities of the Liberation Committee on the ground of self-defence without assuming a priori that colonialism per se is a form of aggression. Whether such defence is sufficiently convincing and reasonably persuasive is a different question.

The core of such this defence is as follows: In order to keep the black majorities in Mozambique, Angola, Rhodesia, South Africa, and South-West Africa politically subservient and powerless, the Portuguese metropolitan government overthrown in 1974 and white minority rulers have resorted to despicable forms of political repression which naturally intensely offend the moral, human, and political sensibilities of the leaders of the independent black African states. Against the assertion that the treatment of

74 Dugard, 'The Organization of African Unity and Colonialism'

one's subjects is a matter of domestic jurisdiction,[75] it can be argued that the practices of colonialism and apartheid strain relations between states, provoke revolt, and create possibilities for a major racial explosion which constitutes a potential threat to world peace.[76] The formulation of Article 51 of the UN Charter, the argument continues, does not exclude the exercise by states of their inherent right of preventive self-defence which is part of the right states enjoy under customary international law. As each state usually claims to be the sole judge of whether circumstances justifying resort to the use of force in self-defence have arisen, the justification of the activities of the Liberation Committee on the grounds of legitimate collective self-defence is quite possible.

It is equally possible to contend that, in taking certain measures such as arms build-up, political repression, and military action, colonial and racist regimes themselves have only been responding in part to the perceived threat represented by the anti-colonial and anti-apartheid OAU; and that in actually responding in kind as Portugal, for example, did against Zambia and Senegal, the colonial and apartheid regimes believed they were acting in self-defence against the intrusion of powerfully organized armed bands operating within their territories from foreign bases.[77] This entitles a state to the right of self-defence within the meaning of Article 51 of the UN Charter.[78] Israel exemplifies this position in relation to the activities of the Palestine Liberation Organization operating from bases in Lebanon and Syria.[79] The Middle East situation is, of course, rather aggravated and complicated by the existing state of armed conflict, and by the problem of Israeli military occupation.

75 Franco Nogueira, *The United Nations and Portugal* (London, 1963), 70-4
76 R.F. Taubenfeld and H.J. Taubenfeld, 'Race, Peace, Law and Southern Africa,' in John Carey, ed., *Race, Peace and Law in Southern Africa* (New York, 1968); McDougal and Reisman, 'Rhodesia and the United Nations: The Lawfulness of International Concern,' *AJIL* LXII (1968), 1-19; Green, 'Rhodesian Oil: Bootleggers or Pirates,' *International Journal* (Toronto) XXI (1965-66), 350-8. For a strong dissent, see C.G. Fenwick, 'Where is there a threat to the Peace? – Rhodesia,' *AJIL* LXI (1967), 753-5
77 For an analysis of the distinction between self-defence and reprisal, see Derek Bowett, 'Reprisal Involving Recourse to Armed Force,' *AJIL* LXVI (1972), 1-36
78 Brownlie, 'International Law and the Activities of Armed Bands,' *ICLQ* VII (1958), 712-35. Contrast the view of Manuel Garcia-Mora, *International Responsibility For Hostile Acts of Private Persons against Foreign States* (The Hague, 1962), 115-20: 'There can of course be no doubt that allowing the formation of irregular bands would justify resort to the Security Council, though resort to self-defence would clearly be unlawful' (120).
79 Theodore Draper, *Israel and World Politics* (New York, 1968), 16, 32, 37

OAU members have not hidden the fact that they have financed and are financing the activities of armed bands operating from the territories of some of them. Even if they claim ignorance of such activities or inability to control them, the presumption under international law is that they bear criminal responsibility for such activities.[80] The 1965 UN Declaration on Non-Intervention prohibits 'subversive, terrorist, or armed activities directed towards the violent overthrow of the regime of another state.'[81] This Declaration was largely inspired by the small new states; the presumption that the Declaration exempts activities in support of the battle for decolonization seems to be evidence of a double standard on the part of the OAU members who incidentally, have also passed an African Declaration on Subversion.[82]

The question then arises as to which of the two arguments is more persuasive. As the UN Charter does not offer any clear-cut guide to the interpretation of the concept of self-defence, an answer to the question would seem to depend largely on individual political perspective. When examining the strategy used by the OAU in its anti-colonial campaign, it is necessary to avoid subordinating the question of the use of force in apparent breach of the UN Charter to the use of force in order to liquidate colonialism. It is not inconsistent to question the legality of the use of force against colonialism while simultaneously recognizing that contemporary trends in international politics have taken a strong anti-colonial direction. The assumption that colonialism per se amounts to aggression requires a more forceful elaboration and a more persuasive defence than now exists if it is to be credible. If one were to assume that the activities of the Liberation Committee are legitimately self-defensive, the question is whether the regional organization has been acting in conformity with the rules of behaviour laid down by the UN Charter for the exercise of the right of self-defence. Under Article 51, measures taken in self-defence are to be immediately reported to the Security Council. There is no record that such report has been made by the OAU.

In defence of the use of force in aid of the anti-colonial campaign of the OAU, a third major claim is sometimes advanced. It is that the OAU in its frontal attack on the institution of colonialism has been doing what the United Nations aims at doing but has not been able to do effectively be-

80 Garcia-Mora, *International Responsibility For Hostile Acts of Private Persons against Foreign States*, 113; Thomas, Thomas, and Salas, *The International Law of Indirect Aggression and Subversion* (Dallas, 1966), 313-31
81 GA. Res. 2131 (xx), 21 December 1965; text in *ILM* v (1966), 374-6
82 Text of the Accra Declaration on Subversion in Brownlie, ed., *Basic Documents on African Affairs* (Oxford, 1971), 16

cause of the vested interests of some of its politically and economically important members. The argument shifts from consideration of the means used to liquidate colonialism to consideration of the goal sought by the OAU. The core of the claim is that the legality of the means employed in aid of the anti-colonial activities of the OAU should be judged in the light of the goal and purpose of the UN in the matter of decolonization. There appears now to be a difference of aim and purpose between the foundation members of the UN and the large number of newly independent countries which have become members, particularly since the mid-1950s. Largely through pressures from the Afro-Asian states and their socialist supporters, decolonization has become a foremost preoccupation of the United Nations.[83]

The claim that so long as the OAU is implementing a major goal of the UN (whatever the means used may be), the former's activities may not be characterized as illegal is similar to the legally contentious, but perhaps politically wise, reasoning of the International Court of Justice in the *Certain Expenses* case. In that case, the Court was called upon to give an advisory opinion on whether certain expenditures authorized by the General Assembly to cover the costs of UN peace-keeping operations in the Middle East and the Congo constituted 'expenses of the Organization' within the meaning of Article 17(2) of the UN Charter. Relying principally on the doctrine of effectiveness in the interpretation of multilateral treaties, the Court, in its majority opinion, declared that 'when the Organization takes action which warrants the assertion that it was appropriate for the fulfilment of one of the stated purposes of the United Nations, the presumption is that such action is not ultra vires the Organization.'[84] The question about whether, in the light of the division of functions and jurisdiction, the organ taking a specific action is in fact legally competent to take such action was apparently put aside. If the reasoning of the World Court is not an irrebuttable one within the context of the relationship between two organs of the same organization,[85] similar reasoning is even more questionable in the context of the relationship between two separate organizations, in this case, between the OAU and the UN. If this reasoning were to be legally incontrovertible, the OAU can similarly claim that the use of force in aid of a purpose of the UN – decolonization and elimination of racism – is not illegal under the UN Char-

83 Claude, *The Changing United Nations* (New York, 1967); David A. Kay, *The New Nations in the United Nations, 1960-67* (New York, 1973)

84 *ICJ Reports* (1962), 168

85 E. Lauterpacht, 'The Legal Effects of Illegal Acts of International Organizations,' in *Cambridge Essays in International Law: Essays in Honour of Lord McNair* (London, 1965), 117; Tunkin, 'The Legal Nature of the United Nations,' 20-25

ter. This will amount to unduly enlarging the scope of exemptions permitted under the principal prohibition against an illegitimate resort to forceful action contained in Article 2(4) of the UN Charter. This was precisely what the United States did in defending the naval quarantine of Cuba in October 1962.

There is an additional reason why what amounts to the 'UN agency' argument can hardly legalize OAU activity. The conception of the OAU as an agency acting on behalf of the United Nations in the matter of decolonization suggests that the regional organization, while acting in this agency-capacity, automatically defines its relationship to the United Nations in terms of Articles 52-54. As the use of force under the direction of the Liberation Committee has neither been authorized by the Security Council nor recommended by the General Assembly acting under the 'Uniting for Peace' Resolution,[86] it is a breach of Article 53(1) of the UN Charter.

THE ABUSES OF POLITICAL INTERPRETATION OF LEGAL NORMS

If international law is properly understood not as a system of neutral rules but as a continuing process of specialized decision making[87] used by governments as an instrument of foreign policy,[88] then the gap between the Charter law of universal-regional relationship and the operating relationship between the United Nations and regional organizations is not surprising. States are not always prone to disregard legal norms in their international relations,[89] but rules of international law have usually been interpreted in the light of national (or regional) policy considerations and in support of particular lines of foreign policy. Dean Acheson remarked in connection with the Cuban missile crisis that 'law simply does not deal with . . . questions of ultimate power – power that comes close to the source of sovereignty . . . No law can destroy the state creating the law. The survival of the state is not a matter of law.'[90]

86 General Assembly Resolution 377 (V), November 1950
87 See generally, Meyers McDougal, 'International Law, Power and Policy,' *Recueil des Cours* LXXXII (1953), part I, 137-258; R.A. Falk, 'New Approaches to the Study of International Law,' *AJIL* LXI (1967), 477-95; Higgins, 'Policy Considerations and the International Judicial Process,' *ICLQ* XVII (1968), 58-84
88 H.C.L. Merillat, ed., *Legal Advisers and International Organizations* (Dobbs Ferry, 1966); also *Legal Advisers and Foreign Affairs* (Dobbs Ferry, 1964)
89 Louis Henkin, *How Nations Behave: Law and Foreign Policy* (New York, 1968)
90 ASIL, *Proceedings* (1963), 14. See also Oliver Lissitzyn, 'Western and Soviet Perspectives on International Law – A Comparison,' *ibid.* (1953), 21-30

With reference to Articles 51 and 53, reflections on the conduct of regional organizations like the OAS, the Warsaw Pact, and the OAU show that the practical effect of political interpretation has been to restrict the scope of UN control over regional organizations which are carrying out 'enforcement measures,' and to encourage the blurring of what should be a fine line between acts of aggression and acts of self-defence. Political interpretation of Articles 51 and 53 which seems clearly more generous to the competence of regional organizations than to the United Nations, has been made to serve national and regional interests, reinforcing the 'law of regional dominance' in international organization for the promotion of peace and security.

7
Regional organization and world order

The maintenance of peace has become the major problem of international law and organization. The cold war, the relative ineffectiveness of the United Nations, the proliferation of regional organizations, and the 'empire-building' character of some regional organizations dominated by super-powers have made problems of inter-organizational co-ordination and control particularly acute since the end of World War II.

The intention of the authors of the League Covenant and the UN Charter was to make the world organization superior to regional organizations in maintaining global order.[1] The different circumstances under which the regional principle came to be expressly admitted into the Covenant and the Charter explain why the law of universal-regional relationship was more systematically formulated in the UN Charter than in the League Covenant.[2] At Paris in 1919, regional organization for promoting peace entered into the political calculation of the authors of the Covenant only as an afterthought.

1 B. Boutros-Ghali, *Contribution a L'Etudes des Ententes Régionales* (Paris, 1949); George Liska, *International Equilibrium* (Cambridge, Mass., 1957); Ronald Yalem, *Regionalism and World Order* (Washington, 1965). What Hersch Lauterpacht said of the League Covenant is true of the UN Charter. He explained that the Covenant was the superior law 'not because there is any hierarchical superiority about the Covenant as a legislative instrument – for there is none,' but because of 'the comprehensiveness of the Covenant which not only limits the right of resort to war but also imposes most far-reaching obligations for the enforcement of the Covenant' ('The Covenant as the "Higher Law," ' *BYBIL* XVII (1936), 59

2 J.M. Yepes, 'Les Accords Régionaux et le Droit International,' *Recueil des Cours* LXXI (1947), part II; 235-344; H. Saba, 'Les Accords Régionaux dans la Charte de L'O.N.U.,' *Recueil des Cours* LXXX (1952), part I, 639-716

But at San Francisco in 1945, international constitution-making from the beginning could not ignore the fact that Churchill and Roosevelt had seemed at one stage to favour the emergence of a regionalized world organization after the war, and that the Latin American Republics desired to protect the integrity of the Inter-American System (which had since 1940 assumed the function of collective defence against armed aggression on the part of any non-American state). Perhaps more importantly, the authors of the UN Charter were very sensitive to the implications of the Yalta voting formula for the operation of the collective security system under the direction of the Security Council.[3] The San Francisco Conference delegates found it necessary to introduce the concept of collective self-defence in order to mediate in the rival claims of universality and regionalism, which are controlled in the UN Charter by a system of operating rules stipulating what the United Nations and regional organizations may or may not do in some defined circumstances. A regional organization will be operating consistently with the United Nations Charter if it conforms with the Charter rules for the performance of specific functions recognized in Articles 51-54.

The establishment of a workable and harmonious relationship between universal and regional organizations which preserves the dominant position of the universal organization is a practical political matter defined by statesmen and foreign policy makers, rather than a theoretical constitutional and legal matter to be debated by scholars. The dominant pattern of international conflict emerging between 1920 and 1939 was neither among the principal regional organizations nor between the League and regional organizations, but among the Great Powers themselves. As the world community was not then ideologically polarized, a predisposition to maintain at all cost the integrity of any regional organization at the expense of the League was not manifest. The compatibility of the operational behaviour of the Little Entente with the duties attached to membership in the League of Nations is hardly surprising since both organizations were committed to the preservation of a territorial status quo based on the Peace Settlement of 1919. What may be surprising is that, in spite of early indications in the 1920s that the United States would not permit the League to extend its jurisdiction to the Western Hemisphere, US policy turned out to be more flexible than expected. The Locarno Pact based itself so completely on League principles, procedures, and machinery, that it may be asked why it was nec-

3 A.L. Camargo, 'Regionalism and International Community,' Carnegie Endowment for International Peace, *Perspectives on Peace, 1910-1960* (New York, 1960), 107-19; W.P. Allen, 'Regional Arrangements and the United Nations,' US Dept of State, *Bulletin* XIV (1946), 925

essary in the first place. The answer could be that experiments in regional organization were regarded as devices for implementing certain obligations of the Covenant which each state could not realistically assume in every case of aggression. During the period 1920 to 1939, proposals for regional security pacts usually emphasized the position of the League as a superior instrument for preserving peace. For instance, while expressly permitting the existence of regional security pacts, the Draft Treaty of Mutual Assistance, drawn up in 1923 but not adopted, provided that '[c]omplementary agreements . . . shall, before being registered, be examined by the [League] Council with a view to determining whether they are in accordance with the principle of the [Draft] Treaty and the Covenant' and authorized the League Council to suggest changes, if necessary, in the texts of agreements submitted to it.[4] There was also an overwhelming consensus among European governments that a European Union must, as the Austrian Government put it, be 'embodied organically in the League of Nations.'[5]

The universal-regional equilibrium was not in practice disturbed in favour of regional organizations in the League days. Since 1945, however, there has been a significant shift in favour of regional organizations, due primarily (but not exclusively) to the East-West ideological cleavage which called into question the dependability of the UN as an effective universal organization. The expansive interpretation now being placed on the powers and competence of regional organizations has also been accompanied by a minimalist construction on the competence and responsibility of the United Nations in the promotion of world peace. The United States and the Soviet Union have found it opportune to challenge the competence of the Security Council to deal with situations in their own spheres of influence. Both powers continue to behave in strict conformity with a rule of behaviour postulated by Kaplan in his loose bi-polar international system: 'All bloc members are to subordinate objectives of universal actor to the objectives of their bloc but to subordinate the objectives of the rival bloc to those of the universal actor.'[6] For all practical purposes, Article 53, prohibiting enforcement action by regional organizations without the prior approval of the Security Council, has become emasculated, and hence has not been the UN

---

4 Art. 6, 7, and 8. See Bruce Williams, *State Security and the League of Nations* (Baltimore, 1927), 151ff
5 'European Federal Union,' *International Conciliation*, no. 265 (1930), 687. See generally, League of Nations, *Documents relating to the Organization of a System of European Union* (Geneva, 1930); F.P. Walters, *A History of the League of Nations* (London, 1967), 432
6 Morton Kaplan, *System and Process in International Politics* (New York, 1957), 38

Charter symbol of the dominance of the United Nations over regional peace agencies.[7]

When the Security Council became the first casualty of the cold war, the right of self-defence (regarded in the text of the UN Charter only as an emergency measure pending action by the Security Council) suddenly acquired new importance. The change of emphasis from collective security under the direction of the Security Council to collective self-defence under regional organizations like the NATO, the Warsaw Pact, the SEATO, the ANZUS Treaty Alliance, and the Inter-American Treaty of Reciprocal Assistance has given the task of distinguishing between the impermissible use of force and permissible self-defence great significance.[8] The urgency of the task is highlighted by cases like the Soviet justification of the Warsaw Pact invasion of Czechoslovakia in 1968 as a self-defensive action. It is doubtful if the intensification of efforts to define aggression with the object of extending the area in which a victim of the threat or use of force runs the risk of itself being guilty of an illegal use of force in its counter-measures provides a much-needed solution. The situation appears hopeless because the Security Council, which can theoretically stop alleged self-defensive use of force by a state or a regional organization and can also pronounce on the legality of that use is constantly under the threat of the veto power from any of its permanent members.

A further consequence of the East-West schism and the resulting loose bi-polar structure of the international society is that it has inadvertently permitted some measure of recklessness by regional organizations composed of militarily weak and economically underdeveloped states. Members of the Organization of African Unity appear to regard obligations imposed

---

7 J.W. Halderman, *The United Nations and the Rule of Law* (Dobbs Ferry, 1966), 37ff; Inis Claude, Jr, 'The OAS, the UN and the United States,' *International Conciliation*, no. 547 (March 1964); G.I.A.D. Draper, 'Regional Arrangements and Enforcement Actions,' *REDI* XX (1964), 18, 20-3; R. St J. Macdonald, 'The Developing Relationship Between Superior and Subordinate Political Bodies at the International Level,' *CYbIL* III (1964), 54; Asbjorn Eide, 'Peace-keeping and Enforcement by Regional Organizations,' *Journal of Peace Research* III (1966), 124-45; Michael Akehurst, 'Enforcement Action by Regional Agencies,' *BYBIL* XLII (1967), 175-227; R. Simmonds, 'Peace-keeping by Regional Organizations: A Critique of the Experience of the Inter-relationships between the Organization of American States and the UN Organization Within the Context of Collective Security,' *University of Ghana Law Journal* XI (1974)

8 Wilfried Schaumann, 'The Maintenance of Peace as the Central Problem of Modern International Law,' *Law and State* V (1972), 123; D.W. Bowett, *Self-Defence in International Law* (Manchester, 1958)

by the Addis Ababa Charter to liquidate colonialism in all its manifestations in Africa as superior to the obligations of UN membership enjoining peaceful relations with all states. The employment of the self-defence argument to validate the use of force by the OAU in aid of the campaign of decolonization in Southern Africa is an example of an overstretched interpretation of the limits of regional action permitted under the UN Charter. The contention that self-determination is a legal right which can legitimately be defended by the use of force is a product of the reformist attitudes of the Afro-Asian states towards rules of international law which they believe have not taken sufficient account of their vital national interests.[9]

CO-ORDINATION AMONG INTERNATIONAL ORGANIZATIONS

The Commission to Study the Organization of Peace posed a crucial question when it asked: 'How might the rivalry between two great regional arrangements – the Soviet System and the North Atlantic Organization – tending toward a bipolarization of power in the world, be moderated so as to permit the United Nations to function more effectively in the maintenance of collective security?'[10] However, a proper relationship between regional organizations is no less essential than that between universal and regional organizations in resolving the problem of co-ordination in international organization.[11] There is now a multiplicity of regional organizations in the world whose relationship to more limited-membership organizations within the same region is equally important.

The constitutional law of the OAU, the Council of Europe, and the OAS nowhere expressly purports to be the 'higher law' for the more limited-

9 Jorge Castenada, 'The Underdeveloped Nations and the Development of International Law,' *International Organization* XV (1961), 38; Richard Falk, 'New States and International Legal Order,' *Recueil des Cours* CXVIII (1966), part II, 7-103; R.P. Annand, 'Attitudes of the Asian-African States Towards Certain Problems of International Law,' *ICLQ* XV (1966), 55-71; Okon Udokang, 'The Role of the New States in International Law,' *Archiv des Völkerrechts* XV (1971), 145-96

10 Commission to Study the Organization of Peace, Eighth Report, *Regional Arrangements for Security and the United Nations* (New York, 1953), 11

11 C.W. Jenks, 'Coordination: A New Problem of International Organization,' *Recueil des Cours* LXXVII (1950), part II, 157-301; and also 'Coordination in International Organization: An Introductory Survey,' *BYBIL* XXVIII (1951), 29-89; R.J. Dupuy, 'Le Droit des Relations entre les Organisations Internationales,' *Recueil des Cours* C (1960), part II, 457-589; H.G. Schermers, *International Institutional Law. 2: Functioning and Legal Order* (Leydem, 1972), chap 12

membership groupings of states in Africa, Western Europe, and the Western Hemisphere. The law of these organizations does not deal with relationships to other organizations in the region. The issue of subcontinental regionalism was raised by many African leaders at the inaugural Conference of the OAU in May 1963 but the Addis Ababa Charter did not record any measures on it. At its First Extra-Ordinary Session in Dakar in August 1963, the OAU Council of Ministers recognized the utility of subcontinental regional co-operation in economic and social terms within the context of the OAU Charter.[12] In addition to assuming the superiority of the OAU over other subcontinental organizations, the Dakar Resolution seems to have conceded to the OAU a special political responsibility for pacific settlement of disputes, without of course prohibiting other subcontinental organizations from seeking to promote peace among their members. The harmonious relationship suggested by the Dakar Resolution has not always materialized. It is, for instance, often claimed that the African and Malagasy Common Organization linking together the French-speaking African states has been used on several occasions to stultify the efforts of the OAU.[13]

The problem of co-ordinating the activities of international organizations in Western Europe would have been extremely acute without the deliberate adoption of the principle of partial functional specialization by various organizations and the policy of institutional rationalization by the Council of Europe. For instance, the Statute of the Council of Europe has deliberately excluded matters relating to defence from its competence, and the Council itself has taken over social and cultural functions performed by the Western European Union (WEU).[14] It is the North Atlantic Treaty Organization, with largely West European membership, that has been primarily preoccupied with questions of defence. The 1957 Report of the Committee of Three on Non-Military Co-operation in NATO has warned that it would not serve the interest of NATO to duplicate the operating functions of other international organizations designed for various forms of economic co-operation.[15] The European Economic Community (EEC), the European Free Trade Association, and the Organization for European Economic Co-operation (OEEC) are primarily responsible for promoting international eco-

12 Organization of African Unity, *Basic Documents of the Organization of African Unity* (Addis Ababa, 1963), 33

13 R.S. Rana, 'OCAM: An Experiment in Regional Cooperation,' *Africa Quarterly* VIII (1968), 158-65; Albert Tevoedjre, *Pan-Africanism in Action: An Account of the UAM* (Cambridge, Mass., 1965)

14 A.H. Robertson, *The Council of Europe* (London, 1961), 227

15 US Dept of State, *Bulletin* XXXVI (1957), 18

nomic co-operation in Western Europe. Applying the principle of functional specialization has tended to minimize the danger of duplication of functions among these organizations.

One aspect of the policy of institutional rationalization is the assumption by the Council of Europe of the role of a co-ordinating agency vis-à-vis other organizations. As Jenks has pointed out, 'when claiming to act as a co-ordinating body for all forms of Western European regional co-operation, including co-operation in respect of matters entrusted previously to other bodies, the Consultative Assembly [of the Council of Europe] relies on its parliamentary character as justifying its claim to review the action of intergovernmental bodies.'[16] Another aspect of institutional rationalization that has emerged is the custom under which the OEEC, the EEC, and the WEU have agreed to send their annual reports to the Consultative Assembly of the Council of Europe.[17]

In the Western Hemisphere, the Organization of American States exists side by side with the Latin American Free Trade Association (LAFTA), composed of Mexico and all of South America excluding Guayana, and the Central American Common Market (CACM), made up of Guatemala, Honduras, Nicaragua, El Salvador, and Costa Rica.[18] Created largely on the initiative of the United Nations Economic Commission for Latin America, both LAFTA and CACM are structurally autonomous of the OAS but are functionally related to its economic activities.

The 1961 Charter of Punta del Este,[19] which is the economic face of the OAS, expressly takes cognizance of both LAFTA and CACM and considers them appropriate instruments for the creation of a Latin American Common Market. In their 1967 Punta del Este Declaration, the Presidents of American States laid down broad plans for the creation, beginning from 1970, of a Latin American Common Market 'based on the complete development and progressive convergence of the Latin American Free Trade Association and of the Central American Common Market, taking into account the interest of the Latin American countries not yet affiliated with these systems.'[20]

LAFTA and CACM deal with international regional economic co-operation which Latin American Republics allege is not given sufficient emphasis

16 Jenks, 'Coordination: A New Problem of International Organization,' 169
17 Robertson, *The Council of Europe*, 221 *et seq*
18 Robert W. Gregg, ed., *International Organization in Western Hemisphere* (Syracuse, 1968)
19 *Ibid.*, 239
20 *Meeting of American Chiefs of State, Punta del Este, Uruguay, April 12-14, 1967* (Washington, 1967), 58

within the framework of the OAS, which has shown special concern for the problems and activities of these two economic groupings in order to ensure their success. The United States is well aware that her Latin American economic policy can determine the success or failure of OAS's Alliance for Progress and of the economic integration efforts made by the Latin American Republics. The awareness that inter-organizational co-ordination would depend on the character of US policy most probably led Governor Rockefeller in 1969 to recommend in his Report, *Quality of Life in the Americas*, the appointment of Assistant Secretaries of Western Hemisphere Affairs for the CACM nations, the LAFTA group of states, and for the Caribbean states.[21] The Latin American Republics have not allowed the imperatives of economic self-help and advantages of economic co-operation among themselves to prevent them from pressuring the US (within the framework of a completely reformed OAS) to liberalize its trade and foreign economic policy towards Latin America. It is in the interest of the Latin American Republics to work towards the achievement of economic co-operation between themselves and the United States within some new development-oriented institutional framework established by the OAS to which they all belong.

The pragmatic search for inter-organizational co-ordination has not been confined to the regional level alone. Since 1945, the question of the forms and procedures of co-operation between the United Nations and regional organization has generated intense political and administrative interest. Generally speaking, two patterns of co-operation have emerged. The older pattern has been the simple administrative practice of mutual exchange of information, observers at each other's meetings, and joint consultation on matters of common interest. A more recent pattern began with the decision of the Security Council to hold a Council meeting in Addis Ababa, the headquarters of the OAU, in order to consider 'questions relating to Africa with which the Security Council is currently seized and the implementation of the Council resolutions.'[22] The proposal was, in its origin, an OAU idea. Bearing in mind that the issues discussed by the Security Council in Addis Ababa (Namibia, Apartheid, and Portuguese colonialism in Africa) have been those very ones which have led OAU members to activities hardly consistent with the obligations of UN membership, the symbolic gesture on the part of the Security Council was obviously designed to foster better rap-

---

21 US Dept of State, *Bulletin* LXI (1969), 512
22 O.O. Ayaga, 'The UN Security Council's African Safari,' *International Studies* (New Delhi) XII (1973)

port between the world organization and the regional peace agency. This was the spirit in which the Security Council members made the trip, in spite of the high financial costs involved. The Council has also met in Panama to consider 'measures for the maintenance and strengthening of international peace and security in Latin America in conformity with the provisions and principles of the Charter.' The meeting was not sponsored by the OAS but by Panama with the support of the 'Latin American group' in the Western Hemisphere, a fact which is not without significance. Again, unlike the Addis Ababa meeting, the debate, which focused on the Panama canal issue, was marked by verbal confrontation between the United States and many Latin American Republics. The Security Council effort to discuss problems peculiar to geographic areas in the field and in a situation of non-crisis seems to reflect a determination on the part of the UN to identify itself more closely with distinct regional problems. It seems likely that the Security Council will in future accept invitations to hold its meetings in other regions.

REGIONAL DOMINATION BY POWERFUL STATES

Membership in regional organizations of very powerful states which have *global* strategic interests cannot but influence the 'internal' and 'external' operation of those regional organizations.[23] At the extreme, membership of a strong world power in a regional organization composed largely of relatively small powers will tend to result in the development of regional hegemonial leadership, creating what looks like, or in practice comes close to, an imperial regional political order. This problem has featured significantly in the relations between the United States and Latin American Republics in the OAS, and between the Soviet Union and her allies in the Warsaw Treaty Organization. Both the OAS and the Warsaw Pact operations have in practice been dominated by the US and the USSR respectively, who have tended to use both organizations to preserve their regional hegemony rather than as impartial instruments for maintaining regional peace.[24]

23 See generally, William Zimmerman, 'Hierarchical Regional Systems and the Politics of System Boundaries,' *International Organization* XXVI (1972), 18-36

24 Claude, 'The OAS, the UN and the United States'; Akindele, 'The Warsaw Pact, the United Nations and the Soviet Union,' *IJIL* XI (1971), 553-71; Thomas M. Franck and Edward Weisband, *World Politics: Verbal Strategy Among the Super Powers* (London 1971); J.S. Nye, 'United States Policy Toward Regional Organization,' *International Organization* XXIII (1969), 719-40; Georg Schwarzenberger, 'Hegemonial Intervention,' *YBWA* XIII (1959), 236-65

Whenever Washington suspected a significant infilteration of communist agents, local or foreign, into the government of any Latin American Republic, it has always organized or aided the overthrow of such a discredited government. President Kennedy warned, in 1961, that 'Should it ever appear that the inter-American doctrine of non-interference merely conceals or excuses a policy of nonaction – if the nations of this hemisphere should fail to meet their commitment against outside Communist penetration – then I want it clearly understood that this Government will not hesitate in meeting its primary obligations, which are to the security of our Nations.'[25] But if the primary purpose of the United States has been to use the OAS in order to give a multilateral framework to her policy of insulating the Western Hemisphere from international communism, the most pressing problem posed for Latin American membership of the OAS is how to safeguard their political independence from possible encroachment from the US. This includes shifting the priority of the regional organization from what most of them regard as excessive preoccupation with security from communism to the acceleration of the economic development of the poorer member-states. As long as the OAS is overwhelmingly dominated by the US, which is in a global competition with the Soviet Union, the regional organization will continue to be used as an instrument of US foreign policy. Furthermore, a regional organization which is vigorously anti-communist will find it difficult to settle impartially disputes between its member-states involving charges of communist infiltration.

The relationship between the Soviet Union and other members of the Warsaw Pact has given the East European regional organization a peculiar neo-imperial character. As the local hegemonial power, the Soviet Union has not shown toleration for deviant political behaviour perceived as undermining the integrity of the socialist system. The Kremlin never permitted Nagy of Hungary to become another Tito, establishing another triumphant test case of national communism. When the Nagy government proclaimed Hungary's neutrality in November 1956 and gave notice of intention to withdraw from the Warsaw Treaty Organization, the Soviet Union moved in with her armed forces, installing a puppet Government in order to secure the political loyalty of the Hungarian government leaders to the Soviet-led socialist world of Eastern Europe.[26] The Kremlin has usually claimed the right to define the limits of tolerable socialist polycentric diversity in East-

25 US Dept of State, *Bulletin* XLIV (1961), 659
26 F. Fejto, *Behind the Rape of Hungary* (New York, 1957); Schwarzenberger, 'Hegemonial Intervention'; J.E. Fawcett, 'Intervention in International Law: A Study of Some Recent Cases,' *Recueil des Cours* CIII (1961), part I, 348-421

ern Europe. Liberalization was reluctantly allowed to proceed in Czechoslovakia, but when the Kremlin felt that liberal reforms under Dubcek provided cover for capitalist-inspired counter-revolutionary forces seeking to subvert the socialist system, it acted swiftly and decisively. The invasion of Czechoslovakia demonstrates that no strategic member state of the Warsaw Pact can be permitted to deviate too much from socialist orthodoxy, let alone to contract out of the Warsaw Pact. The Brezhnev Doctrine subordinating the sovereignty of the individual state of the socialist commonwealth to the international duty of socialist states (defined by the Kremlin) is a good manifestation of the imperial nature of the Warsaw Treaty Organization. In the hands of the Soviet Union, the Warsaw Pact has always been the guardian of an iron-clad status quo which perpetuates the Kremlin's hold over Eastern Europe.

Both the Warsaw Pact and the OAS have been used as foreign policy instruments by the Soviet Union and the United States. More disconcerting is that in cases where resort to and reliance on the regional machinery was preferred by the two super-powers, the choice has usually been permitted to cast doubt on the competence and responsibility of the United Nations.

Since contemporary international political landscape is contoured primarily according to the will of the competing Great Powers, especially the super-powers, it is not surprising that most of the important regional organizations – NATO, SEATO, CENTO, OAS, Warsaw Pact – have been organized around the United States or the Soviet Union. The phenomenon of hegemonial leadership and of regional imperialism is not observable in all of these regional organizations. Where it does not exist, or perhaps exists only in a mild form, as it appears to be the case with the SEATO, NATO, and CENTO, the policies of these regional organizations are still influenced directly or indirectly by the United States. This is reflected in a 'spread effect' whereby 'the alliance behaviour of a superpower in one subsystem can affect the posture of that power's allies in other subsystems' as well as in the 'demonstration effect' of a super-power's influence which helps to establish 'perceptual links' among regional organizations.[27]

REGIONAL ORGANIZATIONS AND NON-MEMBERS

The manner in which the League Covenant and the UN Charter have attempted to deal with the problem of non-membership of the world organi-

---

27 Oran R. Young, 'Political Discontinuities in the International System,' *World Politics* XX (1968), 370-1

zations has not been free of legal controversy.[28] The UN Charter imposes upon members of the world organization the duty to ensure that states which are not members act consistently with the Charter principles so far as may be necessary for the maintenance of international peace. Nowhere does the constitutional law of regional organizations expressly impose similar obligations on members to see that regional non-members conduct their international relations in a peaceful manner. However, Thomas and Thomas, expressing a broad interpretation of the competence of regional organizations, say that 'by ratification of the United Nations Charter, a nation falling within a region in which there is a regional arrangement or agency has indirectly given its consent to intervention by that arrangement or agency in matters in its region relating to the maintenance of international peace . . . Thus if two nonsignatory nations falling within the area of a regional arrangement or agency engage in illegal warfare, collective self-defence might come into play.'[29] The UN Charter offers no legal support for the first part of the claim. A regional treaty is valid only among its signatories.[30] Chapter VIII of the UN Charter can in no sense be construed as suggesting a contrary view. In any case, in international law, the consent of states cannot be presumed.[31] In the event of a dispute between a regional non-member and a signatory to a regional organization, the former cannot be compelled to submit the dispute to mediation or adjudication by the regional organization. But if a regional non-member were to attack or threaten with attack a signatory to a regional collective self-defence arrangement, members of the regional organization would be justified in exercising their right of collective self-defence declared in Article 51 of the UN Charter.

In the event of a conflict between two non-signatory states of a geographical region in which there is a regional organization in operational existence, members of the regional organization may freely consult, but can legally intervene only under two conditions: 1/ if one of the combatants requests assistance from members of the regional organization; and 2/ if

28 Georg Schwarzenberger, *The League of Nations and World Order* (London, 1936), 105-18; Hans Kelsen, *The Law of the United Nations* (New York, 1950); Falk, *The Authority of the United Nations over Non-Members* (Princeton, 1965); Jachen A. Frowein, 'The United Nations and Non-Member States,' *International Journal* (Toronto) XXV (1970), 333-44
29 A. van W. Thomas and A.J. Thomas, *Non-Intervention* (Dallas, 1956), 160
30 Vienna Convention on the Law of Treaties, Art. 34; text in *AJIL* LXIII (1968), 875; Lord McNair, *The Law of Treaties* (Oxford, 1961), 309
31 *SS Lotus* case: *PCIJ*, Series A, no. 10 (1927), 18; M.O. Hudson, *World Court Reports* 2 (New York, 1935), 23 at p. 35

the conflict were considered by any of the signatories to the regional treaty as constituting a threat to its legal interest and security. If the second condition is most likely to result in or provide excuse for a legally questionable use of force by a regional organization against a regional non-member state under the excuse that members are exercising their right of collective self-defence, it is because the concept of self-defence covers the self-defensive use of force in situations of imminent threat of armed attack. The claim implicit in the view of Thomas and Thomas that there is a regional version of Article 2(6) of the UN Charter which permits a regional organization to maintain peace not merely among its members but for the larger geographical region cannot and should not be read into the formulation of Chapter VIII of the UN Charter.

While it is true that no law of regional organizations expressly imposes obligations on member states to ensure that regional non-members conduct their external relations in a peaceful manner, there has always been the danger of regional enforcement action against regional non-members which oppose the regional 'ideological' consensus in a fundamental manner. In the days of the League of Nations, the Hungarian campaign for boundary revision was considered by Czechoslovakia, Rumania, and Yugoslavia as an affront to the consensus among the Little Entente Powers in favour of the 'new' territorial status quo based upon the Treaty of Trianon and the Treaty of Nuielly. Both treaties symbolized the dismemberment of the Austro-Hungarian Empire. The possibility of a collective forceful action against Hungary was raised in connection with the attempted monarchical restoration in 1921 and following the assassination in 1935 of the Yugoslav King, suspected to have been carried out with the connivance of Hungary. The Organization of African Unity continues to organize forceful action against regimes in Southern Africa which refuse to decolonize and which mistreat their black African population. The League of Arab States has been at intermittent war with Israel which belongs to the Middle East but is not a member of the Arab League. In 1962, members of the Organization of American States excluded the communist government of Cuba under Castro from participation in the regional organization. The attitude of these regional organizations towards those non-members accused of challenging the regional 'ideology' has in the past determined and will continue to determine the extent to which regional organizations can behave consistently with UN rules laid down in Articles 51-54 of the Charter. The need to solve this problem was clearly felt by those delegates who, during the debate in the First Committee (Political and Security) of the UN General Assembly in

November 1970 on 'Measures for the Strengthening of International Security,' suggested that all states in a region should participate in regional arrangements on the basis of strict equality and mutual respect.

THE CHALLENGE OF COLD WAR REGIONALISM

The post-1945 challenge of regionalism has been formidable. Writing on the problem of international security in our time, Martin, with the advantage of hindsight, observed:

[T]hose who made the Charter have not been more successful than their predecessors in devising adequate legal guarantees against the dangers inherent in rival alliances. The world was not entitled to expect otherwise. In an imperfectly co-ordinated international society, there will always be dangers that do not respond to purely legal treatment, but call for that kind of safeguard which only superior power can provide. The answer to the problem of regional arrangements lies not in legal rules designed to weaken them; it lies in the political action designed to enhance the military and economic power that can be mobilized from the centre.[32]

The constitutional history of the United Nations shows no record of any attempt to weaken the Charter provisions dealing with regional organizations; it abounds with efforts geared towards strengthening the General Assembly and improving the peace-keeping capability of the world organization.

The universalist response to the increasing challenge of regionalism inspired by the cold war first manifested itself modestly in the proposal of the United States to establish an Interim Committee on Peace and Security.[33] In the course of the General Assembly debate on the American proposal, Sir Hartley Shawcross of the United Kingdom frankly admitted that 'the establishment of this [I]nterim [C]ommittee of the General Assembly is somewhat related to the experience, during the past year or more, of the operation of the Security Council.'[34] Against the opposition of the Soviet Union and its East European allies, the General Assembly voted overwhelmingly in favour of establishing the 'Little Assembly,' as it was called, which was to function continuously and in which every member of the Gen-

32 Andrew Martin, *Collective Security: A Progress Report* (Paris, 1952), 178
33 UN Doc. A/454 (1947)
34 *GAOR*, 2nd Sess., 110th Plenary Mtg (13 November 1947), 789

eral Assembly was to be represented.[35] The Little Assembly was explicitly prohibited from considering matters which were on the agenda of the Security Council. From the Soviet point of view, the political motive behind the creation of the Interim Committee was suspect. The proposal was American and its beneficiary was the General Assembly, dominated (as it was) by the Western Powers. The Soviet Union saw the American proposal as an attempt 'to nullify the Security Council and undermine its foundations.'[36] The value of the Committee remains questionable. The Soviet bloc countries refused to participate in its activities and by 1952 it had ceased to function. The 'Little Assembly' reflects the politically naive view that the United Nations could be strengthened and made more effective in the absence of a developing political *detente* between the two major power camps.

The passing of the celebrated 'Uniting for Peace' Resolution[37] in 1950 was a response to the problem of the Security Council's increasing political impotence. Again, the Resolution was the brain-child of the United States.[38] It was, said Lester B. Pearson, 'our answer to those who would frustrate and make futile the efforts of the Security Council to carry out the task for which it has primary responsibility, the maintenance of international peace and security.'[39] Section A of the Resolution authorizes the General Assembly to recommend measures, including the use of armed force, to maintain international peace if the Security Council has failed to exercise its primary responsibility because of the veto power. For this purpose, an emergency meeting of the General Assembly could be called on twenty-four hours notice at the request of any seven (now nine) members of the Security Council or by a majority of UN members. Section B establishes a Peace Observation Committee to report on any situation which is likely to endanger the maintenance of international peace and security. In Section D a Collective Measures Committee is constituted and empowered to study and report to both the Security Council and the General Assembly on methods for maintaining and strengthening world peace and security, with due regard to collective self-defence and regional arrangements. Under Section C, each UN member is urged to organize, train, and equip units of her armed forces

35 See generally, L.C. Green, 'The "Little Assembly,"' *YBWA* III (1949); Douglas Coster, 'The Interim Committee of the General Assembly: An Appraisal,' *International Organization* III (1949)

36 *GAOR*, 2nd Sess., 110th Plenary Mtg (13 November 1947), 764; Alexander Dallin, *The Soviet Union and the United Nations* (New York, 1962), 55

37 Kelsen, *The Law of the United Nations*, 953, *et seq*

38 L.D. Weiler and A.P. Simons, *The United States and the United Nations* (New York, 1967), 284

39 *UN Bulletin* IX (1950), 515

for United Nations duties. Such units are to be made available in accordance with the constitutional processes of each state and upon the recommendation of the Security Council or of the General Assembly. While the Acheson Plan, as it is popularly known, did seek to strengthen the UN, it did not actually aim at steming the rising tide of regionalism. The formulation of the Resolution itself discourages suggestion of anti-regionalist intent in as much as Sections C and D make deferential references to the integrity of regional security arrangements based on Article 51 of the UN Charter. It is indeed highly probable that political calculation in the Western camp in 1950 was premised on strengthening the West-dominated General Assembly in order to give collective legitimacy and universal character to essentially regional (Western) sponsored operations. The United Nations would then not only retain its theoretical superiority, but would also continue to serve the policy interests of the West.

The Acheson Plan suggested anti-Soviet intention; it is, nevertheless, within the law of the United Nations.[40] The delegates from the Soviet bloc countries confused its pro-Western bias with the question of its constitutionality. The anticipated ascendancy of the General Assembly, following the self-imposed retreat of the Security Council, has not been able to dampen the political appeal of regionalism, and indeed was not really intended for that purpose. The 'Uniting for Peace' Resolution neither redressed the growing disequilibrium in the scale of universal-regional relationship which seemed to favour regional organizations nor did it convert the United Nations into an effective global security system against armed aggression. It added little or nothing to the capacity of the United Nations to maintain peace beyond making it possible to summon an emergency meeting of the General Assembly on very short notice and as soon as the Security Council is prevented from taking necessary action by the veto power.[41]

Another response to the cold war was the successful establishment of ad hoc UN peace-keeping forces in the Middle East (1956), in the Congo

40 J. Andrassy, 'Uniting for Peace,' *AJIL* L (1956), 563-83; Bowett, *United Nations Forces: A Legal Study* (New York, 1964), 290-4; Julius Stone, *Legal Controls of International Conflicts* (New York, 1959), 266ff. For a contrary view, see Kelsen, 'Is the Acheson Plan Constitutional?' *WPQ* III (1950), 527; also *The Law of the United Nations*, 960; G.I. Tunkin, 'The Legal Nature of the United Nations,' *Recueil des Cours* CXIX (1966), part III, 48-56

41 As Green puts it, 'Despite all the sound and fury that accompanied the Caesarean birth of the Interim Committee, instead of some Gargantua being born, what came forth was a mere Tom Thumb ... [I]t is nothing more or less than "a glorified Hampstead Garden Suburb debating society." ' See his 'The Little Assembly,' 187

(1960), and in Cyprus (1964).[42] In these three crisis situations, the claim of the United Nations to be the dominant peace agency met with almost instant, though doubtful long-run, success. The UN Resolutions establishing UNEF, ONUC, and UNFICYP were passed without any dissenting votes.[43] It is a mistake, however, to equate absence of positive dissent from UN members, especially the most powerful ones, with support for improving the peace-keeping capability of the world organization.[44] Obtaining initial support of the major powers in establishing an ad hoc international force was less difficult than securing their continuing support. The constitutional crisis of 1965 demonstrated that the political consensus behind the UN's peace-keeping activities was not as strong as it ought to be if the UN's claim as an effective and dominant international peace agency is to be credible.[45]

In assessing the extent to which the successful creation of ad hoc international forces has contributed to rejuvenating the universalist principle, it is necessary to recognize that the United Nations was using what Dag Hammarskjold called 'preventive diplomacy' and not coercive enforcement against an aggressor state. The purpose of the UN Force in the Middle East was to secure and supervise the cessation of hostilities. The principle underlying Dag Hammarskjold's plan for UNEF and ONUC and U Thant's UNFICYP was that the troops of the permanent members of the Security Council would be excluded from the international forces contrary to the intention of the provisions of Chapter VII of the UN Charter. The purpose for which consensus was achieved in 1956, 1960, and 1964 was not enhancement of the collective capacity of the United Nations to enforce peace by initiating actions against an aggressor, but the more modest one of 'keeping newly arising conflicts outside the sphere of bloc differences,' and hence 'avoiding an extension or achieving a reduction of area into which the bloc

---

42 Rosalyn Higgins, *United Nations Peace-keeping 1946-1967: Documents and Commentary* (London, 1969), 219, *et seq*

43 Bowett, *United Nations Forces*, 290-4

44 In his dissenting Opinion on the *Certain Expenses* case, Judge Koretsky of the USSR pointed out that 'Abstention from the vote on the resolutions [establishing the UNEF and ONUC] cannot be made equal to the Old Roman "non liquet." Another Old Roman rule could be recalled, i.e. if one ought to say "yes," but keeps silent, then that means "no." But that would be excessively logical. Abstention . . . should rather be considered as an expression of unwillingness to participate in these measures (and eventually in their financing as well) and as unwillingness to hamper the implementation of these measures by those who voted "in favour" of them' (*ICJ Reports*, 1962, 151 at p. 279)

45 Claude, 'The Political Framework of the United Nations' Financial Problems,' *International Organization* XVII (1963), 831-59; J. Stoessinger, *The United Nations and the Super-powers* (New York, 1965), 103-13; A.G. Nicholas, 'The United Nations in Crisis,' *International Affairs* (London) XLI (1965), 441-50

conflicts penetrate.'[46] The validity of the distinction was recognized by the International Court of Justice in the *Certain Expenses* case where majority opinion asserted that the operations known as UNEF and ONUC were not enforcement actions within the compass of Chapter VII of the Charter.[47] Consent of the aggressor state is not needed for the deployment of a UN enforcement force, but the consent of the host state has been the basis of UN peacekeeping operations.[48]

The interpretation of UNEF, ONUC, and UNFICYP as 'a manifestation of the view than an organization which is incapable of providing collective security may yet contribute significantly to peace and security if it concentrates on helping states to avoid drifting too near the brink of war, and not on rescuing them from the brink itself'[49] is not intended to belittle the significance of the establishment of these ad hoc forces under a UN command. Rather, it emphasizes that strengthening the peace-keeping capacity of the world organization in this manner falls short of restoring the United Nations (more precisely the Security Council) to the managerial role defined for it in 1945. Nation-states still regard the UN, to use the much-quoted phrases of Dag Hammarskjold, as a 'static conference machinery' rather than as a 'dynamic instrument of governments.'[50]

Two recent developments have bearing on the effectiveness of the United Nations as a universal organization. On 16 December 1970, the General Assembly approved a declaration, 'The Strengthening of International Security,' following a series of debates (reflecting divergent 'group'

46 'Introduction to the Annual Report of the Secretary-General on the work of the Organization, 16 June 1959-15 June 1960,' in *GAOR*, 15th Sess., Suppl. no. 1A (A/4390/Add. 1), 4
47 *ICJ Reports* (1962), 151 at p. 166
48 Higgins, *United Nations Peace-keeping 1946-1967*, 335 *et seq*; J.I. Garvey, 'United Nations Peacekeeping and Host State Consent,' *AJIL* LXIV (1970), 241-69; Bowett, *United Nations Forces*, 124ff
49 Claude, 'The United Nations and the Use of Force,' *International Conciliation*, no. 532, (March 1961), 375
50 'Introduction to the Annual Report of the Secretary-General on the Work of the Organization, 16 June 1960-15 June 1961,' *GAOR*, 16th Sess., Suppl. no. 1A (A/4800/ Add. 1). The model of the UN implicit in the dissenting opinion of Judge Winiarski in the *Certain Expenses* case is quite revealing: 'The intention of those who drafted it [i.e., the UN Charter] was clearly to abandon the possibility of useful action rather than to sacrifice the balance of carefully established fields of competence, as can be seen, for example, in the case of the voting in the Security Council . . . It may be that the United Nations is sometimes not in a position to undertake action which would be useful for the maintenance of international peace and security or for one or other of the purposes indicated in Article 1 of the Charter, but that is the way in which the Organization was conceived and brought into being,' *ICJ Reports* (1962), 151 at p. 230

interests) in the First Committee (Political and Security) begun in October 1969. The declaration reaffirmed, inter alia, the universal and unconditional validity of the purposes of the UN Charter as the basis of relations among states and, more important, urged the Security Council to 'take steps to facilitate the conclusion of the agreements envisaged in Article 43 of the Charter in order to develop fully its capacity for enforcement action as provided for by the Charter.'[51] Another General Assembly resolution, 'Strengthening the Role of the United Nations' (passed on 27 November 1972) reiterated the imperative need to make the UN a more effective instrument for maintaining world peace.[52] There has been a continual search for a workable world order by means of international organization, especially through the United Nations. The gap between goal and achievement reflects the peculiar problems of international politics in a community of diverse sovereign states.

The future effectiveness of the United Nations depends upon the possibility of reducing present political investment in competitive regional defence systems. The existing ideological division of the international community into rival camps does not provide the appropriate political climate in which the United Nations can function as envisaged at San Francisco in 1945. Only when members of the UN are convinced of the dependability and impartiality of the world organization as an effective and supreme international agency can they be expected to abandon their conception of regional organization as *alternative* to the UN. The increasing reliance on regional organizations is a constant reminder that international society is unfortunately not yet ready for an effective universal organization, even though some of its problems are best tackled on the global level. Political realists who are pessimistic about the revitalization and rejuvenation of the Security Council may urge us to begin to readjust our thinking towards stabilizing relations between regional organizations, especially those led by the super-powers, and to disregard the recalcitrant and elusive problem of universal-regional relationship. But there is much to be said in favour of retaining the principle of universality based on dominance by the world organization. A relaxation of great power conflict and a gradual abandonment of excessive veneration for the principle of national sovereignty may make it possible for the Security Council to play the supreme managerial role in the future that was envisaged for it under the 1945 UN Charter.

51 *UN Yearbook* (1970), 101-3
52 *UN Monthly Chronicle* IX (December 1972), 52-5

APPENDIX A
The Covenant of the League of Nations (selected provisions)

Article 10
The Members of the League undertake to respect and preserve as against external aggression the territorial integrity and existing political independence of all Members of the League. In case of any such aggression or in case of any threat or danger of such aggression, the Council shall advise upon the means by which this obligation shall be fulfilled.

Article 11
1 Any war or threat of war, whether immediately affecting any of the Members of the League or not, is hereby declared a matter of concern to the whole League, and the League shall take any action that may be deemed wise and effectual to safeguard the peace of nations. In case any such emergency should arise, the Secretary-General shall, on the request of any Member of the League, forthwith summon a meeting of the Council.
2 It is also declared to be the friendly right of each Member of the League to bring to the attention of the Assembly or of the Council any circumstance whatever affecting international relations which threatens to disturb international peace or the good understanding between nations upon which peace depends.

Article 12
1 The Members of the League agree that if there should arise between them any dispute likely to lead to a rupture they will submit the matter either to arbitration or judicial settlement or to enquiry by the Council, and they

agree in no case to resort to war until three months after the award by the arbitrators or the judicial decision or the report by the Council.

2 In any case under this article the award of the arbitrators or the judicial decision shall be made within a reasonable time, and the report of the Council shall be made within six months after the submission of the dispute.

Article 13

1 The Members of the League agree that whenever any dispute shall arise between them which they recognise to be suitable for submission to arbitration or judicial settlement, and which cannot be satisfactorily settled by diplomacy, they will submit the whole subject-matter to arbitration or judicial settlement.

2 Disputes as to the interpretation of a treaty, as to any question of international law, as to the existence of any fact which, if established, would constitute a breach of any international obligation, or as to the extent and nature of the reparation to be made for any such breach, are declared to be among those which are generally suitable for submission to arbitration or judicial settlement.

3 For the consideration of any such dispute, the court to which the case is referred shall be the Permanent Court of International Justice, established in accordance with Article 14, or any tribunal agreed on by the parties to the dispute or stipulated in any Convention existing between them.

4 The Members of the League agree that they will carry out in full good faith any award or decision that may be rendered, and that they will not resort to war against a Member of the League which complies therewith. In the event of any failure to carry out such an award or decision, the Council shall propose what steps should be taken to give effect thereto.

Article 15

1 If there should arise between Members of the League any dispute likely to lead to a rupture, which is not submitted to arbitration or judicial settlement in accordance with Article 13, the Members of the League agree that they will submit the matter to the Council. Any party to the dispute may effect such submission by giving notice of the existence of the dispute to the Secretary-General, who will make all necessary arrangements for a full investigation and consideration thereof.

2 For this purpose, the parties to the dispute will communicate to the Secretary-General as promptly as possible, statements of their case with all the relevant facts and papers, and the Council may forthwith direct the publication thereof.

3 The Council shall endeavour to effect a settlement of the dispute, and if such efforts are successful, a statement shall be made public giving such facts and explanations regarding the dispute and the terms of settlement thereof as the Council may deem appropriate.

4 If the dispute is not thus settled, the Council either unanimously or by a majority vote shall make and publish a report containing a statement of the facts of the dispute and the recommendations which are deemed just and proper in regard thereto.

5 Any Member of the League represented on the Council may make public a statement of the facts of the dispute and of its conclusions regarding the same.

6 If a report by the Council is unanimously agreed to by the members thereof other than the Representatives of one or more of the parties to the dispute, the Members of the League agree that they will not go to war with any party to the dispute which complies with the recommendations of the report.

7 If the Council fails to reach a report which is unanimously agreed to by the members thereof, other than the Representatives of one or more of the parties to the dispute, the Members of the League reserve to themselves the right to take such action as they shall consider necessary for the maintenance of right and justice.

8 If the dispute between the parties is claimed by one of them, and is found by the Council, to arise out of a matter which by international law is solely within the domestic jurisdiction of that party, the Council shall so report, and shall make no recommendation as to its settlement.

9 The Council may in any case under this article refer the dispute to the Assembly. The dispute shall be so referred at the request of either party to the dispute provided that such request be made within fourteen days after the submission of the dispute to the Council.

10 In any case referred to the Assembly, all the provisions of this article and of Article 12 relating to the action and powers of the Council shall apply to the action and powers of the Assembly, provided that a report made by the Assembly, if concurred in by the Representatives of those Members of the League represented on the Council and of a majority of the other Members of the League, exclusive in each case of the Representatives of the parties to the dispute, shall have the same force as a report by the Council concurred in by all the members thereof other than the Representatives of one or more of the parties to the dispute.

Article 16
1 Should any Member of the League resort to war in disregard of its coven-

ants under Articles 12, 13, or 15, it shall, ipso facto, be deemed to have committed an act of war against all other Members of the League, which hereby undertake immediately to subject it to the severance of all trade or financial relations, the prohibition of all intercourse between their nations and the nationals of the Covenant-breaking State, and the prevention of all financial, commercial or personal intercourse between the nationals of the Covenant-breaking State and the nationals of any other State, whether a Member of the League or not.

2 It shall be the duty of the Council in such case to recommend to the several Governments concerned what effective military, naval or air force the Members of the League shall severally contribute to the armed forces to be used to protect the covenants of the League.

3 The Members of the League agree, further, that they will mutually support one another in the financial and economic measures which are taken under this article, in order to minimise the loss and inconvenience resulting from the above measures, and that they will mutually support one another in resisting any special measures aimed at one of their number by the Covenant-breaking State, and that they will take the necessary steps to afford passage through their territory to the forces of any of the Members of the League which are co-operating to protect the covenants of the League.

4 Any member of the League which has violated any covenant of the League may be declared to be no longer a Member of the League by a vote of the Council concurred in by the Representatives of all the other Members of the League represented thereon.

Article 17

1 In the event of a dispute between a Member of the League and a State which is not a member of the League or between States not members of the League, the State or States not members of the League shall be invited to accept the obligations of membership in the League for the purposes of such dispute, upon such conditions as the Council may deem just. If such invitation is accepted, the provisions of Articles 12 to 16 inclusive shall be applied with such modifications as may be deemed necessary by the Council.

2 Upon such invitation being given, the Council shall immediately institute an enquiry into the circumstances of the dispute and recommend such action as may seem best and most effectual in the circumstances.

3 If a State so invited shall refuse to accept the obligations of membership in the League for the purposes of such dispute, and shall resort to war against a Member of the League, the provisions of Article 16 shall be applicable as against the State taking such action.

4 If both parties to the dispute when so invited refuse to accept the obligations of membership in the League for the purposes of such dispute, the Council may take such measures and make such recommendations as will prevent hostilities and will result in the settlement of the dispute.

Article 20

1 The Members of the League severally agree that this Covenant is accepted as abrogating all obligations or understandings inter se which are inconsistent with the terms thereof, and solemnly undertake that they will not hereafter enter into any engagements inconsistent with the terms thereof.
2 In case any Member of the League shall, before becoming a Member of the League, have undertaken any obligations inconsistent with the terms of this Covenant, it shall be the duty of such Member to take immediate steps to procure its release from such obligations.

Article 21

Nothing in this Covenant shall be deemed to affect the validity of international engagements, such as treaties of arbitration or regional understandings like the Monroe doctrine, for securing the maintenance of peace.

APPENDIX B

Locarno Treaty of Mutual Guarantee between

Germany, Belgium, France, Great Britain and France

Article 1

The High Contracting Parties collectively and severally guarantee, in the manner provided in the following articles, the maintenance of the territorial status quo resulting from the frontiers between Germany and Belgium and between Germany and France and the inviolability of the said frontiers as fixed by or in pursuance of the treaty of peace signed at Versailles on 28 June 1919, and also the observance of the stipulations of Arts. 42 and 43 of the said treaty concerning the demilitarized zone.

Article 2

Germany and Belgium, and also Germany and France, mutually undertake that they will in no case attack or invade each other or resort to war against each other.

This stipulation shall not, however, apply in the case of

1 The exercise of the right of legitimate defence, that is to say, resistance to a violation of the undertaking contained in the previous paragraph or to a flagrant breach of Articles 42 or 43 of the said treaty of Versailles, if such breach constitutes an unprovoked act of agression and by reason of the assembly of armed forces in the demilitarized zone immediate action is necessary.

2 Action in pursuance of Article 16 of the Covenant of the League of Nations.

3 Action as the result of a decision taken by the Assembly or by the Council of the League of Nations or in pursuance of Article 15, paragraph 7, of

the Covenant of the League of Nations, provided that in this last event, the action is directed against a state which was the first to attack.

Article 3
In view of the undertakings entered into in Article 2 of the present treaty, Germany and Belgium and Germany and France undertake to settle by peaceful means and in the manner laid down herein all questions of every kind which may arise between them and which it may not be possible to settle by the normal methods of diplomacy.

Any question with regard to which the parties are in conflict as to their respective rights shall be submitted to judicial decision, and the parties undertake to comply with such decision.

All other questions shall be submitted to a conciliation commission. If the proposals of this commission are not accepted by the two parties, the question shall be brought before the Council of the League of Nations, which will deal with it in accordance with Article 15 of the Covenant of the League.

The detailed arrangements for effecting such peaceful settlement are the subject special agreements signed this day.

Article 4
1 If one of the High Contracting Parties alleges that a violation of Article 2 of the present treaty or a breach of Articles 42 or 43 of the treaty of Versailles has been or is being committed, it shall bring the question at once before the Council of the League of Nations.
2 As soon as the Council of the League of Nations is satisfied that such violation or breach has been committed, it will notify its finding without delay to the powers signatory of the present treaty, who severally agree that in such case, they will each of them come immediately to the assistance of the power against whom the act complained of is directed.
3 In case of a flagrant violation of Article 2 of the present treaty or of a flagrant breach of Articles 42 or 43 of the treaty of Versailles by one of the High Contracting Parties, each of the other Contracting Parties hereby undertakes immediately to come to the help of the party against whom such a violation or breach has been directed as soon as the said power has been able to satisfy itself that this violation constitutes an unprovoked act of aggression and that by reason either of the crossing of the frontier or of the outbreak of hostilities or of the assembly of armed forces in the demilitarized zone immediate action is necessary. Nevertheless, the Council of the League of Nations, which will be seized of the question in accordance with

the first paragraph of this article, will issue its findings, and the High Contracting Parties undertake to act in accordance with the recommendations of the Council provided that they are concurred in by all the members other than the representatives of the parties which have engaged in hostilities.

Article 5

The provisions of Article 3 of the present treaty are placed under the guaranty of the High Contracting Parties as provided by the following stipulations:

If one of the powers referred to in Article 3 refuses to submit a dispute to peaceful settlement or to comply with an arbitral or judicial decision and commits a violation of Article 2 of the present treaty or a breach of Articles 42 or 43 of the treaty of Versailles, the provisions of Article 4 shall apply.

Where one of the powers referred to in Article 3, without committing a violation of Article 2 of the present treaty or a breach of Articles 42 or 43 of the treaty of Versailles, refuses to submit a dispute to peaceful settlement or to comply with an arbitral or judicial decision, the other party shall bring the matter before the Council of the League of Nations, and the Council shall propose what steps shall be taken; the High Contracting Parties shall comply with these proposals.

Article 6

The provisions of the present treaty do not affect the rights and obligations of the High Contracting Parties under the treaty of Versailles or under arrangements supplementary thereto, including the agreements signed in London on 30 August 1924.

Article 7

The present treaty, which is designed to insure the maintenance of peace and is in conformity with the Covenant of the League of Nations, shall not be interpreted as restricting the duty of the League to take whatever action may be deemed wise and effectual to safeguard the peace of the world.

Article 8

The present treaty shall be registered at the League of Nations in accordance with the Covenant of the League. It shall remain in force until the Council, acting on a request of one or other of the High Contracting Parties notified to the other signatory powers three months in advance, and voting at least by a two-thirds majority, decides that the League of Nations insures sufficient protection to the High Contracting Parties; the treaty shall cease to have effect on the expiration of a period of one year from such decision.

Article 9

The present treaty shall impose no obligation upon any of the British dominions, or upon India, unless the Government of such dominion, or of India, signifies its acceptance thereof.

Article 10

The present treaty shall be ratified and the ratifications shall be deposited at Geneva in the archives of the League of Nations as soon as possible.

It shall enter into force as soon as all the ratifications have been deposited and Germany has become a Member of the League of Nations.

The present treaty, done in a single copy, will be deposited in the archives of the League of Nations, and the Secretary-General will be requested to transmit certified copies to each of the High Contracting Parties.

APPENDIX C
The Charter of the United Nations (selected provisions)

Article 1

The Purposes of the United Nations are:

1 To maintain international peace and security, and to that end: to take effective collective measures for the prevention and removal of threats to the peace, and for the suppression of acts of aggression or other breaches of the peace, and to bring about by peaceful means, and in conformity with the principles of justice and international law, adjustment or settlement of international disputes or situations which might lead to a breach of the peace;

2 To develop friendly relations among nations based on respect for the principle of equal rights and self-determination of peoples, and to take other appropriate measures to strengthen universal peace;

3 To achieve international co-operation in solving international problems of an economic, social, cultural, or humanitarian character, and in promoting and encouraging respect for human rights and for fundamental freedoms for all without distinction as to race, sex, language, or religion; and

4 To be a centre for harmonizing the actions of nations in the attainment of these common ends.

Article 2

The Organization and its Members, in pursuit of the Purposes stated in Article 1, shall act in accordance with the following Principles.

1 The Organization is based on the principle of the sovereign equality of all its Members.

2 All Members, in order to ensure to all of them the rights and benefits re-

sulting from membership, shall fulfil in good faith the obligations assumed by them in accordance with the present Charter.

3 All Members shall settle their international disputes by peaceful means in such a manner that international peace and security, and justice, are not endangered.

4 All Members shall refrain in their international relations from the threat or use of force against the territorial integrity or political independence of any state, or in any other manner inconsistent with the Purposes of the United Nations.

5 All Members shall give the United Nations every assistance in any action it takes in accordance with the present Charter, and shall refrain from giving assistance to any state against which the United Nations is taking preventive or enforcement action.

6 The Organization shall ensure that states which are not Members of the United Nations act in accordance with these Principles so far as may be necessary for the maintenance of international peace and security.

7 Nothing contained in the present Charter shall authorize the United Nations to intervene in matters which are essentially within the domestic jurisdiction of any state or shall require the Members to submit such matters to settlement under the present Charter; but this principle shall not prejudice the application of enforcement measures under Chapter VIII.

CHAPTER VI: PACIFIC SETTLEMENT OF DISPUTES

Article 33

1 The parties to any dispute, the continuance of which is likely to endanger the maintenance of international peace and security, shall, first of all, seek a solution by negotiation, enquiry, mediation, conciliation, arbitration, judicial settlement, resort to regional agencies or arrangements, or other peaceful means of their own choice.

2 The Security Council shall, when it deems necessary, call upon the parties to settle their dispute by such means.

Article 34

The Security Council may investigate any dispute, or any situation which might lead to international friction or give rise to a dispute, in order to determine whether the continuance of the dispute or situation is likely to endanger the maintenance of international peace and security.

Article 35

1 Any Member of the United Nations may bring any dispute, or any situa-

tion of the nature referred to in Article 34, to the attention of the Security Council or of the General Assembly.

2 A state which is not a member of the United Nations may bring to the attention of the Security Council or of the General Assembly any dispute to which it is a party if it accepts in advance, for the purposes of the dispute, the obligations of pacific settlement provided in the present Charter.

3 The proceedings of the General Assembly in respect of matters brought to its attention under this Article will be subject to the provisions of Articles 11 and 12.

Article 36

1 The Security Council may, at any stage of a dispute of the nature referred to in Article 33 or of a situation of like nature, recommend appropriate procedures or methods of adjustment.

2 The Security Council should take into consideration any procedures for the settlement of the dispute which have already been adopted by the parties.

3 In making recommendations under this Article, the Security Council should also take into consideration that legal disputes should as a general rule be referred by the parties to the International Court of Justice in accordance with the provisions of the Statute of the Court.

Article 37

1 Should the parties to a dispute of the nature referred to in Article 33 fail to settle it by the means indicated in that Article, they shall refer it to the Security Council.

2 If the Security Council deems that the continuance of the dispute is in fact likely to endanger the maintenance of international peace and security, it shall decide whether to take action under Article 36 or to recommend such terms of settlement as it may consider appropriate.

Article 38

Without prejudice to the provisions of Articles 33 to 37, the Security Council may, if all the parties to any dispute so request, make recommendations to the parties with a view to a pacific settlement of the dispute.

CHAPTER VII: ACTION WITH RESPECT TO THREATS
TO THE PEACE, BREACHES OF THE PEACE, AND ACTS
OF AGGRESSION

Article 39

The Security Council shall determine the existence of any threat to the peace, breach of the peace, or act of aggression and shall make recommendations, or decide what measures shall be taken in accordance with Articles 41 and 42, to maintain or restore international peace and security.

Article 40

In order to prevent an aggravation of the situation, the Security Council may, before making the recommendations or deciding upon the measures provided for in Article 39, call upon the parties concerned to comply with such provisional measures as it deems necessary or desirable. Such provisional measures shall be without prejudice to the rights, claims, or position of the parties concerned. The Security Council shall duly take account of failure to comply with such provisional measures.

Article 41

The Security Council may decide what measures not involving the use of armed force are to be employed to give effect to its decisions, and it may call upon the Members of the United Nations to apply such measures. These may include complete or partial interruption of economic relations and of rail, sea, air, postal, telegraphic, radio and other means of communication, and the severance of diplomatic relations.

Article 42

Should the Security Council consider that measures provided for in Article 41 would be inadequate or have proved to be inadequate, it may take such action by air, sea, or land forces as may be necessary to maintain or restore international peace and security. Such action may include demonstrations, blockade, and other operations by air, sea, or land forces of Members of the United Nations.

Article 43

1 All Members of the United Nations, in order to contribute to the maintenance of international peace and security, undertake to make available to the Security Council, on its call and in accordance with a special agreement or agreements, armed forces, assistance, and facilities, including rights of passage, necessary for the purpose of maintaining international peace and security.

2 Such agreement or agreements shall govern the numbers and types of

forces, their degree of readiness and general location, and the nature of the facilities and assistance to be provided.

3 The agreement or agreements shall be negotiated as soon as possible on the initiative of the Security Council. They shall be concluded between the Security Council and Members or between the Security Council and groups of Members and shall be subject to ratification by the signatory states in accordance with their respective constitutional processes.

Article 44

When the Security Council has decided to use force, it shall, before calling upon a Member not represented on it to provide armed forces in fulfilment of the obligations assumed under Article 43, invite that Member, if the Member so desires, to participate in the decisions of the Security Council concerning the employment of contingents of that Member's armed forces.

Article 45

In order to enable the United Nations to take urgent military measures, Members shall hold immediately available national air-force contingents for combined international enforcement action. The strength and degree of readiness of these contingents and plans for their combined action shall be determined, within the limits laid down in the special agreement or agreements referred to in Article 43, by the Security Council with the assistance of the Military Staff Committee.

Article 46

Plans for the application of armed force shall be made by the Security Council with the assistance of the Military Staff Committee.

Article 47

1 There shall be established a Military Staff Committee to advise and assist the Security Council on all questions relating to the Security Council's military requirements for the maintenance of international peace and security, the employment and command of forces placed at its disposal, the regulation of armaments, and possible disarmament.
2 The Military Staff Committee shall consist of the Chiefs of Staff of the permanent members of the Security Council or their representatives. Any Member of the United Nations not permanently represented on the Committee shall be invited by the Committee to be associated with it when the

efficient discharge of the Committee's responsibilities requires the participation of that Member in its work.

3 The Military Staff Committee shall be responsible under the Security Council for the strategic direction of any armed forces placed at the disposal of the Security Council. Questions relating to the command of such forces shall be worked out subsequently.

4 The Military Staff Committee, with the authorization of the Security Council and after consultation with appropriate regional agencies, may establish regional subcommittees.

Article 48

1 The action required to carry out the decisions of the Security Council for the maintenance of international peace and security shall be taken by all the Members of the United Nations or by some of them, as the Security Council may determine.

2 Such decisions shall be carried out by the Members of the United Nations directly and through their action in the appropriate international agencies of which they are members.

Article 49

The Members of the United Nations shall join in affording mutual assistance in carrying out the measures decided upon by the Security Council.

Article 50

If preventive or enforcement measures against any state are taken by the Security Council, any other state, whether a Member of the United Nations or not, which finds itself confronted with special economic problems arising from the carrying out of those measures shall have the right to consult the Security Council with regard to a solution of those problems.

Article 51

Nothing in the present Charter shall impair the inherent right of individual or collective self-defence if an armed attack occurs against a Member of the United Nations, until the Security Council has taken the measures necessary to maintain international peace and security. Measures taken by Members in the exercise of this right of self-defence shall be immediately reported to the Security Council and shall not in any way affect the authority and responsibility of the Security Council under the present Charter to take at any time such action as it deems necessary in order to maintain or restore international peace and security.

CHAPTER VIII: REGIONAL ARRANGEMENTS

Article 52

1 Nothing in the present Charter precludes the existence of regional arrangements or agencies for dealing with such matters relating to the maintenance of international peace and security as are appropriate for regional action, provided that such arrangements or agencies and their activities are consistent with the Purposes and Principles of the United Nations.

2 The Members of the United Nations entering into such arrangements or constituting such agencies shall make every effort to achieve pacific settlement of local disputes through such regional arrangements or by such regional agencies before referring them to the Security Council.

3 The Security Council shall encourage the development of pacific settlement of local disputes through such regional arrangements or by such regional agencies either on the initiative of the states concerned or by reference from the Security Council.

4 This Article in no way impairs the application of Articles 34 and 35.

Article 53

1 The Security Council shall, where appropriate, utilize such regional arrangements or agencies for enforcement action under its authority. But no enforcement action shall be taken under regional arrangements or by regional agencies without the authorization of the Security Council, with the exception of measures against any enemy state, as defined in paragraph 2 of this Article, provided for pursuant to Article 107 or in regional arrangements directed against renewal of aggressive policy on the part of any such state, until such time as the Organization may, on request of the Governments concerned, be charged with the responsibility for preventing further aggression by such a state.

2 The term enemy state as used in paragraph 1 of this Article applies to any state which during the Second World War has been an enemy of any signatory of the present Charter.

Article 54

The Security Council shall at all times be kept fully informed of activities undertaken or in contemplation under regional arrangements or by regional agencies for the maintenance of international peace and security.

Article 107

Nothing in the present Charter shall invalidate or preclude action, in relation to any state which during the Second World War has been an enemy of any signatory to the present Charter, taken or authorized as a result of that war by the Governments having responsibility for such action.

APPENDIX D

Charter of the Organization of American States
(selected provisions)

CHAPTER V: PACIFIC SETTLEMENT OF DISPUTES

Article 23

All international disputes that may arise between American States shall be submitted to the peaceful procedures set forth in this Charter, before being referred to the Security Council of the United Nations.

Article 24

The following are peaceful procedures: direct negotiation, good offices, mediation, investigation and conciliation, judicial settlement, arbitration, and those which the parties to the dispute may especially agree upon at any time.

Article 137

None of the provisions of this Charter shall be construed as impairing the rights and obligations of the Member States under the United Nations.

Inter-American Treaty of Reciprocal Assistance
(selected provisions)

Article 1

The High Contracting Parties formally condemn war and undertake in their international relations not to resort to the threat or the use of force in any manner inconsistent with the provisions of the Charter of the United Nations or of this treaty.

Article 2

As a consequence of the principle set forth in the preceding Article, the High Contracting Parties undertake to submit every controversy which may arise between them to methods of peaceful settlement and to endeavour to settle any such controversy among themselves by means of the procedures in force in the Inter-American System before referring it to the General Assembly or the Security Council of the United Nations.

Article 3

1 The High Contracting Parties agree that an armed attack by any State against an American State shall be considered as an attack against all the American States and, consequently, each one of the said Contracting Parties undertakes to assist in meeting the attack in the exercise of the inherent right of individual or collective self-defence recognized by Article 51 of the Charter of the United Nations.

4 Measures of self-defence provided for under this Article may be taken until the Security Council of the United Nations has taken the measures necessary to maintain international peace and security.

The North Atlantic Treaty (selected provisions)

Article 1

The Parties undertake, as set forth in the Charter of the United Nations, to settle any international dispute in which they may be involved by peaceful means in such a manner that international peace and security, and justice, are not endangered, and to refrain in their international relations from the threat or use of force in any manner inconsistent with the purposes of the United Nations.

Article 5

The Parties agree that an armed attack against one or more of them in Europe or North America shall be considered an attack against them all; and consequently they agree that, if such an armed attack occurs, each of them, in exercise of the right of individual or collective self-defence recognized by Article 51 of the Charter of the United Nations, will assist the Party or Parties so attacked by taking forthwith, individually and in concert with other Parties, such action as it deems necessary, including the use of armed force, to restore and maintain the security of the North Atlantic area.

Any such armed attack and all measures taken as a result thereof shall immediately be reported to the Security Council. Such measures shall be terminated when the Security Council has taken the measures necessary to restore and maintain international peace and security.

Article 7

This Treaty does not affect, and shall not be interpreted as affecting, in any

way the rights and obligations under the Charter of the Parties which are
members of the United Nations, or the primary responsibility of the Security Council for the maintenance of international peace and security.

APPENDIX G
The Warsaw Treaty of Friendship, Co-operation, and Mutual Assistance (selected provisions)

Article 1

The Contracting Parties undertake, in accordance with the Charter of the United Nations, to refrain in their international relations from the threat or use of force and to settle their international disputes by peaceful means in such a manner that international peace and security are not endangered.

Article 4

In the event of an armed attack in Europe on one or more of the States Parties to the Treaty by any State or group of States, each State Party to the Treaty shall, in the exercise of the right of individual or collective self-defence, in accordance with Article 51 of the United Nations Charter, afford the State or States so attacked immediate assistance, individually and in agreement with the other States Parties to the Treaty, by all the means it considers necessary, including the use of force. The States Parties to the Treaty shall consult together immediately concerning the joint measures necessary to restore and maintain international peace and security.

Measures taken under this article shall be reported to the Security Council in accordance with the provisions of the United Nations Charter. These measures shall be discontinued as soon as the Security Council takes the necessary action to restore and maintain international peace and security.

APPENDIX H
Pact of the League of Arab States
(selected provisions)

Article 2

The League has as its purpose the strengthening of the relations between the member States; the co-ordination of their policies in order to achieve co-operation between them and to safeguard their independence and sovereignty; and a general concern with the affairs and interests of the Arab countries . . .

Article 5

Any resort to force in order to resolve disputes arising between two or more member states of the League is prohibited . . .

The [League] Council shall mediate in all differences which threaten to lead to war between two member States, or a member state and a third state, with a view to bringing about their reconciliation.

APPENDIX I

Joint Defence and Economic Co-operation Treaty between the States of the Arab League (selected provisions)

Article 1

The Contracting States, in an effort to maintain and stabilize peace and security, hereby confirm their desire to settle their international disputes by peaceful means, whether such disputes concern relations among themselves or with other Powers.

Article 2

The Contracting States consider any act of armed aggression made against any one or more of them or their armed forces, to be directed against them all. Therefore, in accordance with the right of self-defence, individually and collectively, they undertake to go without delay to the aid of the State or States against which such an act of aggression is made, and immediately to take, individually and collectively, all steps available, including the use of armed force, to repel the aggression and restore security and peace. In conformity with Article 6 of the Arab League Pact and Article 51 of the United Nations Charter, the Arab League Council and the UN Security Council shall be notified of such act of aggression and the means and procedure taken to check it.

Article 11

No provision of this Treaty shall in any way affect, or is intended to affect, any of the rights or obligations devolving upon the Contracting States from the United Nations Charter or on the responsibilities borne by the United Nations Security Council for the maintenance of international peace and security.

I Charter of the Organization of African Unity
(selected provisions)

Article I

1 The High Contracting Parties do by the present Charter establish an Organization to be known as the Organization of African Unity.

Article II

1 The Organization shall have the following purposes:

a to promote the unity and solidarity of the African States;

b to co-ordinate and intensify their co-operation and efforts to achieve a better life for the peoples of Africa;

c to defend their sovereignty, their territorial integrity and independence;

d to eradicate all forms of colonialism from Africa; and

e to promote international co-operation, having due regard to the Charter of the United Nations and the Universal Declaration of Human Rights.

Article III

The Member States, in pursuit of the purposes stated in Article II, solemnly affirm and declare their adherence to the following principles:

1 the sovereign equality of all Member States;

2 non-interference in the internal affairs of States;

3 respect for the sovereignty and territorial integrity of each State and for its inalienable right to independent existence;

4 peaceful settlement of disputes by negotiation, mediation, conciliation or arbitration;

5 unreserved condemnation, in all its forms, of political assassination as

well as of subversive activities on the part of the neighbouring State or any other State;

6 absolute dedication to the total emancipation of the African territories which are still dependent;

7 affirmation of a policy of non-alignment with regard to all blocs.

Article XIX
Member States pledge to settle all disputes among themselves by peaceful means and, to this end, decide to establish a Commission of Mediation, Conciliation and Arbitration, the composition of which and conditions of service shall be defined by a separate Protocol to be approved by the Assembly of Heads of State and Government. Said Protocol shall be regarded as forming an integral part of the present Charter.

II Regional groupings

The Council of Ministers Meeting, Dakar, Senegal, 2-11 August 1963:

WHEREAS the setting up of the OAU has given rise to great and legitimate hopes among African peoples;

MINDFUL of the will of these peoples to put an end to the division of African States;

WHEREAS this will was unanimously proclaimed by the Heads of State and Government at the Addis Ababa Conference;

WHEREAS furthermore regional groupings have favoured the achievement of African Unity and the development of co-operation amongst Member States;

WHEREAS also the Charter of the OAU has made provision for economic, cultural, scientific, technical and military specialized institutions in order to strengthen solidarity amongst African peoples and co-operation amongst Member States;

CONSIDERING therefore the need for regional or sub-regional groupings to evolve with a view to their adaptation to the Charter of the OAU;

1 TAKES NOTE of the will of Member States to implement all means in order to bring about this adaptation;

2 RECOMMENDS that any regional grouping or sub-grouping be in keeping with the Charter of the OAU and meet the following criteria;

a Geographical realities and economic, social and cultural factors common to the States;

b Co-ordination of economic, social and cultural activities peculiar to the States concerned;

3 SUGGESTS to the African States signatories of Charters in existence before the setting up of the OAU that they henceforth refer to the Charter of Addis Ababa;

4 INVITES all African States desiring to constitute regional groupings or sub-groupings to conform with the principles set forth above and to contemplate the integration of already existing bodies into the specialized institutions of the OAU;

5 REQUESTS Member States to deposit the statutes of the said groupings at the seat of the OAU before their entry into force.

Selected bibliography

A great deal has been written about international organization. The following bibliographical surveys are especially useful: Jacob Robinson, *International Law and Organization* (Leyden: A.W. Sijthoff, 1967); Alexander Rudzinski, *Selected Bibliography on International Organization* (New York: Carnegie Endowment for International Peace, 1953); G.P. Speeckaert, *Selected Bibliography on International Organization* (Brussels: Union of International Associations, 1965); Ronald J. Yalem, 'The Study of International Organization, 1920-1965: A Survey of Literature,' *Background* XX (1966); Norman J. Padelford, 'A Selected Bibliography on Regionalism and Regional Arrangements,' *International Organization* XX (1956).

The United Nations Institute for Training and Research (UNITAR) has recently launched a research programme on the relationship between the United Nations and non-UN regional organizations. Among the published reports are: Berhanykun Andemicael, *Peaceful Settlement of Disputes among African States: Roles of the United Nations and the Organization of African Unity* (New York: UNITAR, 1972); A.H. Robertson, *The Relations between the Council of Europe and the United Nations* (New York: UNITAR, 1972). Some other relevant UNITAR studies completed but yet to be published are: Andemicael, 'The Relations between the Organization of African Unity and the United Nations'; Aida Luisa Levin, 'The Relations between the Organization of American States and the United Nations in the Peace and Security Field'; F.A.M. Alting von Geusau and Alexander Weilenmann, 'The Relations between the Organization for Economic Cooperation and Development and the United Nations'; F.A.M. Alting von Geusau, 'The Relations between the European Economic Community and the United Nations'; Michael Haas, 'Asian International Organizations and the United Nations'; and Sir Peter Smithers, 'Governmental Control: A Prerequisite for Effective Relations between the United Nations and non-UN Regional Organizations.' The Smithers paper formed the basis of a UNITAR Conference (see *Relations between the United Nations and Non-UN Regional International Organizations*, New York: UNITAR, 1973).

The following bibliography is a selective listing of relevant literature intended to assist interested readers. It contains most of the documents, books, and articles used in the preparation of this volume.

DOCUMENTS AND OFFICIAL PUBLICATIONS

LEAGUE OF NATIONS: *Official Journal*
- *Records of the Assembly*
- *Monthly Summary*
- *Report of the Special Main Committee Set Up to Study the Application of the Principles of the Covenant.* Geneva: 1938.
UNITED NATIONS: General Assembly, *Official Records*
- Security Council, *Official Records*
- United Nations, *Monthly Chronicle*
- United Nations Conference on International Organization, *Documents*, 17 volumes, 1945
ORGANIZATION OF AMERICAN STATES: *Report of the Inter-American Peace Committee on the Controversy between Guatemala, Honduras, and Nicaragua.* Washington: 1954.
- *Applications of the Inter-American Treaty of Reciprocal Assistance, 1948-1956.* Washington: 1957.
- *Meeting of American Chiefs of State, Punta del Este, Uruguay, 1967.* Washington: 1967.
- *Sixth Meeting of Consultation of Ministers of Foreign Affairs, San Jose, Costa Rica, 1960, Final Act.* Washington: 1960.
- *Eighth Meeting of Consultation of Ministers of Foreign Affairs, Punta del Este, Uruguay, 1962, Final Act.* Washington: 1962.
- *Ninth Meeting of Consultation of Ministers of Foreign Affairs, 1964, Final Act.* Washington: 1964.
- *Annual Report of the Secretary-General, 1965.* Washington: 1965.
ORGANIZATION OF AFRICAN UNITY: *Basic Documents of the Organization of African Unity.* Addis Ababa: 1963.
- *Resolutions, Recommendations and Statements adopted by the Ordinary and*

Extra-Ordinary Sessions of the Council of Ministers 1963-1967, Vol. I. Addis Ababa: 1973.

– *Resolutions, Recommendations and Statements adopted by the Ordinary and Extra-Ordinary Sessions of the Council of Ministers 1968-1973, Vol. II.* Addis Ababa: 1973.

– *Resolutions and Statements adopted by the Meeting of the Assembly of Heads of State and Government 1963-1973.* Addis Ababa: 1973.

INTERNATIONAL LAW ASSOCIATION: *Report of the 46th Conference*, Edinburgh: 1954.

– *Report of the 48th Conference*, New York: 1958

– *Report of the 53rd Conference*, Buenos Aires: 1968.

UNITED STATES OF AMERICA: *Foreign Relations of the United States* State Department, *Bulletin*

– *Charter of the United Nations: Report to the President on the Results of the San Francisco Conference.* Washington: 1945.

CANADA: *Report on the United Nations Conference on International Organization.* Ottawa: 1945.

NEW ZEALAND: *Report on the Conference held at San Francisco 25 April-26 June.* Wellington: 1945.

UNITED KINGDOM: *The Covenant of the League of Nations with a Commentary Thereon.* Cmd 151 (1919).

– *Papers respecting the Proposals for a Pact of Security Made by the German Government on 9 February 1925.* Cmd 2435 (1925).

– *International Treaty for the Renunciation of War as an Instrument of National Policy, Paris, 27 August 1928.* Cmd 3410 (1929).

– *Dumbarton Oaks Conversations on World Organization: Statement of Tentative Proposals.* Cmd 6560 (1944).

– *A Commentary on the Dunbarton Oaks Proposals for the Establishment of a General International Organization.* Cmd 6571 (1944).

– *A Commentary on the Charter of the United Nations Signed at San Francisco on the 26th June, 1945.* Cmd 6666 (1945).

– *Security Council Proceedings on Czechoslovakia 21-23 August 1968.* Cmd 3757 (1968).

BOOKS

ANABTAWI, M.F. *Arab Unity in Terms of Law.* The Hague: Martinus Nijhoff, 1963.

ASAMOAH, O.Y. *The Legal Significance of the Declaration of the General Assembly of the United Nations.* The Hague: Martinus Nijhoff, 1966.

BAADE, H.W., ed. *The Soviet Impact on International Law*. Dobbs Ferry, New York: Oceana Publications, 1965.

BECKETT, SIR ERIC. *The North Atlantic Treaty, The Brussels Treaty and the Charter of the United Nations*. London: Stevens & Sons, 1950.

BENTWICH, N. and A. MARTIN. *A Commentary on the Charter of the United Nations*. 2nd edition. London: Routledge & Kegan Paul Ltd., 1968.

BETHLEN, S. *The Treaty of Trianon and European Peace*. London: Longmans, 1934.

BOULDING, K. *Conflict and Defense: A General Theory*. New York: Harper and Row, 1962.

BOUTROS-GHALI, B. *L'Organisation de l'Unité Africaine* Paris: Librairie Armand Colin, 1969.

– *Contribution à l'Etude des Ententes Regionales*. Paris: A. Pedone, 1949.

– *Contribution à Une Théorie Générale des Alliances*. Paris: Pedone, 1963.

BOWETT, D.W. *Self-Defence in International Law*. Manchester: Manchester University Press, 1958.

– *The Law of International Institutions*. New York: Praeger, 1963.

– *United Nations Forces: A Legal Study*. New York: Praeger, 1964.

– *The Search for Peace*. London: Routledge & Kegan Paul, 1972.

BROWNLIE, I. *Principles of Public International Law*. Oxford: Clarendon Press, 1966.

– *International Law and the Use of Force*. London: Oxford University Press, 1963.

– ed. *Basic Documents on African Affairs*. Oxford: Clarendon Press, 1971.

BRZEZINSKI, Z.K. *The Soviet Bloc: Unity and Conflict*. Cambridge: Harvard University Press, 1960.

CALOGEROPOULOS - Stratis, *La Grèce et les Nations Unies*. New York: Manhattan Publishing Company, 1957.

CANYES, M. *The Organization of American States and the United Nations*. Washington: Pan American Union, 1963.

CANTORI, L.J. and S.L. SPIEGEL, eds. *The International Politics of Regions: A Comparative Approach*. Englewood Cliffs, New Jersey: Prentice-Hall Inc., 1970.

CARNEGIE ENDOWMENT FOR INTERNATIONAL PEACE. *Perspectives on Peace, 1910-1960*. New York: Praeger, 1960.

CAREY, J., ed. *The Dominican Republic Crisis 1965*. Dobbs Ferry, New York: Oceana Publications, Inc., 1967.

– *Race, Peace and Law in Southern Africa*. Dobbs Ferry: Oceana Publications, 1968.

CARR, E.H. *Nationalism and After*. London: Macmillan, 1965.

CASTANEDA, J. *Mexico and the United Nations*. New York: Manhattan Publishing Company, 1958.

– *The Legal Effects of the United Nations Resolutions*. New York: Columbia University Press, 1969.

CERVENKA, Z. *The Organization of African Unity and Its Charter*. New York: Praeger, 1969.

CHAYES, A. *The Cuban Missile Crisis, 1962*. London: Oxford University Press, 1974.

CHURCHILL, W. *The Second World War*. 4: *The Hinge of Fate* Boston: Houghton Mifflin, 1950.

CLAUDE, I.L., JR. *Swords into Plowshare: The Problems and Progress of International Organization*. 3rd edition, rev. New York: Random House, 1964.

– *The Changing United Nations*. New York: Random House, 1967.

COMMISSION TO STUDY THE ORGANIZATION OF PEACE. *Regional Arrangements for Security and the United Nations*. New York: 1953.

CONWELL-EVANS, T.P. *The League Council in Action*. London: Oxford University Press, 1929.

CONNELL-SMITH, G. *The Inter-American System*. London: Oxford University Press, 1966.

COOPER, R.M. *American Consultation in World Affairs*. New York: Macmillan, 1934.

CORDIER, A., ED. *Columbia Essays in International Affairs*. III: *The Dean's Paper, 1967*. New York: Columbia University Press, 1968.

COULOUMBIS, T. *Greek Political Reaction to American and NATO Influences*. New Haven: Yale University Press, 1966.

DALLIN, A. *The Soviet Union and the United Nations*. New York: Praeger, 1962.

DE ARECHAGA, E.J. *Voting and the Handling of Disputes in the Security Council*. New York: Columnia University Press, 1950.

DOXEY, M. *Economic Sanctions and International Enforcement*. London: Oxford University Press for the Royal Institute of International Affairs, 1971.

DRAPER, T. *Israel and World Politics*. New York: The Viking Press, Inc., 1968.

– *The Dominican Revolt: A Case Study in American Policy*. New York: Commentary, 1968.

DREIER, J.C. *The Organization of American States and the Hemisphere Crisis*. New York: Harper & Row, 1962.

DUNN, F.S. *The Practice and Procedure of International Conferences*. Baltimore: Johns Hopkins University Press, 1929.

EDEN, A. *Full Circle*. London: Frank Cass and Company, 1960.

EMERSON, R. *Self-Determination Revisited in the Era of Decolonization*. Cambridge: Center for International Affairs, Harvard University, 1964.

FALK, R.A. *The Authority of the United Nations over Non-Members*. Princeton: Center of International Studies. 1965.

FEJTO, F. *Behind the Rape of Hungary*. New York: David McKay Company, Inc., 1957.

FISHER, R., ed. *International Conflict and Behavioral Sciences*. New York: Basic Books, 1964.

FLEMING, D.F. *The United States and the League of Nations 1918-1920*. New York: Putnam, 1932.

– *The United States and World Organization 1920-1923*. New York: Columbia University Press, 1938.

FODA, E. *The Projected Arab Court of Justice*. The Hague: Martinus Nijhoff, 1957.

FRANCK, T.M. and EDWARD WEISBAND. *World Politics: Verbal Strategy Among the Super Powers*. London: Oxford University Press, 1971.

GARCIA-MORA, M. *International Responsibility for Hostile Acts of Private Persons against Foreign States*. The Hague: Martinus Nijhoff, 1962.

GARCIA-AMADOR, F.V. *The Inter-American System*. Dobbs Ferry, New York: Oceana Publications, Inc., 1966.

GARNER, W.R. *The Chaco Dispute: A Study in Prestige Diplomacy*. Washington: Public Affairs Press, 1966.

GOODRICH, L.M., E. HAMBRO, and A.P. Simons. *Charter of the United Nations Commentary and Documents*. 3rd and revised edition. New York: Columbia University Press, 1969.

GOODWIN, G.L. *Britain and the United Nations*. New York: Manhattan Publishing Company, 1957.

GOODWIN, G.L. and SUSAN STRANGE. *Research on International Organization*. London: Heinemann, 1968.

GREGG, R.W., ed. *International Organization in Western Hemisphere*. Syracuse: Syracuse University Press, 1968.

GRZYBOWSKI, K. *The Socialist Commonwealth of Nations Organizations and Institutions*. New Haven: Yale University Press, 1964.

HALDERMAN, J.W. *The United Nations and the Rule of Law*. Dobbs Ferry, New York: Oceana Publications, Inc., 1966.

HIGGINS, R. *The Development of International Law Through the Political Organs of the United Nations*. London: Oxford University Press, 1963.

– *Conflict of Interest: International Law in a Divided World*. London: Bodley Head Ltd, 1965.

- ed. *United Nations Peace-keeping, 1946-1967: Documents and Commentary*. London: Oxford University Press, 1969.
HILL, N. *The Public International Conferences*. Standford: Standford University Press, 1929.
HOSKYNS, C., ed. *The Organization of African Unity and the Congo Crisis, 1964-65*. Dar-es-Salaam: Oxford University Press, 1969.
- *The Ethiopia-Somalia-Kenya Dispute, 1960-67*. Dar-es-Salaam: Oxford University Press, 1969.
HOUSTON, J.A. *Latin America in the United Nations*. New York: Carnegie Endowment for International Peace, 1956.
HUDSON, M.O. *The Verdict of the League: Colombia and Peru at Leticia*. Boston: World Peace Foundation, 1933.
- *International Tribunals*. Washington: Carnegie Endowment for International Peace, 1944.
- *World Court Reports*. New York: Carnegie Endowment for International Peace, 1943.
HUGHES, C.E. *Our Relations to the Nations of the Western Hemisphere*. Princeton: Princeton University Press, 1928.
HULL, C. *The Memoirs of Cordell Hull*. 2 volumes. New York: Macmillan, 1948.
INDIAN SOCIETY OF INTERNATIONAL LAW. *Asian-African States: Texts of International Declarations*. New Delhi: Asia Publishing House, 1965.
INSTITUTE ON WORLD ORGANIZATION. *World Organization: A Balance Sheet of the First Great Experiment*. Washington: American Council on Public Affairs, 1942.
- *Regionalism and World Organization*. Washington: Public Affairs Press, 1944.
IRELAND, G. *Boundaries, Possessions, and Conflicts in Central and North America and the Caribbean*. Cambridge, Mass: Harvard University Press, 1941.
JEBB, G. *Halfway to 1984*. New York: Columbia University Press, 1966.
JENKS, C.W. *The Common Law of Mankind*. London: Stevens and Sons 1958.
- *The World Beyond the Charter*. London: Allen and Unwin, 1969.
JENNINGS, R.Y., ed. *Cambridge Essays in International Law: Essays in Honour of Lord McNair*. London: Stevens and Sons, 1965.
JESSUP, P.C. *A Modern Law of Nations*. Hamden: Anchorn Books Inc., 1968.
JOHNSON, H.S. *Self-Determination Within the Community of Nations*. Leyden: A.W. Sijhoff, 1967.
JONES, S.S. *The Scandinavian States and the League of Nations*. Princeton: Princeton University Press, 1939.

JOSE, J.R. *An Inter-American Peace Force within the Framework of the Organization of American States: Advantages, Impediments, Implications.* Metuchen: Scarecrow Reprint Corporation, 1970.

KAHNG, T.J. *Law, Politics and the Security Council.* The Hague: Martinus Nijhoff, 1964.

KAPLAN, M. *System and Process in International Politics.* New York: John Wiley & Sons, 1957.

KAY, D.A. *The New Nations in the United Nations 1960-67.* New York: Columbia University Press, 1973.

KELCHNER, W.H. *Latin American Relations With the League of Nations.* Boston: World Peace Foundation, 1929.

KELSEN, H. *The Law of the United Nations.* New York: Praeger, 1950.

KENNEDY, R.F. *Thirteen Days: A Memoir of the Cuban Missile Crisis.* New York: Norton & Company, 1969.

KOO, W. *Voting Procedures in International Political Organizations.* New York: Columbia University Press, 1947.

KUKANOV, M. *NATO - Threat to World Peace.* Moscow: Progress, 1971.

LA FOY, M. *The Chaco Dispute and the League of Nations.* Ann Arbor: Edwards Brothers, Inc., 1946.

LANDHEER, B. *On the Sociology of International Law and Society.* The Hague: Martinus Nijhoff, 1968.

LAWSON, R. *International Regional Organizations: Constitutional Foundations.* New York: Praeger, 1962.

LEFEVER, E.W. *Crisis in the Congo: A United Nations Force in Action.* Washington: Brookings Institution, 1965.

LIPSKY, G., ed. *Law and Politics in the World Community.* Berkeley: University of California Press, 1953.

LISKA, G. *International Equilibrium. A Theoretical Essay on the Politics and Organization of Security.* Cambridge: Harvard University Press, 1957.

LODGE, H.C. *The Senate and the League of Nations.* New York: Charles Scribner, 1925.

MACDONALD, R.W. *The League of Arab States. A Study in the Dynamics of Regional Organization.* Princeton: Princeton University Press, 1965.

MACHRAY, R. *The Little Entente.* London: Allen & Unwin Ltd, 1929.

MANNING, C.A. *The Policies of the British Dominions in the League of Nations.* London: Oxford University Press, 1932.

MARBURG, T. *The Development of the League of Nations Idea.* New York: 1932.

MARTIN, A. *Collective Security: A Progress Report.* Paris: UNESCO, 1952.

MAZRUI, A.A. *Towards a Pax Africana.* London: Weidenfeld and Nicolson 1967.

MCDOUGAL, M.S. and F.P. FELICIANO. *Law and Minimum World Public Order: The Legal Regulation of International Coercion.* New Haven: Yale University Press, 1961.

MCNAIR, LORD. *The Law of Treaties.* Oxford: Clarendon Press, 1961.

MECHAM, J.L. *The United States and Inter-American Security, 1889-1960.* Austin: University of Texas Press, 1961.

MERILLAT, H.C.L. ed. *Legal Advisers and Foreign Affairs.* Dobbs Ferry, New York: Oceana Publications, 1964.

– *Legal Advisers and International Organizations.* Dobbs Ferry, New York: Oceana Publications, 1966.

MILLER, D.H. *The Drafting of the Covenant.* 2 volumes. New York: Putnam, 1928.

MILLER, L.B. *World Order and Local Disorder: The United Nations and Internal Conflicts.* Princeton: Princeton University Press, 1967.

– *Cyprus: The Law and Politics of Civil Strife.* Cambridge, Mass: Harvard University Press, 1968.

MILLER, L.H. *Organizing Mankind: An Analysis of Contemporary International Organization.* Boston: Holbrook Press, Inc. 1972.

MORLEY, F. *The Society of Nations: Its Organization and Constitutional Development.* Washington: Brookings Institutions, 1932.

NOGUEIRA, F. *The United Nations and Portugal.* London: Sidwick and Jackson, 1963.

NYE, JR, *Peace in Parts: Integration and Conflict in Regional Organization.* Boston: Little, Brown and Company, 1971.

– ed. *International Regionalism.* Boston: Little, Brown and Company, 1968.

OJUKWU, C.O. *Biafra.* 2 volumes. New York: Harper & Row, 1969.

PACY, J.S. 'Hungary, The League of Nations and the Assassination of King Alexander of Yugoslavia: A Case Study of the Resolution of an International Political Crisis.' Unpublished Ph.D. thesis, The American University, 1971.

PEASLEE, A.J., ed. *International Governmental Organizations: Constitutional Documents.* 2 volumes. Revised second edition. The Hague: Martinus Nijhoff, 1961.

PERKINS, D. *A History of the Monroe Doctrine.* Revised edition. Boston: Little, Brown and Company, 1955.

– *A History of the Monroe Doctrine.* Revised edition. Boston: Houghton Mifflin, 1958.

PETERSON, H. *Argentina and the United States, 1810-1920.* New York: State University of New York Press, 1964.

RAJAN, M.S. *The United Nations and Domestic Jurisdiction.* New York: Asia Publishing House, 1961.

RAPPARD, W. *The Quest for Peace Since the World War.* Cambridge, Mass: Harvard University Press, 1940.

RAY, J. *Commentaire du Pacte de la Société des Nations.* Paris: Sirey, 1930.

REDDY, T.R. *India's Policy in the United Nations.* Rutherford: Fairleigh Dickinson University Press, 1968.

REINSCH, P.S. *Public International Unions.* Boston: Ginn and Company, 1911.

REMINGTON, R.A. *The Warsaw Pact: Case Studies in Conflict Resolution.* Cambridge: MIT Press, 1971.

RICHES, C.A. *The Unanimity Rule and the League of Nations.* Baltimore: Johns Hopkins University Press, 1933.

ROBERTSON, A.H. *The Council of Europe.* London: Stevens & Sons, 1961.

ROSS, A. *Constitution of the United Nations: Analysis of Structure and Function.* New York: Rinehart & Company, 1950.

ROTBERG, R.I. and A.A. MAZRUI, eds. *Protest and Power in Black Africa.* New York: Oxford University Press, 1970.

ROUT, L.R. *The Politics of the Chaco Peace Conference, 1935-1939.* Austin: University of Texas Press, 1969.

ROYAL INSTITUTE OF INTERNATIONAL AFFAIRS. *International Sanctions.* London: Oxford University Press, 1938.

– *United Nations Documents, 1941-1945.* London: Oxford University Press, 1946.

– *Documents on Regional Organizations Outside Western Europe, 1940-1949.* London: Oxford University Press, 1950.

RUSSELL, R.B. *A History of the United Nations Charter.* Washington: Brookings Institution, 1958.

RUSSETT, B.M. *International Regions and the International System.* Chicago: Rand McNally and Company, 1967.

SCHERMERS, H.G. *International Institutional Law.* 2 volumes. Leyden: A.W. Sijthoff, 1972.

SCHWARZENBERGER, G. *The League of Nations and World Order: A Treatise on the Principle of Universality in the Theory and Practice of the League of Nations.* London: Constable & Co. Ltd, 1936.

– *Power Politics.* 3rd edition. London: Stevens and Sons, 1964.

– *International Law* 2. London: Stevens & Co., 1968.

SCOTT, J.B., ed. *The International Conferences of American States, 1889-1929.* New York: Oxford University Press, 1931.

– *The International Conferences of American States, First Supplement, 1933-1940.* Washington: Carnegie Endowment for International Peace, 1940.

SHOTWELL, J.T. *War as an Instrument of National Policy*. New York: Harcourt, Brace, 1929.

SIMPSON, J.L. and H. FOX, *International Arbitration*. London: Stevens & Sons, 1959.

SINGH, N. *Termination of Membership in International Organization*. London: Stevens and Sons, 1957.

SLATER, J. *The OAS and the United States Foreign Policy*. Columbus: Ohio State University Press, 1967.

– *Intervention and Negotiation: The United States and the Dominican Revolution*. New York: Harper & Row, 1970.

SMITH, H.A. *The Crisis in the Law of Nations*. London: Stevens and Sons, 1947.

SOHN, L.B. *The United Nations in Action*. Brooklyn: Foundation Press, Inc., 1968.

STARKE, J.G. *The ANZUS Treaty Alliance*. Melbourne: Melbourne University Press, 1965.

STEGENGA, J.A. *The United Nations Force in Cyprus*. Columbus: Ohio University Press, 1968.

STONE, J. *Legal Controls of International Conflict*. New York: Rinehart & Company, 1959.

– *Aggression and World Order*. Berkeley: University of California Press, 1958.

STOESSINGER, J.G. *The United Nations and the Superpowers*. New York: Random House, 1965.

SWIFT, R.N., ed. *Annual Review of the United Nations Affairs, 1965-1966*. Dobbs Ferry, New York: Oceana Publications, 1967.

TEVOEDJRE, A. *Pan-Africanism in Action: An Account of the UAM*. Cambridge, Mass: Harvard University Centre for International Affairs, 1965.

THARP, JR. P.A. *Regional International Organizations: Structures and Functions*. New York: St Martin's Press, 1971.

THOMAS, A.W. and A.J. THOMAS, *Non-Intervention*. Dallas: Southern Methodist University Press, 1956.

– *The Organization of American States*. Dallas: Southern Methodist University Press, 1963.

THOMAS, A.W. and A.J. THOMAS, and SALAS, *The International Law of Indirect Aggression and Subversion*. Dallas: Southern Methodist University Press, 1966.

TONDEL, L.M. JR, ed. *The Inter-American Security System and the Cuban Crisis*. Dobbs Ferry, New York: Oceana Publications, 1964.

TOUVAL, S. *The Boundary Politics of Independent Africa*. London: Oxford University Press for Harvard University Press, 1973.

– *Somali Nationalism.* Cambridge: Harvard University Press, 1963.

TUNKIN, G.I. *Droit International Public.* Paris: A. Pedone, 1965.

UNIVERSITY OF ANKARA, *Turkey and the United Nations.* New York: Manhattan Publishing Company, 1961.

VANDENBERG A. JR, ed. *The Private Papers of Senator Vandenberg.* Boston: Houghton Mifflin, 1952.

WAINHOUSE, D. *International Peace Observation.* Baltimore: Johns Hopkins University Press, 1966.

WALTERS, F.P. *A History of the League of Nations.* London: Oxford University Press, 1967.

WEHN, P.B. 'Germany and the Treaty of Locarno-1925.' Unpublished Ph.D. thesis, Columbia University, 1968.

WEILER, L.D. and A.P. SIMONS. *The United States and the United Nations.* New York: Manhattan Publishing Company, 1967.

WHITAKER, A.P. *The Western Hemisphere Idea: Its Rise and Decline.* Ithaca: Yale University Press, 1954.

WHITEMAN, M.M. *Digest of International Law* 5. Washington: US Government Printing Office, 1956.

– *Digest of International Law* 13. Washington: US Government Printing Office, 1968.

WIDSTRAND, C.G., ed. *African Boundary Problems.* Uppsala: Scandinavian Institute of African Studies, 1969.

WILLIAMS, B. *State Security and the League of Nations.* Baltimore: Johns Hopkins University Press, 1927.

WILLIAMS, J.F. *Some Aspects of the Covenant of the League of Nations.* London: Oxford University Press, 1934.

WILSON, F. *The Origins of the League Covenant.* London: Hogarth Press, 1928.

WINKLER, H.R. *The League of Nations Movement in Great Britain, 1914-1919.* Metuchen: Scarecrow Reprint Corporation, 1967.

WOLFERS, A. *Britain and France Between Two Wars: Conflicting Strategies of Peace Since Versailles.* Hamden: Archon Books, 1963.

WOOD, B. *The United States and Latin American Wars, 1932-1942.* New York: Columbia University Press, 1966.

WOOLF, L.S. ed. *The Framework of a Lasting Peace.* London: Allen and Unwin Ltd, 1917.

WRIGHT, Q. *International Law and the United Nations.* New Delhi: Asia Publishing House, 1960.

XYDIS, S. *Cyprus: Conflict and Conciliation, 1954-1958.* Columbus: Ohio University Press, 1967.

YALEM, R.J. *Regionalism and World Order*. Washington: Public Affairs Press, 1965.
- *Regional Subsystems and World Politics*. Tuscon: University of Arizona, 1970.
YOUNG, O.R. *The Intermediaries: Third Parties in International Crises*. Princeton: Princeton University Press, 1967.
ZIMMERN, A. *The League of Nations and the Rule of Law 1918-1935*. London: Macmillan, 1936.

ARTICLES

AKEHURST, M. 'Enforcement Action by Regional Agencies, With Special Reference to the Organization of American States,' *British Year Book of International Law* XLII (1967)
AKINDELE, R.A. 'The Organization of African Unity and the United Nations,' *Canadian Yearbook of International Law* IX (1971).
- 'The Warsaw Pact, the United Nations and the Soviet Union,' *Indian Journal of International Law* XI (1971).
- 'Regionalist Challenge and Universalist Response: Trends in post-1945 International Organization of Peace and Security,' *Indian Yearbook of International Affairs* XVIII (1972).
ALEXANDROWICZ, C.H. 'The Afro-Asian World and the Law of Nations (Historical Aspects),' *Recueil des Cours* CXXIII (1968) part I.
ALGER, C.F. 'Problems in Global Organization,' *International Social Science Journal* XXII (1970).
ALLEN, W.P. 'Regional Arrangements and the United Nations,' US Department of State, *Bulletin* XIV (2 June 1946).
AMERICAN SOCIETY OF INTERNATIONAL LAW. 'World Security and Regional Arrangements,' *Proceedings of the American Society of International Law*, (1950).
- 'Diverse Systems of World Public Order Today,' *Proceedings of the American Society of International Law* (1959).
ANAND, R.P. 'Attitudes of the Asian-African States Towards Certain Problems of International Law,' *International and Comparative Law Quarterly* XV (1966).
ANDRASSY, J. 'Uniting for Peace,' *American Journal of International Law* L (1956).
ARMSTRONG, H.F. 'After the Assassination of King Alexander,' *Foreign Affairs* XIII (1935).
ARREGUI, J.R. 'Le Régionalisme dans l'Organisation Internationale,' Hague *Recueil des Cours* LIII (1935) part III.

AYAGA, O.O. 'The UN Security Council's African Safari,' *International Studies* (New Delhi) XII (1973).

BAILEY, S.D. 'New Light on Abstentions in the Security Council,' *International Affairs* (London) L (1974).

BARLIANT, R. 'The OAS Peace and Security System,' *Stanford Law Review* XXI (1969).

BAROCH, C.T. 'The Soviet Doctrine of Sovereignty,' *Bulletin* (Institute for the Study of the USSR) XVIII (1971).

BARON, D. 'The Dominican Republic Crisis of 1965: A Case-Study of the Regional vs. the Global Approach to International Peace and Security,' in Andrew W. Cordier, ed., *Columbia Essays in International Affairs*. III: *The Dean's Papers, 1967*. New York: Columbia University Press, 1968.

BEBR, G. 'Regional Organizations: A United Nations Problem,' *American Journal of International Law* XLIX (1955).

BENES, E. 'The Little Entente,' *Foreign Affairs* I (1922).

– 'After Locarno: The Problem of Security Today,' *Foreign Affairs* IV (1926).

BERCHARD, E. 'The Multilateral Treaty for the Renunciation of War,' *American Journal of International Law* XXIII (1929).

BISSCHOP, W.R. 'The Locarno Pact,' *Transactions of the Grotius Society* XI (1925).

BLAKESLEE, G. 'The Japanese Monroe Doctrine,' *Foreign Affairs* XI (1932-33).

BLUM, Y.Z. 'Indonesia's Return to the United Nations,' *International and Comparative Law Quarterly* XVI (1967).

BORELLA, F. 'Le Régionalisme Africain en 1964,' *Annuaire Français de Droit International* X (1964).

– 'Le Régionalisme Africain et l'Organisation de l'Unité Africaine,' *Annuaire Français de Droit International* IX (1963).

BOUTROS-GHALI, B. 'Le Principe d' Egalite des Etats et les Organizations Internationales,' *Recueil des Cours* C (1960) part II.

– 'La Crise de la Ligue Arabe,' *Annuaire Français de Droit International* XIV (1968).

– 'Régionalisme et Nations Unies,' *Revue Egyptienne de Droit International* XXIV (1968).

– 'The Arab League, 1945-1970,' *Revue Egyptienne de Droit International* XXV (1969).

– 'The Addis Ababa Charter,' *International Conciliation*, no. 546 (January 1964).

BOWETT, D.W. 'Reprisal Involving Recourse to Armed Force,' *American Journal of International Law* LXVI (1972).

BRIERLY, J.L. 'The Covenant and the Charter,' *British Yearbook of International Law* XXIII (1946).

BROWNLIE, I. 'International Law and the Activities of Armed Bands,' *International and Comparative Law Quarterly* VII (1958).

C [Elihu Root?]. 'The Monroe Doctrine,' *Foreign Affairs* II (1923-24).

CADOUX, D. 'La Superiorité du Droit des Nations Unies sur le Droit des Etats Membres,' *Revue Générale de Droit International Public* XXX (1959).

CALOYANNI, M.A. 'The Balkan Union, the Balkan Conferences, and the Balkan Pact,' *Transactions of the Grotius Society* XIX (1933).

– 'The Balkan Union, the Balkan Conferences and the Balkan Pact,' *Transactions of the Grotius Society* XX (1934).

CAMARGO, A.L. 'Regionalism and the International Community,' in Carnegie Endowment for International Peace, *Perspectives on Peace 1910-1960*. New York: Praeger, 1960.

CAMPBELL, J.S. 'The Cuban Crisis and the UN Charter: An Analysis of the United States Position,' *Stanford Law Review* XVI (1963-64).

CASTAGNO, A.A. 'The Somali-Kenya Controversy,' *Journal of Modern African Studies* II (1964).

CASTANEDA, J. 'Pan Americanism and Regionalism: A Mexican View,' *International Organization* X (1956).

– 'The Underdeveloped Nations and the Development of International Law,' *International Organization* XV (1961).

CHAYES, A. 'Law and the Quarantine of Cuba,' *Foreign Affairs* XLI (1963).

– 'The Legal Case for the US Action on Cuba,' US Department of State, *Bulletin* XLVII (1962).

CHIME, S. 'The Organization of African Unity and African Boundaries,' in Carl Gosta Widstrand, ed. *African Boundary Problems*. Uppsala: Scandinavian Institute of African Studies, 1965.

CLAUDE, I.L. JR. 'The OAS, the UN and the United States,' *International Conciliation*, no. 547 (March 1964).

– 'The United Nations and the Use of Force,' *International Conciliation*, no. 532, (March 1961).

– 'The Political Framework of the United Nations' Financial Problems,' *International Organization* XVII (1963).

CLEMENS, W.C. JR. 'The Future of the Warsaw Pact,' *Orbis* XI (1968).

COSTER, D. 'The Interim Committee of the General Assembly: An Appraisal,' *International Organization* III (1949).

DAVIS, C.R. and C. CHRISTOL. 'Maritime Quarantine: The Naval Interdiction of Offensive Weapons and Associated Material, 1962,' *American Journal of International Law* LVII (1963).

DE ARECHAGA, E.J. 'La Coordination des Systems de L'O.N.U. et le l'Organisation des Etats Americains Pour de Règlement Pacifique des Différends et la Securité,' Hague *Recueil des Cours* CXI (1964) part I.

– 'Le traitement des différends internationaux par le Conseil de Securité,' Hague *Recueil des Cours* LXXXV (1954) part I.

DE YTURRIAGA, J.A. 'L'Organisation de l'Unité Africaine et les Nations Unies,' *Revue Générale de Droit International Public* XXXVI (1965).

DEGAN, D.V. 'Commission of Mediation, Conciliation and Arbitration of the OAU,' *Revue Egyptienne de Droit International* XX (1964).

DINH, N.Q. 'La légitime défense d'aprè la Charte des Nations Unies,' *Revue Générale du Droit International Public* XIX (1948).

DRAPER, G.I.A.D. 'Regional Arrangements and Enforcement Action,' *Revue Egyptienne de Droit International* XX (1964).

DUGARD, C.J.R. 'The Organization of African Unity and Colonialism: An Inquiry into the Plea of Self-Defence as a Justification for the Use of Force in the Eradication of Colonialism,' *International and Comparative Law Quarterly* XVI 4th Series (1967).

DUGGAN, S.P. 'Latin America, the League and the United States,' *Foreign Affairs* XII (1934).

DUPUY, R.J. 'Aggression indirecte et intervention solicitée: A propos de l'affaire Libanaise,' *Annuaire Française de Droit International* V (1959).

– 'Le Droit des Relations entre les Organisations Internationales,' Hague *Recueil des Cours* C (1960), part II.

– 'Les Etats-Unis, L'O.E.A. et L'O.N.U. à Saint-Dominque,' *Annaire Français de Droit International* XI (1965).

EAGLETON, C. 'The Jurisdiction of the Security Council Over Disputes,' *American Journal of International Law* XXXX (1946).

– 'The North Atlantic Defence Pact,' *Columbian Journal of International Affairs* III (1949).

EHRLICH, T. 'Cyprus, The "Warlike Isle": Origins and Elements of the Current Crisis,' *Standford Law Review* XVIII (1965-66).

EIDE, A. 'Peace-keeping and Enforcement by Regional Organizations,' *Journal of Peace Research* III (1966).

ELIAS, T.O. 'The Commission of Mediation, Conciliation and Arbitration of the Organization of African Unity,' *British Yearbook of International Law* XXXX (1964).

– 'The Charter of the Organization of African Unity,' *American Journal of International Law* LIX (1965).

– 'The Nigerian Crisis in International Law,' *Nigerian Law Journal* V (1971).

EMERSON R. 'Self-Determination,' *American Journal of International Law* LXV (1971).

ENGEL, S. 'League Reform: An Analysis of Official Proposals and Discussions, 1936-1939,' *Geneva Studies* XI (1940).

FALK, R.A. 'New Approaches to the Study of International Law,' *American Journal of International Law* LXI (1967).

– 'New States and International Legal Order,' *Recueil des Cours* CXVIII (1966) part II.

FAWCETT, J.E.S. 'Intervention in International Law: A Study of Some Recent Cases,' Hague *Recueil des Cours* CIII (1961) part II.

– 'Council of Europe Action on Greece,' *World Today* (November 1969).

FEINBERG, N. 'L'Admission de Nouveaux Membres à la Société des Nations et à l'Organisation des Nations Unies,' *Recueil des Cours* LXXX (1952) part I.

FENWICK, C. G. 'Jurisdictional Questions involved in the Guatemalan Revolution,' *American Journal of International Law* XLVIII (1954).

– 'Where is there a threat to the Peace? - Rhodesia,' *American Journal of International Law* LXI (1967).

FERGUSON, Y.H. 'The Dominican Intervention of 1965: Recent Interpretations,' *International Organization* XVII (1973).

FISCHER, G. 'Quelques problèmes juridiques découlant de l'Affaire Tchecoslovaque,' *Annuaire Français de Droit International* XIV (1968).

FLORY, M. 'Les implications juriduques de l'affaire de Goa,' *Annuaire Francais de Droit International* VIII (1962).

FOX, H. 'The Settlement of Disputes by Peaceful Means and the Observance of International Law – African Attitudes,' *International Relations* III (1968).

FROWEIN, J.A. 'The United Nations and Non-Member States,' *International Journal* (Toronto) XXV (1970).

FURNISS, E.S. 'A Re-examination of Regional Arrangements,' *Columbia Journal of International Affairs* IX (1955).

GARCIA-AMADOR, F. 'The Dominican Situation: The Jurisdiction of Regional Organization,' *Americas* XVII (1965).

GARVEY, J.I. 'United Nations Peacekeeping and Host State Consent,' *American Journal of International Law* LXIV (1970).

GINSBURGS, G. 'Socialist Internationalism and State Sovereignty,' *Year Book of World Affairs* XXV (1971).

– 'The Constitutional Foundation of the "Socialist Commonwealth". Some Theoretical and Organizational Principles,' *Year Book of World Affairs* XXVII (1973).

GOLDMAN, M.G. 'Action by the Organization of American States: When is Security Council Authorization Required under Article 53 of the United Nations Charter?' *University of California Los Angeles Law Review* X part 2 (1962-63).

GOODHART, A.L. 'The North Atlantic Treaty of 1949,' *Recueil des Cours* LXXIX (1951) part II.

GOODMAN, R.M. 'The Invasion of Czechoslovakia: 1968,' *International Lawyer* IV (1969).

GOODRICH, L.M. 'San Francisco in Retrospect,' *International Journal* (Toronto) XXV (1970).

– 'Regionalism and the United Nations,' *Columbia Journal of International Affairs* III (1949).

GREEN, L.C. 'The Security Council in Action,' *Year Book of World Affairs* II (1948).

– 'Membership in the United Nations,' *Current Legal Problems* II (1949).

– 'The "Little Assembly,"' *Year Book of World Affairs* III (1949).

– 'The Security Council in Retreat,' *Year Book of World Affairs* VIII (1954).

– 'The Double Standard of the United Nations,' *Year Book of World Affairs* XI (1957).

– 'Armed Conflict, War and Self-Defence,' *Archiv des Völkerrechts* VI (1957).

– 'New States, Regionalism and International Law,' *Canadian Yearbook of International Law* V (1967).

– 'The Impact of the New States on International Law,' *Israel Law Review* IV (1969).

– 'Gentleman's Agreements and the Security Council,' *Current Legal Problems* XIII (1960).

– 'Representation in the Security Council: A Survey,' *Indian Yearbook of International Affairs* XI (1962).

– 'Indonesia, the UN and Malaysia,' *Journal of Southeast Asia History* VI (1965).

– 'Rhodesian Oil: Boot leggers or Pirates,' *International Journal* (Toronto) XXI (1965-66).

GROSS, L. 'Progress Towards Universality of Membership in the United Nations,' *American Journal of International Law* L (1956).

– 'Voting in the Security Council: Abstention from Voting and Absence from Meeting,' *Yale Law Journal* LX (1951).

GRZYBOWSKI, K. 'International Organizations from the Soviet Point of View,' *Law and Contemporary Problems* XXIX (1964).

HAAS, E.B. 'The United Nations and Regionalism,' *International Relations* (London) III (1970).
– 'Regionalism, Functionalism and Universal Organization,' *World Politics* VIII (1955).
HAAS, E.B. and E.T. ROWE. 'Regional Organizations in the United Nations: Is there Externalisation?,' *International Studies Quarterly* XVII (1973).
HALDERMAN, J.W. 'Regional Enforcement Measures and the United Nations,' *Georgetown Law Journal* LII (1961).
HARRIS, W.R. 'Legal Aspects of Indonesia's Withdrawal from the United Nations,' *Harvard International Law Club Journal* VI (1964-5).
HERZ, J.H. 'The Rise and Demise of the Territorial State,' *World Politics* IX (1957).
HIGGINS, R. 'Policy Considerations and the International Judicial Process,' *International and Comparative Law Quarterly* XVII (1968).
HIGHLEY, A.E. 'The First Sanctions Experiment,' *Geneva Studies* IX (1938).
HILL, N.L. 'Post-War Treaties of Security and Mutual Guarantee,' *International Conciliation*, no. 224 (1928).
HILL, S.M. 'The Growth and Development of International Law in Africa,' *Law Quarterly Review* XVI (1900).
HOFFMANN, S. 'In Search of a Thread: the UN in the Congo Labyrinth,' *International Organization* XVI (1962).
HOUBEN, P. 'Principles of International Law Concerning Friendly Relations and Cooperation Among States,' *American Journal of International Law* LXI (1967).
HUDSON, M.O. 'The Chaco Arms Embargo,' *International Conciliation* no. 320 (1936).
HYDE, C.C. 'Legal Aspects of the Japanese Pronouncement in Relation to China,' *American Journal of International Law* XXVIII (1934).
IJALAYE, D.A. 'Some Legal Implication of the Nigerian Civil War,' *Proceedings of the First Annual Conference of the Nigerian Society of International Law – 1969*. Lagos, nd.
– 'Was "Biafra" at Any Time a State in International Law?' *American Journal of International Law* LXV (1971).
INTERNATIONAL LAW ASSOCIATION, 'Charter of the United Nations,' *Report of the Forty-Eighth Conference, New York, 1958*. London: 1959.
– 'Report on Problems of a United Nations Force,' *Report of the Forty-Ninth Conference, Hamburg, 1960*. London: 1961.
– 'Report on Some Aspects of the Principle of Self-Defence in the Charter of the United Nations,' *Report of the Forty-Eighth Conference, New York, 1958*. London: 1959.

- 'Report on Self-Defence Under the United Nations and the Use of Prohibitive Weapons,' *Report of the Fiftieth Conference, Brussels, 1962*, London: 1963.
JACOBSON, J. 'The Conduct of Locarno Diplomacy,' *Review of Politics* XXXIV (1972).
JENKS, C.W. 'Some Constitutional Problems of International Organization,' *British Year Book of International Law* XXII (1945).
- 'Coordination: A New Problem in International Organization,' Hague *Recueil des Cours* LXXVII (1950) part II.
- 'Coordination in International Organization: An Introductory Survey,' *British Year Book of International Law* XXIX (1951).
JONES, C. 'The Question of Tacna Arica,' *Transactions of the Grotius Society* XV (1930).
KAIN, R.S. 'The Chaco Dispute and the Peace System,' *Political Science, Quarterly* L (1935).
KAISER, K. 'The Interaction of Regional Subsystems: Some Preliminary Notes on Recurrent Patterns and Role of Superpowers,' *World Politics* XXI (1968).
KAY, D.A. 'The Impact of African States on the United Nations,' *International Organization* XXIII (1969).
KELCHNER, W.H. 'The Relations of the Union of American Republics to the World Organization,' US Department of State, *Bulletin* II (1940).
KELSEN, H. 'Legal Technique in International Law: A Textual Critique of the League Covenant,' *Geneva Studies* X (1939).
- 'The Principle of Sovereign Equality of States as a Basis for International Organization,' *Yale Law Journal* LIII (1944).
- 'Is the Acheson Plan Constitutional?' *World Political Quarterly* III (1950).
- 'Is the North Atlantic Treaty in Conformity with the Charter of the United Nations?' *Osterreichische Zeitscherift Für Offentliches Recht* III (1951).
KERLEY, E. 'The Powers of Investigation of the United Nations Security Council,' *American Journal of International Law* LV (1961).
KEY, D. MCK. 'The Organization of American States and the United Nations: Rivals or Partners?' US Department of State, *Bulletin* XXXI (1954).
KHADDURI, M. 'The Arab League as a Regional Arrangement,' *American Journal of International Law* XL (1946).
KISS, A. 'L'Admission des Etats Comme Membres du Conseil de L'Europe,' *Annuaire Français de Droit International* IX (1963).
KORBONSKI, A. 'The Warsaw Pact,' *International Conciliation* no. 573 (May 1969).

KRISHNAN, V.M. 'African State Practice Relating to Certain Issues of International Law,' *Indian Year Book of International Affairs* XIV (1965).

KUNZ, J.L. 'L'Article XI du Pacte de la Société des Nations,' Hague *Recueil des Cours* XXXIX (1932) part I.

– 'Individual and Collective Self-Defense in Article 51 of the Charter of the United Nations,' *American Journal of International Law* XLI (1947).

– 'General International Law and the Law of International Organizations,' *American Journal of International Law* XLVII (1953).

LASSWELL, H.D. and M.S. MCDOUGAL. 'The Identification and Appraisal of Diverse Systems of Public Order,' *American Journal of International Law* LIII (1959).

LAUTERPACHT, H. 'The Covenant as the "Higher Law," ' *British Year Book of International Law* XVII (1936).

LEVIE, H.S. 'Some Constitutional Aspects of Selected Regional Organizations: A Comparative Study,' *Columbian Journal of Transnational Law* V (1966).

LIANG, Y. 'Regional Arrangements and International Security,' *Transactions of the Grotius Society* XXXI (1945).

– 'Abstention and Absence of a Permanent Member in Relation to the Voting Procedure in the Security Council,' *American Journal of International Law* XLIV (1950).

LISSITZYN, O. 'Western and Soviet Perspectives on International Law – A Comparison,' *Proceedings of the American Society of International Law* (1953).

LIVINGSTON, F. 'Withdrawal from the United Nations – Indonesia,' *International and Comparative Law Quarterly* XIV (1965).

LOEBER, D.A. 'The Legal Structure of the Communist Bloc,' *Social Research* XXVII (1960).

LONDON, K.L. 'The "Socialist Commonwealth of Nations": Pattern for Communist World Organization,' *Orbis* III (1960).

LOWENTHAL, A.F. 'The Dominican Intervention in Retrospect,' *Public Policy* XVIII (1969).

MACDONALD, R. ST J. 'The Organization of American States in Action,' *University of Toronto Law Journal*, XV (1963-64).

– 'The Developing Relationship between Superior and Subordinate Political Bodies at the International Level: A Note on the Experience of the United Nations and the Organization of American States,' *Canadian Yearbook of International Law* II (1964).

– 'The Resort to Economic Coercion by International Political Organizations,' *University of Toronto Law Journal* XVII (1967).

MAZRUI, A.A. 'The United Nations and Some African Political Attitudes,' *International Organization* XVIII (1964).

MCDOUGAL, M.S. 'International Law, Power and Policy,' *Recueil des Cours* LXXXII (1953), part I.

– 'The Soviet-Cuban Quarantine and Self-Defence,' *American Journal of International Law* LVIII (1963).

MCDOUGAL, M., and REISMAN, 'Rhodesia and the United Nations: The Lawfulness of International Concern,' *American Journal of International Law* LXII (1968).

MCLAREN, J.P.S. 'The Dominican Crisis: An Inter-American Dilemma,' *Canadian Yearbook of International Law* IV (1966).

MCWHINNEY, E., 'The "New" Countries and the "New" International Law: The United Nations Special Conference on Friendly Relations and Cooperation Among States,' *American Journal of International Law* LX (1966).

MEEKER, L.C. 'Defensive Quarantine and the Law,' *American Journal of International Law* LVII (1963).

– 'The Dominican Situation in the Perspective of International Law,' US Department of State, *Bulletin* LIII (1965).

MEYERS, B.D. 'Intra-Regional Conflict Management by the Organization of African Unity,' *International Organization* XXVIII (1973).

MEZERIK, A.G., ed. 'Invasion and Occupation of Czechoslovakia and the UN,' *International Review Service* XIV (1968).

MICHALAK, S.J. 'The League of Nations and the United Nations in World Politics – A Plea for Comparative Research on Universal International Organizations,' *International Studies Quarterly* XV (1971).

MILLER, L.B. 'Regional Organization and the Regulation of Internal Conflict,' *World Politics* XIX (1967).

MITCHELL, R.J. 'The Brezhnev Doctrine and Communist Ideology,' *Review of Politics* XXXIV (1972).

MOHAN, J. 'Ghana, the Congo and the United Nations,' *Journal of Modern African Studies* VII (1969).

MOWER, A.G. 'Observer Countries: Quasi Members of the United Nations,' *International Organization* XX (1966).

MUSHKAT, M. 'The African Approach to Some Basic Problem of Modern International Law,' *Indian Journal of International Law* VII (1967).

NAWAZ, M.K. 'The Meaning and Range of the Principle of Self-Determination,' *Duke Law Journal* V (1965).

NICHOLAS, A.G. 'The United Nations in Crisis,' *International Affairs* (London) XLI (1965).

NYE, J.S. 'United States Policy Toward Regional Organization,' *International Organization* XXIII (1969).

OSNITSKAYA, G. 'The Downfall of Colonialism and International Law,' *International Affairs* (Moscow, January 1961).

OSUSKY, S. 'The Little Entente and the League of Nations,' *International Affairs* XIII (1934).

PADELFORD, N.J. 'Regional Organizations and the United Nations,' *International Organization* VIII (1954).

– 'Recent Developments in Regional Organization,' *Proceedings of the American Society of International Law* (1955).

PARTAN, D.G. 'The Cuban Quarantine: Some Implications for Self-Defense,' *Duke Law Journal* III (1963).

PIKE, F.B. 'Guatemala, the United States and Communism in the Americas,' *Review of Politics* XVII (1955).

PINDIC, D. 'Some Observation concerning Regionalism in the Contemporary International Law,' *Eastern Journal of International Law* III (1971).

POLLUX [EDVARD HAMBRO?]. 'The Interpretation of the Charter,' *British Yearbook of International Law* XXIII (1946).

POTTER, P.B. 'The League of Nations and Other International Organizations,' *Geneva Studies* V (1934).

– 'Universalism versus Regionalism in International Organization,' *American Political Science Review* XXXVII (1943).

PRADHAN, R.C. 'The OAU and the Congo Crisis,' *Africa Quarterly* V (1965).

RAMOLEFE, A.M.R., and A.J.G.M. SANDERS. 'The Structural Pattern of African Regionalism,' *Comparative and International Law Journal of Southern Africa* IV (1971).

RANA, R.S. 'OCAM: An Experiment in Regional Cooperation,' *African Quarterly* VIII (1968).

REMINGTON, R.A. 'The Warsaw Pact: Communist Coalition Politics in Action,' *Year Book of World Affairs* XXVII (1973).

ROBERTSON, A.H. 'Revision of the Charter of the Organization of American States,' *International and Comparative Law Quarterly* VII (1968).

ROBINSON, J. 'Metamorphosis of the United Nations,' Hague *Recueil des Cours* XCVIII (1958) part II.

ROMANIECKI. 'Sources of the Brezhnev Doctrine of Limited Sovereignty and Intervention,' *Israel Law Review* V (1970).

RUDZINSKI, A.W. 'Admission of New Members. The United Nations and the League of Nations,' *International Conciliation* no. 480 (April 1952).

SABA, H. 'Les Accords Régionaux dans la Charte de L'O.N.U.,' Hague *Recueil des Cours* LXXX (1952) part I.

SALMON, J. 'La Convention Européenne pour le Règlement Pacifique des Différends,' *Revue Générale de Droit International Public* XXX (1959).

SCHACHTER, O. 'The Quasi-Judicial Role of the Security Council and of the General Assembly,' *American Journal of International Law* LVIII (1964).

SCHAUMANN, W. 'The Maintenance of Peace as the Central Problem of Modern International Law,' *Law and State* V (1972).

SCHEMAN, L.R. 'Admission of States to the Organization of American States,' *American Journal of International Law* LVIII (1964).

SCHICK, F.B. 'Peace on Trial – A Study of Defence in International Organization,' *Western Political Quarterly* II (1949).

– 'The North Atlantic Treaty and the Problem of Peace,' *Juridical Review* CLII (1950).

SCHWARZENBERGER, G. 'The Impact of the East-West Rift on International Law,' *Transactions of the Grotius Society* XXXVI (1950).

– 'Hegemonial Intervention,' *Year Book of World Affairs* XXIII (1959).

– 'Reflections on the Law of International Institutions,' *Current Legal Problems* XIII (1960).

SCHWELB, E. 'Withdrawal from the United Nations: The Indonesian Intermezzo,' *American Journal of International Law* LXI (1967).

SIMMONDS, R. 'Peace-keeping by Regional Organizations: A Critique of the Experience of the Inter-relationships between the Organization of American States and the UN Organization within the Context of Collective Security,' *University of Ghana Law Journal* XI (1974).

SOHN, L.B. 'The Role of International Institutions as Conflict-Adjusting Agencies,' *University of Chicago Law Review* XXVIII (1961).

– 'The Function of International Arbitration Today,' *Recueil des Cours* CVIII (1963) part I.

SOWARD, F.H. 'Canada and the League of Nations,' *International Conciliation* no. 283 (1932).

SPENCER, J. 'The Monroe Doctrine and the League Covenant,' *American Journal of International Law* XXX (1936).

SWEETSER, A. 'The Practical Working of the League of Nations: A Concrete Example,' *International Conciliation*, no. 249 (1929).

TAFT, H.W. 'The Monroe Doctrine,' *League of Nations* II (1919).

TAKAKI, Y. 'World Peace Machinery and the Asian Monroe Doctrine,' *Pacific Affairs* V (1932).

TAYLOR, P.B. JR. 'The Guatemalan Affairs: A Critique of United States Policy,' *American Political Science Review* L (1956).

THOMAS, A.W. and A.J. THOMAS, 'Democracy and the Organization of American States,' *Minnesota Law Review* XLVI (1961-62).

TOUVAL, S. 'The Organization of African Unity and African Borders,' *International Organization* XXI (1967).

TUNKIN, G.I. 'Coexistence and International Law,' Hague *Recueil des Cours* XCV (1958) part III.

– 'The Legal Nature of the United Nations,' Hague *Recueil des Cours* CXIX (1966) part III.

UDOKANG, O. 'The Role of the New States in International Law,' *Archiv des Völkerrechts* XV (1971).

UMOZURIKE, U.O. 'International Law and Colonialism in Africa,' *East African Law Journal* III (1970).

VALLAT, F.A. 'The General Assembly and the Security Council of the United Nations,' *British Yearbook of International Law* XXIX (1952).

VAN KLEFFENS, E.N. 'Regionalism and Political Pacts,' *American Journal of International Law* XLIII (1949).

VERDROSS, A. 'General International Law and the United Nations Charter,' *International Affairs* XXX (1954).

VIGNES, D. 'La place des pactes de défense dans la société internationale actuelle,' *Annuaire Français de Droit International* V (1959).

VON FREYTAG-LORINGHOVEN, A. 'Les Ententes Régionales,' Hague *Recueil des Cours* LVI (1936) part II.

WALDOCK, C.H.M. 'The Regulation of the Use of Force by Individual States in International Law,' Hague *Recueil des Cours* LXXXI (1952) part II.

WEBSTER, SIR CHARLES. 'The Making of the Charter of the United Nations,' in his *The Art and Practice of Diplomacy*. London: Chatto & Windus, 1961.

WHITE, R.T. 'Regionalism vs. Universalism in the League of Nations,' *Annals of International Studies* (Geneva), no. 1 (1970).

WHITEMAN, K. 'The OAU and the Nigerian Issue,' *World Today* (November 1968).

WILCOX, F.O. 'Regionalism and the United Nations,' *International Organization* XIX (1965).

WILD, P.B. 'The Organization of African Unity and the Algerian-Moroccan Border Conflict: A Case Study of New Machinery for Peaceful Settlement of Disputes,' *International Organization* XX (1966).

WILK, K. 'International Law and Global Ideological Conflict: Reflections on the Universality of International Law,' *American Journal of International Law* XLV (1951).

WILSON, L.C. 'International Law and the United States Cuban Quarantine of 1962,' *Journal of Inter-American Studies* VII (1965).

WINDSOR, P. 'NATO and the Cyprus Crisis,' *Adelphi Papers* no. 14 (November 1964).

WOOLSEY, L.H. 'The Leticia Dispute between Colombia and Peru,' *American Journal of International Law* XXVII (1933).

– 'The Leticia Dispute between Colombia and Peru,' *American Journal of International Law* XXIX (1935).

– 'The Settlement of Chaco Dispute,' *American Journal of International Law* XXXIII (1939).

WRIGHT, Q. 'Territorial Propinquity,' *American Journal of International Law* XII (1919).

– 'United States Intervention in the Lebanon,' *American Journal of International Law* LIII (1959).

– 'The Goa Incident,' *American Journal of International Law* LVI (1962).

– 'The Cuban Quarantine,' *American Journal of International Law* LVII (1963).

YEPES, J.M. 'Les Accords Régionaux et le Droit International,' Hague *Recueil des Cours* LXXI (1947) part II.

YALEM, RONALD. 'Regionalism and World Order,' *International Affairs* XXXVIII (1962).

YOUNG, O.R. 'The United Nations and the International System,' *International Organization* XXII (1968).

– 'Political Discontinuities in the International System,' *World Politics* XX (1968).

ZIMMERMAN, W. 'Hierarchical Regional Systems and the Politics of Systems Boundaries,' *International Organization* XXVI (1972).

Index